Farm Management Pocketbook

by

JOHN NIX

with Paul Hill

THIRTIETH EDITION

(2000)

SEPTEMBER 1999

Copies of this book may be obtained from Wye College Press,
Wye College, near Ashford, Kent, TN25 5AH.
(Tel. 01233-812401 ext. 285; Fax. 01233-813320)

PRICE £9.00
(6 to 11 copies: £8.75)
(12 to 49 copies: £8.50)
(50 to 199 copies: £8.25)
(200-499 copies: £8.00)
(Over 500 copies: £7.50)

ISBN 0 86266 210 9

Farm Management
Pocketbook

FOREWORD TO THE FIRST EDITION

This booklet is intended for farmers, advisers, students and everyone else who, frequently or infrequently, find themselves hunting for data relating to farm management—whether it is for blunt pencil calculations on the back of an envelope or for feeding into a computer. The material contained is based upon the sort of information which the author finds himself frequently having to look up in his twin roles as adviser and teacher in farm management. There are several excellent handbooks already in existence, but this pocketbook endeavours to cover a wider field and thus to be substantially more comprehensive. It is intended that most of the data herein contained will have a national application, although there is inevitably some bias towards conditions in the south-eastern half of the country.

The development of farm planning techniques in recent years has outstripped the quality and quantity of data available. It is hoped that this booklet will go a little further in supplying the type of information required. It cannot, however, claim to be the ultimate in this respect. For example, there are many variations in labour requirements according to farm conditions and sizes and types of machine used and there are many more variations in sheep and beef systems than are dealt with here. More detailed data on these lines are gradually becoming available from various sources. It is hoped further to refine the material in this booklet and to keep it up to date in subsequent editions, as the information becomes available. As a help towards this end, any comments or criticisms will be gratefully received.

The author wishes to thank his many friends and colleagues who have given him so much time and help in compiling this information.

John Nix
October, 1966

First published October 1966

Thirtieth Edition   September 1999

FOREWORD TO THE THIRTIETH EDITION

Considerable revisions and additions have been made to several sections of this edition, including short rotation coppice, most of the so-called "minority crops", vineyards, ostriches, golf etc. Everything has been updated that can be updated. A summary of the Agenda 2000 provisions is included and future area and headage payments are estimated.

These "best estimates" for the year 2000 (made in mid-summer 1999) show a dismal picture for farm profitability, which will surprise no one. Some improvement in world prices, together with some weakening of the pound, are badly needed if many farmers are to be saved from being forced to give up — especially those with small farms, poorish land and substantial borrowings. Belt-tightening can only go so far. Naturally, largish-scale owner-occupiers on good land, with few or no borrowings, will continue, but with a lot less money to spend on the farm or themselves. An industry that is obliged largely to depend on paying little or nothing for the land, capital and management it uses — and in many cases much of the manual labour too — is a despondent industry. It is sad to have to write this for what is another "anniversary edition". However, what is misery for some means opportunities and challenges for others and times will undoubtedly improve and perhaps before very long.

As indicated, most of the figures are predicted forward one year, *i.e.* to 2000. *Thus the crops data relate to the 2000 harvest, i.e. the 2000/2001 marketing year* (N.B. not just, in the case of product prices, those prevailing at or just after harvest time). *The livestock data relate either to the 2000 calendar year (e.g. for milk production) or to 2000/2001 (e.g. for winter finished beef), as appropriate.* In a few cases current (*i.e.* mid-1999) figures are given, where it seemed particularly difficult to try to forecast ahead. The year to which the figures relate is normally stated.

The figures for yields and prices assume a "normal", or average, season, based on trends, *e.g.* for potatoes, looking 18-24 months ahead to 2000/2001, no one can predict what the *actual* average yield and price for that particular year will be. Similarly with pig production: no attempt is made to predict the *actual* position of the pig cycle during 2000 — only what the average trend figure is likely to be, in neither an "up" or "down" stage, given estimated changes in the relevant indices.

The data in this book should always be used with caution. *The figures should be adjusted as appropriate according to circumstances and price and cost differences.* As far as possible the assumptions in the tables are set out so as to enable this to be done fairly readily.

The principal author wishes to thank all those who assisted with this edition. In particular, and as for many years, Paul Hill has revised many important sections. In addition Angela Edwards has been of considerable assistance in revising and expanding a substantial number of enterprises.

John Nix
July, 1999

CONTENTS

I. GENERAL

1. THE USE OF GROSS MARGINS

Definition. The Gross Margin of an enterprise is its enterprise output less its variable costs. Enterprise output includes the market value of production retained on the farm. The variable costs must (a) be specific to the enterprise and (b) vary in proportion to the size of the enterprise, *i.e.* number of hectares or head of stock. The main items of variable costs are: Crops: fertilizer, seed, sprays, casual labour and contract work specific to the crop. Non-Grazing Livestock: concentrate feed, vet. and med., marketing expenses. Grazing Livestock: as for non-grazing livestock, plus forage crop variable costs.

Points to Note about the concept are as follows:

1. The gross margin is in no sense a profit figure. The so-called "fixed costs" (rent, labour, machinery, general overheads — see pages 157-161) have to be covered by the total farm gross margin before arriving at a profit.

2. The gross margin of an enterprise will differ from season to season, partly because of yield and price differences affecting output and partly because variable costs may vary, *e.g.* the number and type of sprays required. Different soils and other natural factors, as well as level of management, will also cause differences between farms.

3. Items of variable cost may vary from farm to farm, *e.g.* some farmers use casual labour (a variable cost) to plant and pick their potatoes, others use only regular labour (a fixed cost); some farmers employ a contractor to combine their cereals (a variable cost), others employ their own equipment (a fixed cost); some employ a contractor to cart their sugar beet to the factory (a variable cost), others have their own lorry (a fixed cost). These differences must be borne in mind in making inter-farm comparisons.

4. Provided points 2 and 3 are borne in mind, comparison of gross margins (particularly averages over several seasons) with standards can be a useful check on technical efficiency.

5. The other main usefulness of gross margins lies in farm planning. This is not simply a matter of substituting high gross margin enterprises for low gross margin enterprises. The gross margin is only one relevant feature of an enterprise, although an important one. It says nothing about the call the enterprise makes on the basic farm resources—labour at different times of the year, machinery, buildings, working capital requirements, etc. All these factors and more have to be taken into account in the planning process.

6. This is not to argue that these other costs should be allocated. Complete allocation of many farm expenses is only possible on an arbitrary basis, since they are shared by two or more, possibly all, farm enterprises. Allocation can therefore be completely misleading when making planning decisions. The same is true even when regular labour and machinery are employed specifically on certain enterprises, if such costs are calculated on a per hectare or per head basis. This is because when enterprises are substituted, expanded, contracted or deleted the variable costs for each enterprise will vary roughly in proportion to the size of that enterprise, but other costs will not, except possibly for fuel and some repair costs. Most "fixed" costs may stay the same, others will change — but not smoothly in small amounts at a time. Either the same regular labour force will cope with a revised plan or a smaller or larger number of men will be needed. The same is true of tractors, other machines and buildings. Such cost changes must of course be taken into account, but allocating these costs on a per hectare or per head basis will not aid, and may positively confuse, planning decisions. The only point of making such calculations is for efficiency comparisons, *e.g.* labour costs per cow.

7. Allocating fixed costs at a flat rate (*e.g.* per hectare) for all enterprises, deducting this from the gross margin and hence calculating a "net profit" from each enterprise can also be misleading. It ignores the whole problem of enterprise inter-relationships, differences between enterprises in total and seasonal requirements for labour, machinery and capital, and other factors such as different quality land on the same farm.

8. Changes in the scale of an enterprise may well affect its gross margin per unit, *e.g.* increasing the area of winter wheat from 30 per cent to 50 per cent on a farm will mean more second and third crop wheats being grown and a smaller proportion of the crop being drilled under the best conditions; hence yields will in all probability fall. Even if yields remain the same, variable costs (*e.g.* fertilizer use) will probably increase.

9. Gross margins used for planning future changes should also take account of possible changes in price, and the effect of changes in production techniques.

Low, Average and High Levels

The three performance and production levels given for most crop and livestock enterprises are meant for the most part to indicate differences in natural factors, soil productivity, and/or managerial skill, *given the level of variable cost inputs.* They refer, at each level, to *an average over several years* taking *trends* into account. The evidence on the effect of significantly higher or lower levels of variable inputs on gross margins is conflicting and highly uncertain, depending on many factors, including soil type, and will vary from season to season.

2. COMPLETE ENTERPRISE COSTINGS

Requests are occasionally made for this book to include "complete" enterprise costings, by which is meant the allocation of *all* costs to each individual enterprise, not only the variable costs as in the calculation of gross margins.

In the early days of farm business management teaching and research this was the preoccupation of most of those specialising in the subject. The system was, however, abandoned by nearly all practising farm economists in the 1950s. The main reasons are given in item 6 of the previous section explaining gross margins. Much meaningless and arbitrary allocation of "joint costs" is required, (attempting "to allocate the unallocatable"), and the results are often misleading in making farm decisions. Furthermore, it requires a considerable amount of record-keeping — in allocating labour on a mixed farm, tractor and machinery costs, telephone bills and so on. Few farmers are prepared to spend the required time and money to do this, nor do they need to.

Another problem in "complete enterprise costing" is where to stop. Should interest on capital be included, whether borrowed or not? Further problems of asset valuation and allocation are involved if so. What of management and marketing supplied by the farmer? Should these be for free, as is usually assumed in such cases?

Variations between farms in their financial situations are considerable as, for instance, between the farmer who owns all his land without any mortgage and has no other borrowings and the one with both a rent to pay for all his land and heavy borrowings in addition.

In some situations, e g in some company-owned farms, farm managers are obliged to supply such data to their employers, whether they want to or not. Also, if enterprise costs are used for price fixing purposes governments, or price negotiators, usually require some such attempt to be made, whatever the difficulties and shortcomings of the methodology employed.

The above problems arise when "costs per tonne" or "costs per litre" are calculated. Wheat can be calculated to cost anything between £50 and £150 a tonne according to just what costs are included, how they are calculated (allocated) and the yield level assumed.

This is not to decry the efforts that are sometimes made in this direction. Particularly when product prices are falling it seems a natural thing to want to do — to calculate "unit costs" to compare with prices received. Sometimes they do make clearer particular costs that need investigating and by that means economies that might be made, and they always attract interest. For these reasons costs per litre of milk are included in this edition for the first time, although the calculation of some of the "fixed cost" items is difficult. If a farm has only one enterprise such calculations on that farm are obviously straightforward. However, even on solely dairy farms followers are usually reared, which is a second enterprise to milk production.

If required *a* cost per tonne of wheat (and other combinable crops) can be readily calculated by adding the fixed costs per hectare of mainly cereals farms (according to size range, given on page 159) to the variable costs per hectare given in the enterprise gross margin data and dividing by the selected yield.

The allocation of specific labour (*e.g.* a full-time cowman), machinery (*e.g.* a potato harvester) and buildings (*e.g.* a grain store) is relatively simple and can provide useful information both for purposes of efficiency comparisons and partial budgeting. For some enterprises on many mixed farms, however, there are few, if any, such specific items and the question of the other so-called fixed cost items remains if a full costing is attempted.

3. TOTAL FARM GROSS MARGIN

No attempt is made in this book to compile total gross margins for the whole farm, based on the forecasts made for individual enterprises for 2000, since the possible permutations in terms of enterprise combinations and performance levels are endless. Nor has it ever been the intention in the Pocketbook to include "historical data", except for some of the material in the Agristats section. Hence total farm survey results, which are inevitably a year or two old by the time they are collated, analysed and published, are not included. Their usefulness for any particular farm is bound to be limited, particularly if the farm systems are broadly defined and cover much of the United Kingdom.

Furthermore, such data are published annually on a regional basis, covering the wide range of farm types and size ranges in each particular part of the country.

Easily the main source in the United Kingdom is the Farm Business Survey, carried out for and financed by MAFF in England and Wales, the Scottish Office and the Department of Northern Ireland. The annual reports are readily available from the departments that do the work. The names of the publications and the relevant University, College or Department are given below. The addresses and telephone numbers are given on page 238.

North:	Farming in Northern England (University of Newcastle-upon-Tyne).
Yorkshire:	Farming in Yorkshire (Askham Bryan College).
North-West:	An Economic Review of Farming in the North West (University of Manchester).
East Midlands:	Farming in the East Midlands (University of Nottingham).
Eastern Counties:	Report on Farming in the Eastern Counties (University of Cambridge).
South-East	Farm Business Statistics for South East England (Wye College, University of London).
South:	Farm Business Data (University of Reading).
South-West:	Farm Incomes in South West England (and Farm Management Handbook) (University of Exeter).
Wales:	Farm Business Survey in Wales (University of Wales, Aberystwyth).

Data for Scotland and Northern Ireland are available from the Scottish Agricultural College and Department of Agriculture, Northern Ireland respectively. Their addresses too are given on page 238.

III AGENDA 2000 AND AREA/HEADAGE PAYMENTS

AGENDA 2000

The Agenda 2000 reforms were finally agreed in March 1999. Some remaining details were agreed subsequently. The UK position in mid-July 1999 is as described below. Some points and details have yet to be decided by the governments of individual member states, including the UK, or have yet to be made quite clear.

When the euro was introduced, in early January 1999, its value was 71 pence. Despite continual forecasts that the £ sterling would weaken, by mid-July the euro was worth barely 65 pence. At the final proof stages of preparing this book, however, the £ had in fact begun to fall (early August) — but whether this will continue and, if so, to what extent, is impossible to say.

ARABLE CROPS

The present cereals intervention price of 119.19 euros/tonne will be reduced by15% in two steps to 110.25 (£74.40) from 1ˢᵗ July 2000 and 101.31 (£68.40) from 1ˢᵗ July 2001. Monthly increments to remain as at present.

Cereals area payments will rise from the present 54.34 euros/tonne to 58.67 in 2000 and 63 from 2001 onwards. (Durum wheat supplements to continue as at present).

Oilseeds area payments will fall to 81.74 euros/tonne in 2000, 72.37 in 2001 and 63 from 2002 onwards (i.e. the same rate as cereals).

As with linseed, proteins and set-aside the area payments are calculated by multiplying the euros/tonne by the regional cereals yield.

Cuts in the payments for exceeding base areas and a given average world price level will still apply in 2000 and 2001, but there will be a minimum payment equal to the payment for cereals.

Linseed area payments will fall from the present 105.10 euro/tonne to 88.26 in 2000, 75.63 in 2001 and 63 from 2002 onwards (i.e. the same rate for cereals).

Protein crops area payments will fall from the present 78.49 euros/ tonne to 72.5 from 2000 onwards, i.e. a supplement to the cereals etc. payments remains.

Set-aside area payments will fall from the present 68.83 euros/tonne to 58.67 in 2000 (i.e. the same rate as cereals) and 63 from 2001 onwards (i.e. again the same rate as cereals).

Further Details

The relevant euro value will in future not be taken as that on the "operative date", e.g. 1ˢᵗ July, but on the average daily quoted rates in the preceding month.

Arable area payments will be made between 16ᵗʰ November and 31ˢᵗ January from 2000 onwards; (up to 31ˢᵗ March in the case of non-food crops on set-aside).

Payments will continue to be reduced if regional base areas are exceeded, but penalty set-aside has been abolished. The regional base areas will be the average area under eligible crops in the years 1989 to 1991.

Member states retain the option of having separate base areas for maize. A new option is for making area payments on grass silage in states where maize is not a "traditional" crop. Payment rate to be as for cereals, within a separate sub-base area. UK's position currently unclear.

The (effectively compulsory) set-aside "default rate" is 10% from 2000 to 2006, but a different rate may still be agreed each year. Small producer exemption continues to apply, with a voluntary set-aside option. Voluntary set-aside will continue; member states are able to set a maximum area, which cannot be less than 10% and may be up to 100%. A mandatory EU-wide *ceiling* on aid payments was not agreed, but remains an option for member states, with proceeds diverted to some rural development measures. Individual member states may include provisions on environmental conditions and *modulation*. Re the latter, member states have been given discretion to reduce direct payments by up to 20% according to labour force or overall prosperity criteria and/or the total amount of aid received by farmers. The funds saved can be used for additional support for agri-environment and forestry measures, HLCAs and early retirement schemes (otherwise they have to be returned to Brussels); however, matching funds have to be found from national sources. It seems unlikely that modulation will be adopted in the UK.

Agrimonetary Compensation

These supplements to the area payment are not part of Agenda 2000, but are relevant to UK payments in 2000 and 2001. They are compensation for revaluation of the currency between 1ˢᵗ July 1998 and 1ˢᵗ July 1999. The 11.5% "freeze" has gone. However, UK farmers receive a minimum of 75p/euro for livestock and arable payments in 1999. This is totally EU funded.

In 2000 the compensation is cut to two-thirds of the difference between the UK euro value and 75p/euro, i.e. two thirds of 7.5p if the value in 2000 were to be 67.5p. In 2001 the compensation will be cut to one-third of the difference. However, only 50% of the compensation in 2000 and 2001 is EU funded, the other half comes from MAFF, which is not obliged to make the payment. Compensation payments are linked to the claimant, not the holding; hence whoever makes the claim in 1999 will be entitled to compensation in subsequent years.

Further 3-year sequences of possible compensation may be triggered if the euro rate is less favourable than the previous two Julys, but the whole of this is optional for member states.

AREA PAYMENTS

Area payments, in euros per hectare, are calculated by multiplying prescribed regional (cereals) yields per hectare by payment rates expressed in euros per tonne. These regional yields for the UK are as follows:

England	Scotland (non LFA)	Scotland (LFA)	Wales (non LFA)	Wales (LFA)	Northern Ireland (non LFA)	Northern Ireland (LFA)
5·89	5·67	5·21	5·17	5·05	5·22	5·03

(Separate regional yields used until this year for oilseed rape will no longer apply under Agenda 2000 regulations).

The euros per tonne are as follows for the years from 1999 onwards:

	1999	2000	2001	2002†
Cereals	54·34	58·67	63	63
Oilseeds	—*	81·74	72·37	63
Linseed	105·10	88·26	75·63	63
Proteins	78·49	72·5	72·5	72·5
Set-aside	68·83	58·67	63	63

† And subsequent years.
* Different calculation (separate oilseed yield and euros/tonne).

The following are the euros per hectare and the payments in £ per hectare (per acre) — to the nearest £ — for 1999 onwards. It has to be stressed that the payment figures for 2000 onwards can only be highly speculative, since they will depend on the unpredictable future value of the euro and, at least to some extent, other MAFF/EC decisions and details at present unknown. They do not take account of any deductions for exceeding base areas or (for oilseed rape) prescribed world price levels (except for, in 1999, base area overshoots of 1·4% in England and 7·07% in Scotland non-LFA), or any constraints imposed according to previous crop areas.

The euro value assumed is 67·5 pence and agrimonetary compensation (which may in fact be phased in differently than is assumed here) paid at 2·5p per euro in 2000, 1·25p per euro in 2001 and nothing thereafter. Thus a total of 70p per euro is assumed for 2000, 68·75p for 2001 and 67·5p for 2002 onwards. The level of agrimonetary compensation assumes that only half the sum available (i.e. that supplied by the EU) is paid, i.e. that the UK government does not pay the other half.

England

	1999 euros	£	2000 euros	£	2001 euros	£	2002† euros	£
Cereals	320·06	238 (96)	345·57	242 (98)	371·07	255 (103)	371·07	250 (101)
Oilseeds	—	421 (170)	481·45	337 (136)	426·26	293 (119)	371·07	250 (101)
Linseed	619·04	461 (187)	519·85	364 (147)	445·46	306 (124)	371·07	250 (101)
Proteins	462·31	344 (139)	427·02	299 (121)	427·02	294 (119)	427·02	288 (117)
Set-aside	405·41	302 (122)	345·57	242 (98)	371·07	255 (103)	371·07	250 (101)

Scotland (non-LFA)

	1999 euros	£	2000 euros	£	2001 euros	£	2002† euros	£
Cereals	308·11	216 (88)	332·66	233 (94)	357·21	246 (99)	357·21	241 (98)
Oilseeds	—	445 (180)	463·47	324 (131)	410·34	282 (114)	357·21	241 (98)
Linseed	595·92	418 (169)	500·43	350 (142)	428·82	300 (121)	357·21	241 (98)
Proteins	445·04	312 (126)	411·08	288 (116)	411·08	283 (114)	411·08	277 (112)
Set-aside	390·03	274 (111)	332·66	233 (94)	357·21	246 (99)	357·21	241 (98)

Scotland (LFA)

	1999 euros	£	2000 euros	£	2001 euros	£	2002† euros	£
Cereals	283·11	214 (87)	305·67	214 (87)	328·23	226 (91)	328·23	222 (90)
Oilseeds	—	394 (159)	425·87	298 (121)	377·05	259 (105)	328·23	222 (90)
Linseed	547·57	414 (167)	459·83	186 (75)	394·03	271 (110)	328·23	222 (90)
Proteins	408·93	309 (125)	377·72	264 (107)	377·72	260 (105)	377·72	255 (103)
Set-aside	358·60	271 (110)	305·67	214 (87)	328·33	226 (91)	328·23	222 (90)

Wales (non-LFA)

	1999		2000		2001		2002†	
	euros	£	euros	£	euros	£	euros	£
Cereals	280·94	212 (86)	303·32	212 (86)	325·71	224 (91)	325·71	220 (89)
Oilseeds	—	436 (176)	422·60	296 (120)	374·15	257 (104)	325·71	220 (89)
Linseed	543·37	410 (166)	456·30	319 (129)	391·01	269 (109)	325·71	220 (89)
Proteins	405·79	306 (124)	374·82	262 (106)	374·82	258 (104)	374·82	253 (102)
Set-aside	355·85	269 (109)	303·32	212 (86)	325·71	224 (91)	325·71	220 (89)

Wales (LFA)

	1999		2000		2001		2002†	
	euros	£	euros	£	euros	£	euros	£
Cereals	274·42	207 (84)	296·28	207 (84)	318·15	219 (89)	318·15	215 (87)
Oilseeds	—	436 (176)	412·79	289 (117)	365·47	251 (102)	318·15	215 (87)
Linseed	530·75	401 (162)	445·71	312 (126)	381·93	263 (106)	318·15	215 (87)
Proteins	396·37	299 (121)	366·12	256 (104)	366·12	252 (102)	366·12	247 (100)
Set-aside	347·59	263 (106)	296·28	207 (84)	318·15	219 (89)	318·15	215 (87)

Northern Ireland (non-LFA)

	1999		2000		2001		2002†	
	euros	£	euros	£	euros	£	euros	£
Cereals	283·65	214 (87)	306·26	214 (87)	328·86	226 (91)	328·86	222 (90)
Oilseeds	—	405 (164)	426·68	299 (121)	377·77	260 (105)	328·86	222 (90)
Linseed	548·62	414 (168)	460·72	323 (131)	394·79	271 (110)	328·86	222 (90)
Proteins	409·72	309 (125)	378·45	265 (107)	378·45	260 (105)	378·45	255 (103)
Set-aside	359·29	271 (110)	306·26	214 (87)	328·86	226 (91)	328·86	222 (90)

Northern Ireland (LFA)

	1999		2000		2001		2002†	
	euros	£	euros	£	euros	£	euros	£
Cereals	273·33	206 (84)	295·11	207 (84)	316·89	218 (88)	316·89	214 (87)
Oilseeds	—	405 (164)	411·15	288 (116)	364·02	250 (101)	316·89	214 (87)
Linseed	528·65	399 (162)	443·95	311 (126)	380·42	262 (106)	316·89	214 (87)
Proteins	394·80	298 (121)	364·67	255 (103)	364·67	251 (101)	364·67	246 (100)
Set-aside	346·21	261 (106)	295·11	207 (84)	316·89	218 (88)	316·89	214 (87)

†And subsequent years.

In the crop gross margin tables below the rounded figures for England in 2000 are used.

BEEF
(including headage payments)

The present intervention price will be reduced by 20% in three equal annual steps from 1st July 2000. Private storage aid will replace intervention from 1st July 2002, but safety net intervention will remain as a provision after 1st July 2002 if market prices fall below a set level.

As regards direct payments, a phased increase in the suckler cow premium and the beef special premium will start from 2000 to reach the final target date in 2002. A new slaughter premium is to be introduced, with national ceilings. A national ceiling on claims is to be introduced for the suckler cow premium (1·7 million rights).

From 2000, up to 20% of an individual's suckler cow claims to be made on heifers, with possibly a minimum age; but this has still to be confirmed.

The national ceiling for beef special premium claims in the UK has been increased by 100,000 units to 1·52 millions; this will remain while the ban on live calf exports continues.

The payments in euros/head, with a euro value of 67·5p, plus agrimonetary compensation (see above) of 2·5p in 2000 and 1·25p in 2001 (no compensation is assumed for 2002), to the nearest £0·5/head in brackets, are as follows (though note that the value of the euro in 2001 and 2002 is even more problematical than in 2000):

	2000	2001	2002 plus
Beef special premium[1]			
Steers[2]	122 (£85·5)	136 (£93·5)	150 (£101)
Young bulls[3]	160 (£112)	185 (£127)	210 (£142)
Slaughter premium[4]			
Adult cattle	27 (£19)	53 (£36·5)	80 (£54)
Calves	17 (£12)	33 (£22·5)	50 (£34)
Suckler cow premium	163 (£114)	182 (£125)	200 (£135)

[1] Minimum age for claiming reduced to 7 months for first claim and 19 months for second; payable at 9 and 21 months respectively.
[2] Claimable twice in lifetime of steer.
[3] Claimable once in lifetime of bull.
[4] Claimable on steers, heifers, young bulls, cows and calves (minimum age 1 month); eligible up to 7 months old and 160 kg dw; subject to a retention period of two months; there will be a national ceiling on claims, set at 1995 slaughterings; full details still to be agreed.

Provision exists for the payment of an *additional premium* on top of one or all of the headage premia: the so-called "national envelope": about £14 millions in 2000, double this in 2001 and treble in 2002, in the UK. The government can distribute this sum as it wishes: an addition to the suckler premium is thought to be most likely (about £8 a head in 2000 if so).

Extensification premium. Member states may choose between a simple supplement of 100 euro (£70) per premium where the stocking density is below 1·4 livestock units (LU)/ha and a two tier system which, in 2000 and 2001, is 33 euro (£23) if between 1·6 and 2 LU/ha and 66 (£46) if less than 1·6. The measurement of stocking density will be tightened up in terms of the type of crop allowed in the calculation and heifers over 6 months old will be included (at 0·6 LU). This will make the new extensification premia more difficult to achieve than at present.

(The maximum stocking rate (2·0 LU/forage ha) for the payment of the full beef special premium on all cattle on the holding remains, but the present stocking rate calculation still applies.)

Hill Livestock Compensatory Allowances (which are not part of Agenda 2000) are to change from being headage based to being area based. Payment levels can be decided at national level within set limits. It will probably take until 2001 for these changes to be implemented (see further pages 91-92).

MILK

Dairy reform has been delayed until 2005/2006. Quotas look certain to continue until at least 2008; some increases in quota have been made but these do not apply to the UK. A review is planned for 2003; there is a fairly widespread view that there could be another reform as early as 2002/03.

III ENTERPRISE DATA

1. CASH CROPS

WINTER WHEAT

Production level	Low	Average	High
Yield: tonnes per ha (tons per acre)			
Feed	6·25 (2·5)	7·75 (3·1)	9·25 (3·7)
Milling	5·7 (2·25)	7·05 (2·8)	8·4 (3·35)
Price per tonne (Feed/Milling):			
£70/£77	£	£	£
Sale Value	440 (178)	545 (221)	650 (263)
Area Payment	240 (97)	240 (97)	240 (97)
OUTPUT:	680 (275)	785 (318)	890 (360)
Variable Costs:			
Seed		47·5 (19)	
Fertilizer		82·5 (33·5)	
Sprays		115 (46·5)	
TOTAL VARIABLE COSTS		245 (99)	
GROSS MARGIN per ha (acre) ...	435 (176)	540 (219)	645 (261)

Notes

1. *Prices.* Market prices for cereals continued at a low level during the 1998/99 marketing year. The average feed wheat price for the 2000 harvest crop is taken to be £70 tonne, rising from £65 at harvest to £77·50 in May/June 2001. The average milling price is taken to be £77/tonne after allowing for a proportion of rejects; £77 is simply the "break-even" price that gives the same output/ha as feed wheat at the price assumed for the latter; the average premium was well above the £7/tonne (10%) assumed in both 1997/98 and 1998/99 but in some years it is significantly less.

   In mid 1999, at a euro value of 65p, the November 1999 *intervention price* for eligible cereals (which excludes much feed wheat) was £78·12/tonne, increasing by 66p (1 ecu)/month to £82·02 in May 2000. For the 2000 harvest the basic intervention price will be 110 euros/tonne, compared with 119 for the 1999 crop.

   Area Payment. See pages 5 to 9 for the Agenda 2000 decisions, the assumptions made re the euro value and agrimonetary compensation and the payments consequentially assumed for year 2000. The rounded figure for England has been used for all the cereal crops in this edition.

2. *Yields.* The overall average yield, for *all* winter wheat, is taken as 7·6 tonnes/ha (3·025 tons (60·5 cwt.)/acre).

3. *Feed v. Milling.* It is assumed that the yield of milling wheat *averages* 9% below that of feed wheat (the difference could be greater on high-yielding land and less on moderate quality land and also tends to be greater on second than on first wheats). The assumed milling premium of approximately £7/tonne is that needed to give the same gross margin for both, given this assumed difference in yield. Although higher costs for fertiliser and sprays might be expected for milling wheats such survey data as exists indicates little difference in variable costs in practice. Obviously different relative yields and premiums will give different gross margins: these can be readily calculated. The actual premium in any one season varies according to quality and scarcity. The best breadmaking wheat achieves substantially higher premiums; grade 2 varieties normally achieve a premium of only a few pounds a tonne but their average yields are higher than grade 1 varieties. Not all wheat grown for milling achieves a

premium and more care is required. The proportion of the UK wheat area sown with milling varieties has risen from only some 20% a few years ago to around 34% (grade 1 and 2 varieties combined) for the 1999 harvest, following the high premiums in recent years.

4. *First v. Second (Feed) Wheats.* The evidence concerning the effect of different types and lengths of rotational breaks on subsequent cereal yields is inevitably variable, given the differences between seasons (weather effects), soils, varieties etc. The table below (for *feed* wheat only) assumes a yield reduction of approximately 7·5% for second wheats compared with first and higher fertilizer and seed costs as shown; (the later the sowing date the less the yield gap tends to be). The same price and area payment is assumed as in the initial table. Only average and high levels are shown. Third wheats could yield 10-15% below second wheats; variable costs are likely to be similar.

Production level	Average		High	
Year (after break)	First	Second	First	Second
Yield: tonnes per ha (tons per acre)	8·25 (3·3)	7·65 (3·05)	9·75 (3·9)	9·00 (3·6)
	£	£	£	£
OUTPUT (inc. Area Payment) ...	820 (332)	775 (314)	925 (374)	870 (352)
VARIABLE COSTS	235 (95)	255 (103)	235 (95)	255 (103)
GROSS MARGIN per ha (acre) ...	585 (237)	520 (211)	690 (279)	615 (249)

5. *Straw* is not included above. Average yield is approx. 3·5 tonnes per hectare (range 2·5 to 5); value £10 to £50 per tonne according to region and season; variable costs (string) approx. £1·75 per tonne. In 1995, 70% of the area of wheat straw in England and Wales was baled and 30% ploughed in or cultivated; (later data are unavailable). Standing straw (sold for baling): anything from no value to £150/ha (£60/acre), according to type of crop, season and area of the country/local demand: average around £40/ha (£16/acre).

6. *Seed and Fertilizer.* From survey data, updated. Seed rates and fertilizer applications vary according to soil, season, variety, farm policy, etc. Seed 35 to 40% farm-saved (single dressing £70/tonne). Seed rate averages around 190 kg/ha, price range mainly £180-£260/tonne.

7. *Sprays.* Amounts variable according to season, variety, policy, etc. Typical breakdown: herbicides 38%, fungicides 46%, insecticides 3%, growth regulators 8%, other 5%.

8. If a *Contractor* is employed, extra variable costs (£ per hectare) will be approximately as follows:

Spraying:	£11 (material included above)
Drilling:	£21
Combining:	£75 (excluding carting)
	£90 (including carting)
Drying:	£60 to £100 (according to yield and moisture content; transport one way is included; *this assumes that* $^2/_3$ of the crop needs to be dried in an average season).
Baling Straw:	£45 (including string).

9. *Fuel and Repairs* (per hectare): grain £90, straw £32.

10. *Specialized Equipment Prices:* see pages 138-141.

11. *Labour:* see pages 120-122.

N.B.—Approximately 75% of home-grown wheat is used for feed, 20% for milling and 5% for seed.

SPRING WHEAT

Production level	Low	Average	High
Yield: tonnes per hectare (tons per acre)...	4·25 (1·7)	5·25 (2·1)	6·25 (2·5)
	£	£	£
Price per tonne: £75			
Sale Value	300 (122)	370 (150)	440 (178)
Area Payment	240 (97)	240 (97)	240 (97)
OUTPUT	540 (219)	610 (247)	680 (275)
Variable Costs:			
Seed		62·5 (25·5)	
Fertilizer		55 (22)	
Sprays		72·5 (29·5)	
TOTAL VARIABLE COSTS		190 (77)	
GROSS MARGIN per ha (acre)	350 (142)	420 (170)	490 (198)

Notes

1. *Price:* In general, see Winter Wheat (page 12). A higher proportion of spring wheat is sold for milling compared with winter wheat. The average price taken above, for the 2000 harvest, (£75/tonne), assumes approximately two-thirds sold for milling, one-third for feed.

2. *Straw.* See Winter Wheat, page 13.

3. If a *Contractor is* employed, extra variable costs (£ per hectare) will be as shown for Winter Wheat above.

4. *Fuel and Repairs* (per hectare): grain £85, straw £30.

5. *Specialized Equipment Prices:* see pages 138-141.

6. *Labour:* see pages 121-122.

N.B.—Normally only 1 or 2% of the UK wheat area is spring sown; the percentage is naturally higher following a particularly wet autumn. The percentage is even lower in Scotland (1% or less) than in England and Wales.

WINTER BARLEY

Production level						Low	Average	High
Yield: tonnes per ha (tons per acre)								
Feed ...	...	...	...	...	...	5·1 (2·05)	6·35 (2·55)	7·6 (3·05)
Malting	...	...	...	...	...	4·3 (1·7)	5·35 (2·15)	6·4 (2·55)

Price per tonne (Feed/Malting): £68/£81			£	£	£
Sale Value (Feed and Malting)	...	...	345 (140)	430 (174)	515 (209)
Area Payment	...	...	240 (97)	240 (97)	240 (97)

OUTPUT (Feed and Malting)...	...	...	585 (237)	670 (271)	755 (306)

Variable Costs:					Feed	Malting
Seed	...	...	...	...	45 (19)	50 (20)
Fertilizer	...	...	...	...	72·5	60
Sprays	...	...	...	...	87·5	95

TOTAL VARIABLE COSTS	...	...	...	205 (83)	205 (83)

GROSS MARGIN per ha (acre)	...	...	380 (154)	465 (188)	550 (223)

1. *Prices and Area Payment.* See Winter Wheat (page 12) for CAP support details, but note intervention is available for feed barley. The average feed barley price for the 2000 harvest crop (*i.e.* 2000/2001 marketing year) is taken to be £68/tonne, rising from £63 at harvest to £75 in May/June 2001. The malting price (£81/tonne) assumes a premium over feed of £13/tonne, which is what is required to equate the output and hence the gross margin for feed barley given the same total variable costs per hectare and the assumed yield difference. This allows for malting varieties sown that do not reach malting standards. The *actual* premium obtained over feed barley varies according to season and quality: for the best malting barleys the premium is usually at least £25 and in some years can even reach £50 plus. These higher prices for quality are normally available even at harvest time, when the differential over feed has normally exceeded £15. However, premiums have been low in recent years.

2. *Straw* not included. Average yield is approx. 2·75 tonnes per hectare, value £12·50 to £55 per tonne according to region and season, variable cost (string) approximately £1·50 per tonne. In 1995, 96% of the area both of winter barley straw and of spring barley straw in England and Wales was baled; (later data are unavailable). Standing straw (sold for baling): anything from no value to £150/ha (£60/acre) according to crop, season and area of the country (local demand): average around £45/ha (£18/acre).

3. *Fertilizer* Costs on continuous barley will be approximately £15 higher. *Seed* includes 35 to 40% farm-saved; amounts vary around 180kg/ha according to soil, conditions etc.

4. *Sprays.* Amounts variable according to season, variety, policy, etc. Typical breakdown: herbicides 39%, fungicides 44%, growth regulators 13%, other 4%.

5. If *Contractor* employed, extra variable costs as shown for Winter Wheat (p. 12, note 8).

6. *Fuel and Repairs* (per hectare): grain £90. straw £32.

7. *Specialized Equipment Prices:* see pages 138-141.

8. *Labour:* see pages 120-122.

SPRING BARLEY

Production level	Low	Average	High
Yield: tonnes per ha (tons per acre)			
Feed	4·4 (1·75)	5·5 (2·2)	6·6 (2·65)
Malting	3·7 (1·45)	4·7 (1·85)	5·6 (2·25)

Price per tonne (Feed/Malting): £68/£81	£	£	£
Sale Value (Feed and Malting)	300 (122)	375 (152)	450 (182)
Area Payment	240 (97)	240 (97)	240 (97)

OUTPUT (Feed and Malting)	540 (219)	615 (249)	690 (279)

Variable Costs:	Feed	Malting
Seed	50 (20)	55 (22)
Fertilizer	62·5 (25·5)	52·5 (21·5)
Sprays	47·5 (19·5)	52·5 (21·5)

TOTAL VARIABLE COSTS	160 (65)	160 (65)

GROSS MARGIN per ha (acre)	380 (154)	455 (184)	530 (214)

Notes: As for Winter Barley above.

The UK percentage of winter barley has steadily risen, from 56% of the total barley area in 1993 to 62% in 1998. In 1997 and 1998 the percentage for England was nearly 80% and for England and Wales 75-77%; for Scotland and Northern Ireland it was just over 20%. Naturally the proportion of spring barley increases following a wet autumn. The relative profitability of spring versus winter crops were improved when flat area payments were introduced in 1993, in that the flat rate area payments per hectare mean a higher payment *per tonne* for lower yielding crops: this effect has been slightly augmented by the Agenda 2000 CAP reform changes (reduced price support but higher area payment).

WINTER OATS

Production level	Low	Average	High
Yield: tonnes per ha (tons per acre)	5·25 (2·1)	6·75 (2·7)	8·25 (3·3)

Price per tonne (Feed/Milling): £69/£72

Sale Value	£	£	£
Feed ...	360 (146)	465 (188)	570 (231)
Milling	380 (154)	485 (196)	595 (241)
Area Payment	240 (97)	240 (97)	240 (97)
OUTPUT Feed	600 (243)	705 (285)	810 (328)
OUTPUT Milling	620 (251)	725 (293)	835 (338)

Variable Costs:	
Seed ...	45 (18)
Fertilizer	60 (24·5)
Sprays	60 (24·5)
TOTAL VARIABLE COSTS	165 (67)

GROSS MARGIN per ha (acre)

	Low	Average	High
Feed ...	435 (176)	540 (218)	645 (261)
Milling	455 (184)	560 (226)	670 (271)

1. Prices. See Winter Wheat (page 12) for CAP support details. Prices are the assumed averages for the 2000 harvest crop, *i.e.* the whole 2000/2001 marketing year. Roughly half the UK oat crop goes for milling and half for feed. Conservation grade milling oats may obtain a premium of £10/tonne.
2. Straw is not included above. Average yield is 3·5 tonnes per hectare; value £10 to £50 per tonne according to region and season; variable costs (string) approximately £1·50 per tonne. In 1995, 73% of the area of oat straw in England and Wales was baled; (later data are unavailable).
3. If a *Contractor* is employed, extra variable costs will be as shown for Winter Wheat (p. 13, note 8).
4. *Fuel and Repairs* (per hectare): grain £85, straw £32.
5. *Labour:* see pages 120-122.

SPRING OATS

Production level	Low	Average	High
Yield: tonnes per ha (tons per acre)	4·0 (1·6)	5·0 (2·0)	6·25 (2·5)

Price per tonne (Feed/Milling): £69/£72

Sale Value	£	£	£
Feed ...	275 (112)	345 (140)	430 (174)
Milling	290 (118)	360 (146)	450 (182)
Area Payment	240 (97)	240 (97)	240 (97)
OUTPUT Feed ...	515 (209)	585 (237)	670 (271)
OUTPUT Milling	530 (215)	600 (243)	690 (279)

Variable Costs:	
Seed ...	60 (24)
Fertilizer	47·5 (19·5)
Sprays	47·5 (19·5)
TOTAL VARIABLE COSTS	155 (63)

GROSS MARGIN Per ha (acre)

	Low	Average	High
Feed ...	360 (146)	430 (174)	515 (208)
Milling	375 (152)	445 (180)	535 (216)

Notes: As for winter oats above.

N.B.—The proportion of winter oats in Great Britain was 75% of the total oats area in 1995 and 80% in 1996; the proportion increases from north to south: it was thus 90% and 92% in England and Wales in 1995 and 1996 respectively but 26% and 34% in Scotland. Oats now account for less than 3% of the total UK cereals area (98,200 ha were grown in 1998). The risk of lodging and thus difficult harvesting remains a drawback.

OILSEED RAPE

Winter Rape

Production level				Low	Average	High
Yield: tonnes per ha (tons per acre)			...	2·5 (1)	3·25 (1·3)	4·0 (1·6)
				£	£	£
Sale Value (£115/tonne)	...	...	...	290 (117)	375 (151)	460 (186)
Area Payment	...	...	...	335 (136)	335 (136)	335 (136)
OUTPUT	...	...	...	625 (253)	710 (287)	795 (322)
Variable Costs:						
Seed ...	...	...	...		32·5 (13)	
Fertilizer	...	...	...		92·5 (37·5)	
Sprays	...	...	...		110 (44·5)	
TOTAL VARIABLE COSTS	...	...			235 (95)	
GROSS MARGIN per ha (acre)		...	...	390 (158)	475 (192)	560 (227)

Spring Rape

Production level				Low	Average	High
Yield: tonnes per ha (tons per acre)			...	1·5 (0·6)	2·0 (0·8)	2·5 (1)
				£	£	£
Sale Value (£115/tonne)	...	...	...	175 (71)	230 (93)	290 (117)
Area Payment	...	...	...	335 (136)	335 (136)	335 (136)
OUTPUT	...	...	...	510 (207)	565 (229)	625 (253)
Variable Costs:						
Seed ...	...	...	...		35 (14)	
Fertilizer	...	...	...		57·5 (23·5)	
Sprays	...	...	...		52·5 (21·5)	
TOTAL VARIABLE COSTS	...	...			145 (59)	
GROSS MARGIN per ha (acre)		...	...	365 (148)	420 (170)	480 (194)

1. *Prices.* The price assumed for the 2000 crop, £115/tonne, is the average for the whole of the 2000/2001 marketing season, ranging from £105-110 at harvest to £120-125 at its peak. For the 1998 harvest crop prices were high, at £150 to £160 a tonne from August to September, but slumped after February 1999 to little over £100/tonne by harvest time that year.

   Area Payment. See pages 5 to 9 for the Agenda 2000 decisions, the assumptions made re the euro value and agrimonetary compensation and the payments consequently assumed for year 2000, disregarding any deductions. At the price level assumed no cut on the basis of world price levels would occur. There may be no cut because of overshooting of base areas as the area of oilseed rape grown is likely to fall, caused by the reductions made in "basic" area payments. The rounded figure for England has been used in the table above.

2. Winter crops are mainly sown between 10th August and 10th September (before the end of August if possible). Spring-sown crops are best sown between late March and mid-April. Winter crops normally are harvested between late July and mid-August, spring-sown crops in the first half of September. With spring-sown crops inputs are lower, pigeons are less trouble and the late summer/autumn workload is eased; however, the later harvesting tends to clash with the winter wheat harvest, there is less time to prepare the ground for, and drill, the following winter cereal crop, and spring droughts are a potential hazard to establishment; above all, yields average only 60% of those of winter rape; hence less than 10% of the total oilseed rape crop is spring-sown. The proportion of the total area sown with *hybrid winter rape* is increasing rapidly; the seed is more expensive but an average increase in yield of 0·5 tonnes/ha is claimed by its plant breeders.

3. *Seed.* Approximately 35% farm-saved.

4. *Sprays.* Variable with season, etc. Typically: herbicides 65%, fungicides 25%, insecticides 10%.

5. *Labour:* see page 128.

18

TURNIP RAPE

Spring-sown. Two-thirds is grown in Scotland, where it comprises two-thirds of the spring rape area. Average yields about 20% (0·4-0·5 tonne/ha) below spring swede rape, but substantially earlier to harvest, has fast early growth, giving good weed suppression; has good resistance to shedding. Savings in variable costs (seed, nitrogen and herbicides) of around £50/ha (£20/acre) and lower drying costs likely, but vulnerable to sclerotina and pollen beetle. Its advantages increase further north and in more extreme growing areas. Winter turnip rape now being tried: can be drilled up to ten days later than winter swede rape.

LINSEED

Production level	Low	Average	High
Yield: tonnes per ha (tons per acre): ...	1·0 (0·4)	1·4 (0·55)	1·8 (0·725)
	£	£	£
Sale Value (£100/tonne)	100 (40)	140 (56)	180 (73)
Area Payment...	365 (148)	365 (148)	365 (148)
OUTPUT	465 (188)	505 (204)	545 (221)
Variable Costs:			
Seed		75 (30·5)	
Fertilizer		32·5 (13)	
Sprays		62·5 (25·5)	
TOTAL VARIABLE COSTS		170 (69)	
GROSS MARGIN per ha (acre)	295 (119)	335 (135)	375 (152)

The *price* assumed, £100/tonne, is the average for the 2000 harvest crop, *i.e.* the whole of the 2000/2001 marketing season. Prices are very variable; they have varied from £110 to £165 in recent years.

Area payments. See pages 5 to 9 for the Agenda 2000 decisions, the assumptions made re the euro value and agrimonetary compensation and the payments consequentially assumed for the year 2000. The rounded figure for England has been used in the above table.

From 1,165 ha in 1984 the UK area increased to 150,000 ha (94% of the total EU linseed area) in 1993. A considerable reduction occurred afterwards, but a record high area was grown in 1999: around 200,000 ha.

Mainly spring-sown, drilling mid-March to mid-April (best mid-March to end March). Susceptible to frost. Should not be grown more than 1 year in 5. Care needed re level of nitrogen use: too much (over 75 kg/ha) can cause severe lodging, delayed maturity and excessive weed growth — and hence difficult harvesting, poor quality and lower yields; it should be applied early.

Harvesting: normally not before September and can even be after mid-October in a late season. Does not shed. Moisture content most likely 12-16%: must be dried to 9% for storage.

Winter Linseed

Big surge in plantings for the 1997 harvest: around 30,000 ha, but down to about 20,000 the following year. Still too early to generalise re yield compared with spring crops: may average around one-third higher (*i.e.* 2.0 tonnes/ha (0·8 t/acre)). However, crop losses a risk in a harsh winter, *e.g.* frost heave on lighter land; pigeons and rabbits can also be troublesome. Early sowing (early to mid-September) appears best, with higher seed rates; otherwise variable costs similar to spring. Earlier to harvest: mid-August the norm (but therefore clashes with cereals). Average gross margin (with same price, fertiliser and spray assumptions as for the spring crop): approximately £400/ha (£162/acre), *assuming no significant winter loss of crop*, but 1997 harvest crops were generally poor, some as low as 0·5 tonnes/ha, and 1998 crops disappointing.

Linola

Edible linseed: the oil contains more linoleic and less linolenic acid than conventional linseed, like sunflower oil. The area grown is increasing rapidly: first grown on any scale in 1996 (1,600 ha), approximately 12,000 ha in 1998. Spring-sown. Agronomy and yield similar to conventional linseed; good weed control essential. Price higher (based on oilseed rape price), same area payment; grown on contract. Harvest early-mid September.

With same yield and variable costs as conventional linseed and an oilseed rape price of £115/tonne, the average gross margin is £355/ha (£144/acre).

FLAX
(Cut for Industrial Fibre)

Production level					Low	Average	High
Seed							
Yield: tonnes per ha (tons per acre)				...	0·5 (0·2)	0·85 (0·34)	1.3 (0·52)
Price: £ per tonne [1]	...	...	...	...	130	130	130
Seed Output	...	...	...	...	65 (26)	110 (44)	170 (69)
Straw							
Yield: tonnes per ha (tons per acre)				...	1·0 (0·4)	1·5 (0·6)	3·0 (1·2)
Price: £ per tonne [2]	...	...	...	...	20	20	20
Straw Output	...	...	...	...	20 (8)	30 (12)	60 (24)
Area Payment [3]		...	...	...	535 (217)	535 (217)	535 (217)
TOTAL OUTPUT	...	...	...	...	620 (251)	675 (273)	765 (310)
Variable Costs:							
Seed	...	...	...	...	...	135 (55)	
Fertilizer	...	...	...	...	...	30 (12)	
Sprays	...	...	...	...	...	65 (26)	
TOTAL VARIABLE COSTS		...	...	...		230 (93)	
GROSS MARGIN per ha (acre)			...	...	390 (158)	445 (180)	535 (217)

(1) As for linseed

(2) Can be higher depending on quality

(3) Non de-seeded crop £465; (both figures approximate only).

Notes

Flax is the same species as linseed, but the straw is longer. Over the last 4 or 5 years fibre flax has been reintroduced into the UK, not as the traditional, pulled, long fibre variety used for linen textiles but as a cut, combinable crop producing shorter fibres for industrial uses. Most of the UK crop goes for paper. Five processing plants are now in operation. It is a non-food industrial crop attracting EU aid. Natural fibres are biodegradable and renewable and therefore a "green" alternative to synthetic fibres and plastic produced from fossil fuels. The area grown in the UK expanded from 200 ha in 1992 to 20,200 ha in 1996 but has since fallen back, to an estimated 15,500 ha in 1999. Fibre prices are at their lowest level for 20 years.

Advantages to the farmer: it can be grown on IACS eligible or ineligible land, with no set-aside requirement (but it cannot be grown on set-aside land), there is a large area payment, it uses existing farm machinery and equipment and is a good cereal break crop.

To obtain the full area payment a minimum straw yield is required. This was (in tonnes/ha) 1·5 in 1999 and is 2·0 in 2000 and 2·5 in 2001. This is the average straw yield of the area for which an aid application has been made (or the yields from the area of each owner or farmers' contract). It is the tonnage of straw removed from the field and ready for processing divided by the area. The seed yield may now be included, making these minimum yields much easier to achieve. Where the minimum yield is not achieved, the aid payable is reduced by 65%. EU member states may make allowances for below minimum yields due to exceptional weather conditions. Where the straw has been machine processed to some extent in the field, so improving the quality of straw but reducing its weight, this may also be taken into account. No subsidy will be paid until the crop has been processed.

The agronomy is similar to that of linseed but it is harvested earlier. It is spring-sown, suitable for most soil types although lighter soil is preferred. It is a low input crop but weed control is essential. It grows best in areas of high rainfall such as Wales and the South West.

Currently short fibre flax can only be grown under contract with a merchant/processor, using a recognised fibre flax variety. The grower must make a sowing declaration, give notification of harvest, make a harvest declaration, use a minimum cutting height of 10 cm (4 in), and leave the stubble uncultivated for a minimum of 20 days. He receives the subsidy through the merchant or processor. Contracts will not be accepted on land of high conservation value.

There are several harvesting options (described in the previous edition). Currently the preferred option is desiccation followed by combining. The straw is left to rett in the field and then baled. Retting takes 10-21 days, depending on weather conditions. The price paid for straw will reflect quality. The fibre content of a reasonable crop is 20-30%.

Researcher: Angela Edwards.

INDUSTRIAL OILSEED RAPE

Rape for non-food uses may be grown on set-aside land, provided a direct contract with a first *processor* (or collector) is obtained; since 1998, however, the contract has not needed to be signed before the crop is sown and there is now greater flexibility for amending contracts. The non-food product must be worth more than the total value of any food by-products. Only approved varieties may be grown, or high erucic rapeseed.

The full set-aside area payment is paid but no other EU payments can be claimed. If the rules concerning contracts are broken both the set-aside payment and area payments for other crops could be forfeited, and a further penalty imposed.

The first processor or collector has to lodge a security equal to 120% of the set-aside payments on the fields concerned; this is returned provided an equivalent quantity of raw material has been processed into the final end product in the contract. Area aid is only paid after delivery of the crop to the collector and the weight is declared to the Regional Service Centre. Payments are reduced and penalties are imposed if prescribed minimum yields are not achieved: these differ between regions and between winter and spring rape, averaging around 2·15 tonnes/ha for the former and 1·35 for the latter.

Two types of industrial rape are grown: high erucic acid (HEAR) and, mainly, double low, which is primarily spring-sown. The former usually has a lower yield, reckoned to be around 10% for winter-sown and up to 20% for spring-sown; the price is consequently higher: £150 or £160 a tonne contracts were being offered for the 1999 spring-sown crops in January, before the collapse in commercial oilseed rape prices.

The following are estimated gross margins for double low industrial rape for the 2000 harvest, given a price of £100/tonne and slightly lower variable costs (lower seed cost). The set-aside payment is a rounded figure for England, as given on page 8.

Production level				Winter-sown		Spring-sown	
				Average	High	Average	High
Yield (tonnes per ha (tons per acre))			...	3·25 (1·3)	4·0 (1·6)	2·0 (0·8)	2·5 (1)
				£	£	£	£
Sale Value (at £110/tonne)		...	...	325 (132)	400 (162)	200 (81)	250 (101)
Set-aside Payment ...		...	...	240 (97)	240 (97)	240 (97)	240 (97)
OUTPUT ...	...	...	...	565 (229)	640 (259)	440 (178)	490 (198)
VARIABLE COSTS	...	...	...	235 (95)	235 (95)	145 (59)	145 (59)
GROSS MARGIN per ha (acre)		...	...	330 (134)	405 (164)	295 (119)	345 (139)

The additional gross margin compared with set-aside should cover any additional fixed costs incurred on most farms, unless substantial fixed cost savings can be made by adhering to fallow set-aside; also, it is widely believed that subsequent crops benefit more from following oilseed rape than from following a (virtual) fallow.

The area of industrial rape is estimated to have increased four fold in 1999, to over 120,000 ha, owing to growers' fears concerning area payment penalties for commercial crops.

INDUSTRIAL LINSEED

Similar rules apply to those for industrial rape.

Production level ... ... Yield (tonnes per ha (cwt. per acre))...	Average 1·4 (0·55)	High 1·8 (0·725)
	£	£
Sale Value (at £90/tonne)	125 (51)	160 (65)
Set-aside Payment	240 (97)	240 (97)
OUTPUT	365 (148)	400 (162)
VARIABLE COSTS*	150 (61)	150 (61)
GROSS MARGIN per ha (acre)	215 (87)	250 (101)

*Seed £20/ha less than non-industrial linseed.

The price varies a little depending on the details of the contract, which must be signed before the crop is sown. Some contracts include seed supplied at a special price as well as the purchase price. It will be observed that on the assumptions made the average gross margin is less than the set-aside payment.

Acknowledgement. Tony Hardwick (consultant agronomist) gave considerable advice on industrial rape and linseed but the data is the author's sole responsibility.

FIELD BEANS

Winter Beans

Production level ... ... Yield: tonnes per ha (tons per acre) ...	Low 2·8 (1·1)	Average 3·5 (1·4)	High 4·2 (1·675)
	£	£	£
Sale Value (£75/tonne)	210 (85)	265 (107)	315 (127)
Area Payment	300 (121)	300 (121)	300 (121)
OUTPUT	510 (206)	565 (228)	615 (248)
Variable Costs: (3)			
Seed		50 (20·5)	
Fertilizer		12·5 (5)	
Sprays		72·5 (29·5)	
TOTAL VARIABLE COSTS		135 (55)	
GROSS MARGIN per ha (acre)	375 (151)	430 (173)	480 (193)

Notes

1. *Price.* The 2000 harvest (2000/2001 marketing year) price assumed is £75 per tonne. Tannin-free varieties usually fetch about £8 a tonne more but yield some 5% less. Beans for human consumption normally fetch a premium of around £12/tonne.

   Area Payment. See pages 5 to 9 for the Agenda 2000 decisions, the assumptions made re the euro value and agrimonetary compensation and the payments consequentially assumed for the year 2000. The rounded figure for England has been used in the above table.

2. *Physical input.* Seed: 225 kg per hectare, about 60% farm-saved; average cost is approximately £10 less if own seed is sown in alternate years. Fertilizer: 200 kg of no (or low) nitrogen compound where applied, but some crops receive no fertilizer.

3. *Labour:* see page 128.

Spring Beans

Production level	Low	Average	High
Yield: tonnes per ha (tons per acre) ...	2·6 (1·05)	3·2 (1·25)	3·8 (1·5)
	£	£	£
Sale Value (£75/tonne)	195 (79)	240 (97)	285 (115)
Area Payment	300 (121)	300 (121)	300 (121)
OUTPUT	495 (200)	540 (218)	585 (236)
Variable Costs:			
Seed		52·5	
Fertilizer		12·5 (5)	
Sprays		65	
TOTAL VARIABLE COSTS		130 (53)	
GROSS MARGIN per ha (acre)	365 (147)	410 (165)	455 (183)

Notes

1. *Price.* The (2000/2001) price assumed is £75 per tonne. Spring beans contain more protein than winter beans (except for tannin-free varieties), but large-scale compounders appear to make no distinction between them. For area payments see page 8.

Winter versus Spring Beans. It used to be assumed that the yield of winter beans was about 0·5 tonnes per hectare above spring beans *provided* a full crop was obtained, that is, where there was no exceptional damage from frost and birds and, in particular, where there was no severe attack of chocolate spot. Thus, whether the average yield over a period of years was higher or lower than spring beans depended mainly upon the incidence of attacks of chocolate spot, which can write off the crop completely. In drier parts of the Eastern Counties this may be only one year in six or eight but in south-eastern counties the frequency may be substantially higher. NIAB data have shown an average 8% yield advantage for winter over spring beans.

Other points in favour of spring beans are that: cold, wet seedbeds and winter kill can lead to poor establishment of winter beans; the yield difference between autumn- and spring-sown crops is less than for other crops, especially cereals; there is a longer "near-optimal" period during which they can be sown; and there have been substantial genetic improvements in recent years for spring beans but little for winter beans. However, spring beans are vulnerable to droughts in spring and early summer, especially on light land.

The relative area of winter and spring beans is largely determined by the autumn rainfall and recent comparative yields. Currently about two-thirds are winter beans.

DRIED PEAS

Production level	Low	Average	High
Yield: tonnes per ha (tons per acre) ...	3·0 (1·2)	3·8 (1·5)	4·6 (1·85)
	£	£	£
Sale Value (£75/tonne)	225 (91)	285 (115)	345 (139)
Area Payment	300 (121)	300 (121)	300 (121)
OUTPUT *(feed)*	525 (212)	585 (236)	645 (260)
Variable Costs:			
Seed		80 (32·5)	
Fertilizer		12·5 (5)	
Sprays		97·5 (39·5)	
TOTAL VARIABLE COSTS		190 (77)	
GROSS MARGIN per ha (acre)	335 (135)	395 (159)	455 (183)

Notes

1. Dried peas are combine harvested and include peas (especially marrowfats) for human consumption (after processing) and protein peas, for animal feed. About 75% of the crop goes for feed compounding.

2. *Price.* The 2000 harvest year (2000/2001 marketing year) price assumed above (which is for feed peas) is £75 per tonne. Feed peas sold on the open market are subject to wide price variations, particularly as poor samples can fetch very low prices. The price for peas for processing (*e.g.*, marrowfats for canning) for *human consumption* obtain a premium of generally £25 to £50/tonne according to quality (size and colour) and the percentage of wastage, but marrowfat yields are generally 5 to 10% lower than feed varieties; most peas for human consumption are grown on contract. The premium for peas for the pigeon trade is usually around £10/tonne.

   The *area payments* are as for field beans (page 8).

3. *Physical Inputs.* Seed: 200 to 250 kg, about 40% farm-saved. Fertilizer: 250 kg of no nitrogen compound where applied, but some crops receive no fertilizer.

4. *Harvesting* (normally in late July — early August) can be a difficult operation. Most crops are direct combined, although there is a high risk of loss and poor quality, as well as heavy wear and tear on the combine. Drying and handling the crop can be very difficult, much care being needed. Sometimes the crop is desiccated before direct combining, using diquat, to even out maturity and kill green weeds.

5. *Winter Peas:* increasing interest, with new, more frost-resistant, French varieties. About 5,000 ha sown in UK for the 1998 harvest. Earlier to harvest (by 10 to 14 days) and potentially advantageous on droughty soils, but at risk in a severe winter, and disease, weeds and pigeons more of a problem than with spring-sown crops. Average yields may just exceed those of spring crops but inconsistent results to date have led to a small reduction in the area sown.

6. *Labour:* see page 127.

7. *Peas versus Beans* (for feed). *On average,* yields of peas are slightly above those for beans nationally. Peas are normally spring-sown (winter peas are beginning to be tried) and spring beans are easier to manage than peas. Peas are unsuited to heavier soils and are more vulnerable if the weather is wet during flowering and harvest. They are more sensitive to soil compaction and waterlogging. Their yields are thus more variable than for beans. Their seed costs are also much higher. On the other hand, peas for human consumption fetch higher prices than beans and the same used to be true of feed peas also; however the average price for feed beans has exceeded that for feed peas for three of the last four harvest crops. Peas are less sensitive to drought and are normally ready to harvest well before spring beans. From 1990 to 1994 the UK area of beans was more than double that of peas, but after 1994 the area of beans fell sharply, following poor yields, whereas that of peas remained very stable, until rising significantly in 1997. In 1998 the area of field beans in England was 10% above that of dried peas, which was 100,000 ha.

VINING PEAS

Production level					Low £	Average £	High £
OUTPUT (1)	...	...	...	...	875 (354)	1015 (411)	1150 (465)
Variable Costs:							
Seed (1) ...	...	...	...	...		165 (67)	
Fertilizer (2)	...	...	...	...		10 (4)	
Sprays (3) ...	...	...	...	...		75 (30)	
TOTAL VARIABLE COSTS		...	...	...		250 (101)	
GROSS MARGIN per ha (per acre)	...		...		625 (253)	765 (310)	900 (364)

24

1. The table overleaf relates to vining peas grown for Bird's Eye. As the peas are of particularly high quality ("150 minute peas": the maximum time between harvest and freezing) the growers must be within 40 miles of the factory. The price paid is above that paid to other growers, but the yield is lower. Average yield is approximately 4·5 tonnes/ha (1·8/acre) and average price approximately £225/tonne. Harvesting (approximately £55/tonne) and transport (averaging around £25/tonne but varying with distance) are paid for by Bird's Eye, which also subsidises the seed. A pea viner costs nearly £300,000.

   Other growers produce peas of an average lower quality and can be grown further from the factory ("long haul peas"). The yield is higher (averaging just under 6 tonnes/ha [2·4/acre]) but the overall price is lower, allowing for the fact that there is no additional payment for harvesting or transport. The seed is unsubsidised and averages around £185/ha (£75/acre).

   For *petits pois* (Bird's Eye) the average yield is nearly 25% lower as a rule (but was in fact slightly higher in 1998) but the price is 15 to 25% higher.
2. *Fertilizer:* many growers use no fertilizer; it is more often used on light land.
3. *Sprays:* both herbicide and aphicides. There are large seasonal variations according to weather conditions and the need for midge control: average spray costs exceeded £100/ha in 1998.
4. *Labour:* see page 127.
5. Around 40,000 ha are grown in the UK annually.

Acknowledgements. Arthur Fisk, Bird's Eye.

Note:
   For full details (yields, prices, variable costs) of *actual* average past Cash Crop Gross Margins in different parts of the country, see the following annual reports: **Report on Farming in The Eastern Counties of England: University of Cambridge, Agricultural Economics Unit, Department of Land Economy.**
   An Economic Review of Farming in the North West: University of Manchester, Farm Business Unit, School of Economic Studies.
   Farm Management Handbook: University of Exeter, Agricultural Economics Unit.
   (Full addresses on page 238).

MAINCROP POTATOES

		Low	Average	High
Production level	...	Low	Average	High
Yield: tonnes per ha (tons per acre)	...	32·5 (13)	42·5 (17)	52·5 (21)
		£	£	£
OUTPUT	...	2275 (920)	2975 (1205)	3675 (1490)
Variable Costs:				
Seed	...		575 (233)	
Fertilizer	...		200 (81)	
Sprays	...		425 (172)	
Casual Labour for harvesting and grading (3)	...		375 (152)	
Sundries (levy, sacks, etc.)	...	325 (132)	375 (152)	425 (172)
TOTAL VARIABLE COSTS	...	1900 (770)	1950 (790)	2000 (810)
GROSS MARGIN per hectare (acre) ...	...	375 (150)	1025 (415)	1675 (680)

Notes
1. *Prices.* The price assumed above is £75 per tonne for ware and £12·50 for stockfeed (assumed to be 7½ per cent), which is approximately £70 per tonne for the whole crop. The *actual price* in any one season will depend mainly on the national average yield. The five-year *average* GB price for maincrops between 1993/94 and 1997/98 was £103 per tonne (£113 in 2000 money values) but the average annual price varied from £66 to £157 per tonne. The average price for the 1994 and 1995 crops were very high; that for the 1996 crop was very low and for the 1997 crop only a little better; that for the 1998 crop was quite high; that for the 1999 crop looks like being very low.

The average seasonal monthly price indices between 1993/94 and 1997/98 (with each annual price = 100) were as follows: July 103, August 87, September 81, October 81, November 86, December 95, January 102, February 107, March 116, April 129, May 141, June 165. The variation between years is considerable, particularly at the beginning and end of the season.

2. *Physical Inputs.* Seed: 80% planted with certified seed: 2·8 tonnes per hectare at £225-230 per tonne (the price varies widely from season to season); 20% with once-grown seed: 2·4 tonnes per hectare at £140 per tonne. Sprays: herbicide, blight control, and haulm destruction.

3. *Casual Labour.* The figure in the table above is for assistance during harvesting (£100/ha; machine harvesting is assumed) and for grading/riddling (£275/ha); it is assumed that half the labour for the latter is supplied by casuals, half by regulars. Other jobs for which casual labour may be employed are:

Planting:	£110 per hectare
Picking by hand:	£520 per hectare
Grading/Riddling (all):	£520 per hectare (£12·25 per tonne).

4. *Contract mechanical harvesting:* approximately £275/hectare (excl. carting, etc.). Other contract work see page 144.

5. *British Potato Council levy:* £35/ha (£14/acre) for growers, 20p a tonne for first buyers.

6. *Sacks.* Approx. £7·50 per tonne.

7. *Chitting.* Additional annual cost of chitting is approximately £45 per tonne of seed, or £125 per hectare, including depreciation and interest on the chitting house.

8. *Fuel and Repairs (per hectare):* £180.

9. *Specialised Equipment Prices:* see page 141.

10. *Potato Store Costs:* see page 173.

11. *Labour:* see page 124.

In 1998, the percentages of the total potato area in Great Britain planted in maincrop, second early and first early varieties respectively were 65·1, 27·0 and 7·9; in England: 65·5, 26·6 and 7·9; in Scotland: 67·5, 27·4 and 5·1; in Wales: 20·5, 38·9 and 40·6. 19% of the total GB potato area was in Scotland.

EARLY POTATOES

Production level					Low	Average	High
Yield: tonnes per ha (tons per acre):				...	17·5 (7)	22·5 (9)	27·5 (11)
					£	£	£
OUTPUT	...	...	...	...	2500 (1010)	3250 (1315)	4000 (1615)
Variable Costs:							
Seed	...	...	...	...		800 (323)	
Fertilizer	...	...	...	...		165 (66)	
Sprays	...	...	...	...		200 (81)	
Casual labour	...	...	...	...		180 (72)	
Sundries	...	...	...	...		205 (83)	
TOTAL VARIABLE COSTS	...	...	...			1550 (625)	
GROSS MARGIN per ha (acre)		...	...		950 (385)	1700 (690)	2450 (990)

Notes

1. *Prices and Yields.* The price assumed above is an average of £145 per tonne. However, yields increase and prices fall as the season progresses. Thus both depend on the date of lifting, *e.g.* late May to early June, 7 to 12 tonnes per hectare; July, 20 to 30 tonnes per hectare. Prices in late May to mid June are typically three times those in July; the very earliest crops (early May) can even fetch more than £1,000 per tonne, but the price could be down to £500 by mid May and to £250 or even £200 by the end of May. Thus the average output of £3500 given above could also be obtained from 10 tonnes at £325 per tonne, 15 at £217, 20 at £162·50 or 30 at £108.

2. *Casual labour* for planting: £115 per hectare.

3. *Chitting.* See Maincrop Potatoes.

4. *Fuel and Repairs (£ per hectare):* £150.

5. *Labour:* see page 125.

SECOND EARLY POTATOES

Output (average): 40 tonnes/ha (16 tons/acre) @ £65/tonne = £2600 (1050) (lifting July to early September).

Variable Costs: Seed £575 (233), fertilizer £190 (77), sprays £275 (111), casual labour £330 (134), miscellaneous £345 (140); total £1715 (695).

Gross Margin: £885 (355).

Labour: see page 000.

SUGAR BEET

Production level	Low	Average	High
Yield: tonnes per ha (tons per acre)*	40 (16)	52·5 (21)	65 (26)
	£	£	£
OUTPUT	1265 (512)	1660 (672)	2055 (832)
Variable Costs:			
Seed		125 (50)	
Fertilizer		120 (49)	
Sprays		155 (63)	
Transport (Contract)	170 (69)	220 (89)	270 (109)
TOTAL VARIABLE COSTS	570 (231)	620 (251)	670 (271)
GROSS MARGIN per ha (acre)	695 (281)	1040 (421)	1385 (561)

"Adjusted tonnes" at standard 16% sugar content (MAFF)

Notes
1. *Prices.* The "all beet" price for the 2000 crop is assumed to be £35 per clean tonne at the UK 5-year average sugar content of 17·2%; (£31·60 per adjusted tonne of 16%). This consists of £36·17 for A/B contract beet, £8·93 for C beet (net of transport allowance and bonuses) and assumes 82% A/B and 18% C beet (a 1999 estimate); the average transport allowance is £3·30 per clean tonne and 45p/tonne is added for early/late delivery bonuses. All these figures are reduced by approximately 9·75% to give 16·0% adjusted tonne figures.

   The price is varied by 0·9 per cent (1 per cent below 15 per cent sugar content) of the contract price for each 0·1 per cent difference in sugar content.

   In addition, early and late delivery allowances are paid as follows (all dates approximate only). Early delivery: 18% is added to the basic price if crops are delivered on September 15th; this reduces by one percentage point per day till October 10th, when just the basic price is paid. Late delivery: 26th December — 7th January: 0·8% of UK minimum price; thereafter, the rate rises by 0·2% per day.
2. *Effect of Harvesting Date.* As the season progresses, changes occur in the crop before lifting, approximately as follows, on average:

	early Sept. to early Oct.	early Oct. to early Nov.	early Nov. to early Dec.	early Dec. to early Jan.
Yield (tonnes of washed beet per hectare)	up 3·75	up 1·9	up 1·25	up 1·25
Sugar Content (%)	up 1%	up ¼%	down ¼%	down ¾%
Yield of Sugar (kg per hectare)	up 1000	up 375	up 190	down 60

3. *Sprays.* Herbicides normally comprise between 85% and 92·5% of the total cost of spray materials.
4. *Contract* Contract mechanical harvesting costs approx. £155 per hectare excluding carting or £190 per hectare including carting.
5. *Transport.* Contract haulage charges vary widely according to distance from the factory. The figure assumed above is approximately £4 per (unadjusted) tonne of unwashed beet including loading and cleaning (dirt and top tare assumed at 14% in total).
6. *Fuel and Repairs* (per hectare): £160.
7. *Specialized Equipment Prices:* see page 141.
8. *Labour:* see page 126.

HERBAGE SEEDS

		Italian Ryegrass		Early Perennial Ryegrass	
		Average	High	Average	High
Yield (tonnes/ha)	... ...	1·15	1·55	1·2	1·6
Price per 50 kg (£)*	... ...	28		28	
Aid per 50 kg (£)	... ...	7·65		11·25	
OUTPUT		820	1105	940	1255
Variable Costs:					
Seed		70		50	
Fertilizer		75		75	
Sprays		55		55	
Cleaning, etc.		160	215	165	220
TOTAL VARIABLE COSTS		360	415	345	400
GROSS MARGIN per ha		460	690	595	855
GROSS MARGIN per acre... ...		185	280	240	345

		Intermediate Perennial Ryegrass		Late Perennial Ryegrass	
		Average	High	Average	High
Yield (tonnes/ha)	... ...	1·25	1·65	1·1	1·45
Price per 50 kg (£)*	... ...	30		35	
Aid per 50 kg (£)	... ...	11·25		11·25	
OUTPUT		1030	1360	1020	1340
Variable Costs:					
Seed		50		50	
Fertilizer		75		75	
Sprays		55		55	
Cleaning, etc.		170	225	150	200
TOTAL VARIABLE COSTS		350	405	330	380
GROSS MARGIN per ha		680	955	690	960
GROSS MARGIN per acre... ...		275	385	280	390

Prices fell to a very low level in 1999 (only around £16 per 50kg for early and intermediate perennial ryegrass). Prices were high in 1996 and 1997 (e.g. nearly £40 for the same two ryegrasses) and low in 1994 and 1995 — though not nearly as low as in 1999. The prices used in these tables are approximate averages for the last six years, including 1999.

| | | Hybrid Ryegrass | | Kent Wild White Clover & Kent Indig. Perennial Ryegrass | |
		Average	High	Average	High
Yield (tonnes/ha)	... ...	1·15	1·55	0·08(C); 0·5(R)	0·11(C); 0·7(R)
Price per 50 kg (£)	... ...	30		225(C); 30(R)	
Aid per 50 kg (£)	... ...	7·65		27·25(C); 11·25(R)	
OUTPUT		865	1165	815	1130
Variable Costs:					
Seed		70		40	
Fertilizer		75		35	
Sprays		55		35	
Cleaning, etc.		160	215	105	140
TOTAL VARIABLE COSTS		360	415	215	250
GROSS MARGIN per ha		505	750	600	880
GROSS MARGIN per acre... ...		205	305	245	355

Notes

1. The following were the number of hectares entered for certified seed production for the main grasses and clovers in the UK for the 1999 harvest:

Italian Ryegrass	1,085	Cocksfoot	127
Early Perennial Ryegrass ...	330	Timothy	36
Inter. Perennial Ryegrass ...	1,928	Red Fescue	410
Late Perennial Ryegrass ...	2,632	Meadow Fescue	6
Amenity Perennial Ryegrass	1,310	White Clover	25
Hybrid Ryegrass	930	Red Clover	44
Westerwold Ryegrass ...	47	Vetch	50

The ryegrasses total 8,262 ha (20,415 acres)
All herbage seeds total 8,963 ha (22,148 acres)

2. Average *yields* are approximate NIAB recorded averages for cleaned certified seed. The crop is very risky, *i.e.* yields are highly variable, depending especially on the weather at, and precise timeliness of, harvesting. A considerable amount of skill is necessary to attain the "high" levels. Most grasses give their highest yield in their first harvest year, assuming good establishment.

3. *Prices* in the table are estimated prices for certified seed. The actual prices received in any one year are very uncertain (see footnote on page 28). Diploid prices are above tetraploid prices, but yields of diploid are usually lower. The *aid rates* are approximate levels for 2000/2001.

4. No allowance has been made above for by-products. Some crops produce 4 to 5 tonnes of threshed hay, which is, however, of low feeding value. This could be worth £200 or more per hectare. Some grasses, especially spring-sown ryegrass, also provide sub-stantial quantities of autumn and winter grazing. Clovers can be either grazed or cut for hay or silage and do not have to be "shut up" until mid or late May, or, in some cases and seasons, even early June. More grazing (until end of May) and better quality threshed hay is provided with a combination of ryegrass and white clover than with the specialist herbage seed grasses.

5. If the seed crop is to be undersown, specialist growers often reduce the seed rate for the cover crop by up to half and restrict nitrogen dressing: the cereal yield may thus be reduced by up to 0·6 tonnes per hectare. If this is not done the grass seed yield is usually lower in the first year compared with direct drilling, except for ryegrass.

6. *Labour:* see page 129.

Acknowledgement: The basic data for this crop have been provided by D. I. White, Head of Fodder and Oilseeds Section, NIAB, but the price, variable costs and gross margin assumptions and calculations are solely the author's responsibility.

RYE

Production level	Low	Average	High
Yield: tonnes per ha (tons per acre):	4·5 (1·8)	5·75 (2·3)	7·0 (2·8)
	£	£	£
Sale Value (£80/tonne)	360 (146)	460 (186)	560 (227)
Area Payment...	240 (97)	240 (97)	240 (97)
OUTPUT: (Contract price)	600 (243)	700 (283)	800 (324)
Variable Costs:			
Seed		65 (26·5)	
Fertilizer		55 (22)	
Sprays		75 (30·5)	
TOTAL VARIABLE COSTS		195 (79)	
GROSS MARGIN per ha (acre):	405 (164)	505 (204)	605 (245)

Largely grown on light, infertile, sandy or stony soils, where yields are poor for other cereals. Yields would clearly be higher on better soils, but then rye has difficulty in competing with wheat and barley; it could never do so on good wheat land. The average yield in England and Wales in the five years 1994 to 1998 has been 5·6 tonnes/ha (MAFF).

The UK area grown has steadily risen from 5,700 ha in 1993 to 9,700 ha in 1998, mainly in the south, south-east and East Anglia. Rye crispbread is a major outlet. It is also milled into flour, used in mixed-grain bread and muesli. Increasing concern with dieting means that demand is increasing. About two-thirds of UK requirements are imported, mainly from Canada (which produces the highest quality), Denmark, Germany and Spain.

The price assumed above (£80 a tonne) is an estimated 2000 price at harvest for milling. Deductions are made for low quality, particularly if it is only of feed grade (between feed wheat and feed barley price). Only a small percentage of the crop is grown for the free market, which is risky. The area payment is as estimated for England (see page 8).

Rye, which is autumn-sown, is drought tolerant and very hardy, can withstand low temperatures and starts growing early in the spring. It has all-round resistance to wheat and barley diseases, e.g. eyespot, and suffers less from take-all than wheat — hence it is a possible replacement for third or fourth wheat. Its vigour keeps weeds down. Its herbicide, fungicide and fertilizer requirements are lower than for other cereals. Harvested earlier than winter wheat (useful for following with oilseed rape).

Drawbacks: it sprouts in a wet harvest: must thus harvest early, at relatively high moisture content. It grows very tall and lodges easily: hence high levels of nitrogen are not possible; but growth regulators help. Its heavy straw crop means very slow combining (takes about twice as long per hectare as wheat and barley), and difficult straw incorporation. New hybrid varieties, with shorter, stiffer straw, are being developed; these would improve the comparative profitability of rye on better soils.

Drilling: 2nd and 3rd weeks September.

Harvesting: by mid-August (at relatively high moisture content, then dry to 14-15%).

TRITICALE

Production level				Low	Average	High
Yield: tonnes per ha (tons per acre):			...	4·75 (1·9)	6·0 (2·4)	7·25 (2·9)
				£	£	£
Sale Value (£67/tonne)	...	...	...	320 (130)	400 (162)	485 (196)
Area Payment	...	...	...	240 (97)	240 (97)	240 (97)
OUTPUT	...	...	...	560 (227)	640 (259)	725 (293)
Variable Costs:						
Seed	...	...	...		55 (22·5)	
Fertilizer	...	...	...		60 (24·5)	
Sprays	...	...	...		50 (20)	
TOTAL VARIABLE COSTS	...	...			165 (67)	
GROSS MARGIN per ha (acre)		...	...	395 (160)	475 (192)	560 (226)

A "man-made" cross between rye and hard wheat. Combines the hardiness of rye and the marketability of feed wheat. The main use is in pig and poultry rations: it contains a superior quality of protein. Nearly 9,000 ha were grown in England and Wales in 1998: nearly a 50% increase over the area in 1996 and 1997. In Germany the triticale area more than quadrupled after 1991 to over 600,000 ha in 1998 and the area in France now exceeds 200,000 ha.

The *price* of late has been some way below that of feed wheat and the average throughout the 2000/2001 season is taken to be £67 per tonne. The area payment is as estimated for England (see page 8).

Its main scope to date has been on light land, especially thin, drought-prone, poorish, marginal cereal-growing soils, where it frequently outyields wheat or barley, especially the former, and it has lower input requirements. Its yields tend to be more consistent on such soil than those of barley. It tends to do well compared with second and subsequent wheats owing to its resistance to drought and fungal diseases. Given that it is mainly grown on poorer soils the average yield in England and Wales of 5·9 tonnes/ ha in the five years 1994 to 1998 (MAFF) is commendable.

Lower levels of fungicide are needed because of its good disease resistance, except for ergot, but including take-all (making it a possible replacement for a third or fourth wheat, as indicated above). It is a tall crop, which helps to suppress weeds, but it is susceptible to lodging; growth regulators are beneficial. New semi-dwarf varieties are being developed, to overcome straw strength weakness and susceptibility to rust infections.

The crop is best drilled early (September) on very light, drought-prone soils; otherwise October is satisfactory.

Harvesting is at approximately the same time as wheat. There is more straw, which slows combining, and incorporation is very difficult; this is less of a problem on poor soils as there is less straw.

NAKED OATS

Production level	Low	Average	High
Yield: tonnes per ha (tons per acre):	3·5 (1·4)	4·75 (1·9)	6·0 (2·4)
	£	£	£
Sale Value (£110/tonne)	385 (156)	525 (213)	660 (267)
Area Payment	240 (97)	240 (97)	240 (97)
OUTPUT	625 (253)	765 (310)	900 (364)
Variable Costs:			
Seed		60 (24·5)	
Fertilizer		50 (20)	
Sprays		60 (24·5)	
TOTAL VARIABLE COSTS		170 (69)	
GROSS MARGIN per ha (acre)	455 (184)	595 (241)	730 (295)

Naked oats have a higher protein, energy and oil content than "traditional" oats, but the fibre content is lower—as the husk falls off during harvesting. Because of the high oil content it can go rancid if stored too moist, hence contracts require a maximum moisture content of 14% and 12% is recommended for long-term storage. The crop needs priority treatment at harvest.

Between 6,000 and 8,000 ha are grown in the UK at present and the area is steadily increasing. The traditional markets such as for racehorses and dog foods are increasing and the bird food market has been developed, but at least half the crop is now sold for human consumption: for health foods, fancy breads and breakfast cereals.

The (2000/2001) price assumed is £110 per tonne. Contracts offering premiums between 30% and 75% above the average feed wheat/feed barley price, according to husk content, are normally available. One company has offered a single fixed premium of 50% and a no screenings clause. The area payment is as estimated for England (see page 8).

About 85% of the crop is winter sown. NIAB suggests that yields average 25 to 30% less than conventional oats, but survey data over several years is as yet unavailable. Like other oats, the variable inputs are lower than for wheat or barley and the crop provides a break in the take-all cycle.

Naked barley, suitable for roasting, flaking or milling as pearl barley, is getting increasingly in the news. In 1997 it was available on buy-back contracts with a £30/tonne premium over feed grains. Both winter and spring varieties are available. The crop is grown like normal barley, but yields are expected to be some 15% lower.

DURUM WHEAT

		Low	Average	High
Production level		Low	Average	High
Yield: tonnes per ha (tons per acre):	...	3·00 (1·2)	4·00 (1·6)	5·00 (2·0)
		£	£	£
Sale Value (£90/tonne)		270 (109)	360 (145)	450 (182)
Area Payment (including supplementary aid) ...		340 (138)	340 (138)	340 (138)
OUTPUT		610 (247)	700 (283)	790 (320)
Variable Costs:				
Seed			80 (32)	
Fertilizer			65 (26·5)	
Sprays			65 (26·5)	
TOTAL VARIABLE COSTS			210 (85)	
GROSS MARGIN per ha (acre) ...		400 (162)	490 (198)	580 (235)

N.B. Extra drying costs estimated at £8 per tonne.

A Mediterranean crop. Used for pasta, semolina (if high quality) and breakfast cereals. Must be grown under contract. The UK demand is relatively small (60,000 tonnes a year); UK consumption per head is approx. 4% that of Italy and 10% that of France. It started to be grown in England in the late 1970s and built up to 11,000 ha (27,000 acres) in 1984. A series of years of poor yields reduced this to a few hundred hectares by the mid-1990s. In 1992 targeted aid was introduced for traditional producing Mediterranean EU countries and a few others, but not England, where durum had only the same intervention price as common wheat, though the yield was much lower.

After more than five years of campaigning, helped by the increasing consumption of pasta causing higher EU imports, a supplementary aid has been granted to the UK, starting with the 1999 harvest. This is 138·9 euros/ha (*i.e.* £97/ha at 70p/euro including agrimonetary compensation), which is additional to the normal cereals area payment, but is limited to 5,000 ha (12,355 acres); if more than this is grown the 5,000 ha total aid will be spread over the total area, *i.e.* the aid per ha will fall *pro rata*. It must be grown on AAPS eligible land, with proof that a minimum amount of eligible certified seed has been sown. MAFF has to designate eligible areas; these will probably be restricted to southern England.

Yields well above the average given above are often quoted (typically 75% of conventional feed wheat), but the 5-year average yield in Cambridge University's Farm Business Survey in 1988-92 was only 3·55 tonnes/ha, despite averaging 4·83 in the 1992 harvest. Possibly it has been mainly grown on dry, poorish soils.

The (1999 harvest) *price* assumed is £90 per tonne, *i.e.* approximately £20/tonne over feed wheat. Contract prices vary according to quality. The area payment is as estimated for England and the supplement assumes that no more than 5,000 ha are grown.

As with milling wheat, there is a risk of rejection if contaminated with excess foreign seeds, especially self-set cereals from previous crop; thus safer as a first cereal crop. A poor price is obtained (no EU subsidy) if quality is too poor for pasta and thus has to go for feed.

The crop is likely to be grown only in the driest parts of the east/south east, where it can best compete with second and third wheats. It is now mainly (approx. 90%) sown in the spring (March) compared with in the autumn (October) less than 10 years ago. The crop is very sensitive to stress and frost-kill in severe winters; the spring-sown crop is more reliable, and cheaper to grow. The crop has a higher disease resistance than other wheats, except for eyespot and ergot.

Harvest: spring crop usually mid-August. Critical operation: need to harvest as soon as reaches 20% moisture content, or at most 18%: crop very prone to sprouting and quality for semolina reduced if harvest delayed. Must be dried (slowly) to 15%: easier and quicker to dry than normal wheat. The straw is of poorer quality than wheat straw.

MINORITY CROPS

The following crops have limited possibilities at present, if indeed they can be grown successfully at all, but such factors as the breeding of new varieties could alter the position in the future. Some can be grown, but there is a very limited market, *e.g.*, borage.

Borage

Indigenous to Britain (or at least here since Roman times); grown wild and cultivated for centuries. Produced principally for use as a dietary supplement but it may be used in the pharmaceutical industry. The oil has a high gamma linolenic acid (GLA) content — more than twice that of evening primrose. It was first grown as a field crop in the UK in 1983 but demand fell after 1986 owing to over-production of GLA from non-contract crops of evening primrose in other countries. The area grown in the UK is now expanding and is currently around 1,800 ha. It is mainly cultivated in Suffolk, Essex and Yorkshire.

Compared with evening primrose it has the advantages of spring sowing (ideally mid-April), bigger seeds, faster growth and earlier harvesting (mid-August). Its aggressive growth gives good weed control with a high plant density. Low rainfall areas are preferred due to harvesting difficulties in wet conditions. There are no significant pests and diseases, except for powdery mildew. It is combinable, after swathing. Harvesting can be difficult and seed shedding at maturity is a problem. There is no area aid. If the crop is grown for the pharmaceutical industry it may be grown on set-aside but most is destined for food supplements and so cannot. It is highly advisable for a grower to have a contract, as there is virtually no "market" for the crop. Borage is a crop best suited to meticulous farmers prepared to invest some time on the crop.

Yields: from virtually nothing to 0·75 tonnes/ha (6 cwt./acre); average 0·4 (3·2).

Price: Around £2,100 a tonne. Output at assumed average yield, £840/ha (340/acre).

Variable costs (approximately) (£ per ha [acre]): seed 140 (55); fertilizer 50 (20); sprays 25 (10); total £215 (85).

Gross margin: £625/ha (255/acre).

Evening Primrose

Common as a wild flower and garden plant as well as a crop. The seed oil is a good source of essential fatty acids, especially gamma linolenic acid (GLA), which has a wide range of medicinal uses from food supplements to pharmaceuticals. At one time it was suggested that there were 1,000 ha in the UK but the area is currently only 170 ha. Owing to its perceived value to the pharmaceutical industry it was hoped that a strategic argument could be made for growing part of the UK supply at home, possibly using set-aside land, replacing some of the imports being produced using a great deal of hand labour but still very competitively priced. The initiative is no longer being pursued.

It is cultivated in relatively small areas, usually 2-5 ha with 10 ha being the maximum. A wide range of soils are suitable but not acid, high pH or fen. Good drainage is necessary. The crop can be spring sown, in March or April, for harvesting in early to mid-October. This is now the preferred option, although it may give rise to problems with late and unreliable germination and establishment and late and difficult harvest. Alternatively it can be sown in mid-August for harvesting in September/October of the following year, but septoria and botrytis can cause winter kill. Germination and establishment are difficult; seedbed preparation and consolidation are important; the seed is tiny and should be surface sown. Little if any fertilizer is needed unless the soil is very poor. Weed control can be a major problem but control regimes are possible. There are no significant pest or disease problems of the established crop. Uneven ripening and pod shedding can be a problem but non-shedding varieties have been developed. The crop is swathed rather than desiccated. Ideally it should lie in the swath 2-3 weeks but harvest is usually too late to allow it. With shedding varieties cutting time is critical and they should lie in the swath for the minimum time. Combining must be slow to avoid shattering the pods prematurely; seeds need to be dried quickly to 10-12% moisture.

This is a high risk crop which should be grown only on contract. There is no area payment. As for borage, this crop is best suited to meticulous farmers.

Yields: Nothing to 1·0 tonnes/ha (0 to 8 cwt./acre); average 0·7 (5·5).

Price: approx. £1,700 a tonne. Output at assumed average yield, £1,200/ha (£485/acre).

Variable costs (approximately) (£ per ha [acre]): seed 30 (12), fertilizer 50 (20), sprays 100 (40); cleaning 70 (28); total £250 (100).

Gross margin: £950/ha (385/acre).

Hemp (Cannabis)

Now approved for growing in UK for industrial purposes, under licence (costing £300 in 1999, rising to £320 by the year 2000) obtained from the Home Office. Production in the UK is co-ordinated by Hemcore of Essex, which processed about 2,400 ha in 1998 and expects 2,000 ha in 1999 from about 80 growers. The reduction in area is probably a result of new regulations similar to those for flax, stipulating that a contract is essential and the grower receives no subsidy until the fibre is processed and a minimum yield of 2·5 tonne/ha achieved (rising to 3t/ha in 2000).

Hemp can be grown on IACS or non-IACS land and attracts the full area aid of £500/ha. On set-aside land it gets only the set-aside payment.

It is drilled in late April/early May and grows 3 to 3·5m (10-12 feet) tall. Average yields are around 5 tonnes/ha (2t/acre), target yields are 7·5t/ha (3t/acre). The price of the crop ranges from £48 to £70/tonne delivered, the difference depending on *when* the crop is delivered. Because Hemcore requires a year-round supply increments are paid to farmers for storing the crop.

	£/ha	(£/acre)
Output: Yield 5t/ha, Price £55/t	275	(111)
Area Payment (approx.)	500	(202)
Total	775	(313)
Variable costs approx:		
Seed	175	(71)
Fertilizer	50	(20)
Sprays	nil	(-)
Contract swathing and baling	130	(52)
Haulage to factory	50-70 (10/tonne)	(20-30)
Total:	415	(168)
Gross margin:	360	(145)

Outlook said to be good, with new markets being opened up. The core or pith of the plant is used for horse or poultry bedding. Currently over 90% of the fibre is used for paper (mainly cigarette tissue) and the balance made into industrial textiles, but the industrial textiles market is the one forecast to grow. By 2002 the automotive industry must use a minimum percentage of natural or recyclable materials. It is hoped that textile containing hemp fibre, which is already used in car door panels in Germany, will then be more widely adopted in the UK.

France currently grows 14-15,000 ha of hemp and Spain 21,000 ha.

Lupins

A leguminous crop traditionally associated with light land. The protein content is about 40% higher than peas and beans, making lupins a good substitute for soya beans in livestock feed compounds. Some 30,000 tons of lupin products are imported into the UK from Australia each year.

In 1985 1,300 ha of lupins were grown in the UK but the results were so poor that little has been grown since. However, a new winter dwarf determinate variety (with restricted vegetative growth) has been developed which will be available to farmers in autumn 2000. It matures earlier and yields better than existing types and can be harvested by mid-September, with no desiccant needed. It is suitable for all but the heaviest land but is not tolerant to alkaline soils: growth is impaired at a pH greater than 7·0. Unfortunately much of the suitable land in the UK is in the cooler north and west of the country. Although the new varieties do not have such exacting heat requirements they do better in warmer conditions.

The new variety is winter sown: the sowing date is crucial, as the plant must reach a certain stage in development to be frost resistant. In the south, sowing should be done in the middle two weeks of September. It must be sown earlier in the north and can be later in the south-west. A good cereal seedbed will suffice. Broad-leaved weed control is vital. Pre-emergence herbicide should be used, with a second application if necessary. A first-time crop needs a rhizobium inoculant to be added to the crop at the time of drilling. No fertilizer is applied to the crop but P and K at 50-55k/ha should be replaced later. Rust rather than botrytis is now the predominant problem but it can be controlled with a fungicide. A potentially serious disease, anthracnose, which has devastated crops in mainland Europe, has so far been excluded by seed health measures. Bean seed fly is controlled with a pesticide incorporated into the soil at sowing. Harvest is from mid-August to early September.

A big increase in the area grown is forecast.

Output: Yield: 2·4-4·0 t/ha (1·0-1·6t/acre) should be achieved (well above that of earlier years). Price: £95/tonne

	£/ha	(£/acre)	
Area Payment:	300	(121)	
Total:	525-675	(215-275)	
Variable costs:			
Seed	60-70	(24-28)	(approx. only; no prices set as yet).
Fertilizer	15	(6)	
Sprays	100	(40)	
	____	____	
Total:	180	(72)	
	____	____	
Gross margin:	420	170	

Maize for Grain

Little scope with present varieties because, as with Sunflowers, our climate is not warm enough. Did reasonably well in good springs and summers for a while, in southern England, over ten years ago, but results were very poor in late springs and cool summers and harvesting between mid-October and mid-December is grim in a wet autumn/early winter, and drying very costly. Possibly 200 ha are being grown annually in the UK. The short season variety developed so successfully for forage maize can be grown for grain, with some advantage over earlier varieties. However, marketing can be a problem as consignments are too small to interest the major buyers. Some have developed a specialised or local market, *e.g.* feed for pigeons or corn-fed chickens.

Does well to average 4 to 5 tonnes/ha (the average is about double this in France); price for the 2000 crop could be £110 or so a tonne; area payment (England) £240/ha (£97/acre). Seed (125), fertilizer (45) and sprays (20); total approx. £190/ha (£77/acre); drying £100/ha (£40/acre).

Navy Beans

Used for baked beans, for which the UK imports 110,000 tonnes annually from North America. The world price is buoyant. Varieties have now been introduced which are adapted to the soil types and climate of the UK and growers are being contracted to grow the crop for canning to supply two leading supermarkets. The area grown in 1999 is 130 ha but it is predicted to increase to 2,000 ha within two years. There is no EU area aid but the crop can be grown on IACS non-registered land. Requires good fertile land and some care in growing. Sowing mid-May when no further frost risk. Harvest late-August/early-September. Target yield 2·5t/ha but average achieved likely to be less. There may be a premium for the crop if it is GM-free and organically produced.

Output:
Yield	1·8t/ha	(0·73t/acre)
Price	£270/t*	

	£/ha	(£/acre)
Total	485	(196)

*Based on a contract price of £295 set at 3% waste and stain, less £6 per 1% over that; 7% is typical.

Variable Costs:
Seed	85	(34·5)
Fertilizer	60	(24)
Spray	110	(44·5)
Total:	255	(103)

Gross margin:	230	(93)

Soya Beans

Soya is a sub-tropical crop in origin grown mainly in the USA, but some is grown in southern Europe. A considerable quantity is imported into the UK for animal feed. Until recently it was felt unlikely that the crop could ever be successfully grown commercially in the UK as it needed a warmer climate in which to mature. A new variety has now been developed from a conventional plant breeding programme which can be grown in latitudes up to 52° North, *i.e.* in southern England. 380 ha grown in the UK in 1999 and some claim the area could expand to as much as 12,000 ha within a few years. As soya is a legume it could be a good alternative break crop. It is eligible for the oilseed area payment. A premium may be paid for GM free crop.

Sown from mid-April, depending on soil temperature and harvested in September. Target yield is 3t/ha but the average achieved is likely to be less, particularly in early years as producers become familiar with the crop.

Output (year 2000):
Yield	2·5t/ha	(1t/acre)
Price	£135/t (oilseed rape price plus £20)	

	£/ha	(£/acre)
Sales	340	(137)
Area aid	335	(136)
Total:	675	(273)

Variable Costs:
Seed	125	(51)
Fertilizer	50	(20)
Spray	70	(29)
Total:	245	(100)

Gross margin:	430	(173)

Sunflowers

The UK imports the equivalent of about 400,000 tonnes of sunflower seed each year, mainly as sunflower oil. Currently little or none is crushed in the UK. There has been continued interest in sunflowers as both an import replacement and a useful break crop, but a series of late harvests and low yields have discouraged growers. Currently only about 300 ha are grown, producing 500 tonnes of seed, most of it destined for the bird seed market.

A new extra early maturing semi-dwarf hybrid has now been developed which is more suitable to conditions in the UK. This should allow harvesting in early September without significant yield reduction. Yields of 2·2t/ha with oil content of 44% are being canvassed. But the crop still needs a relatively mild climate and is best grown south-east of a line from the Wash to east Dorset. A wide range of soil types are suitable. Sowing is from April to early May when the soil temperature is 7-8°C. Pre-emergence weed control is necessary; at the right plant density weeds should not subsequently be a problem. Sclerotina and botrytis, in a wet season, may affect the crop; on areas of less than 6 ha bird damage can be serious. The crop is dried to 9 or 10% for safe storage. Sunflowers may be grown successfully without fertilizer or sprays; hence could be an attractive option for organic growers.

Until sufficient is grown to make up batches for crushing (1,000 tonnes a time) marketing may be a problem, though human consumption and bird seed do take perhaps 4,000 tonnes annually. UK produced sunflower oil is of a good quality and there is an initiative to produce a premium oil by cold pressing small batches of home produced sunflower seed.

Area aid as for oilseed rape. Drying costs £50/ha.

Output:

Yield (tonnes)	1·8/ha	(0·7/acre)
Price (possibly)	£150	
	£/ha	(£/acre)
Sale Value	270	(109)
Area aid	335	(136)
Total:	605	(245)
Variable Costs:		
Seed	110	(45)
Fertilizer	35	(14)
Sprays	45	(18)
Total:	190	(77)
Gross margin:	415	(168)

Others

Other crops that have been in the news in recent years as possible new crops for the future (or present crops capable of substantial development) include the following: miscanthus (elephant grass, as an energy crop), chickpeas and lentils, fenugreek, meadowfoam, cuphea, peppermint, poppies (for cooking oils, not opium), quinoa, buckwheat and sunwheat (an early maturing short type of sunflower). At present there are no reliable data for these crops on average yield expectations and little on prices or variable costs, when grown on a commercial scale in this country. A number of them are either for the health food market or are sources of oil for industry as replacements for whale oil and light mineral oil. Research continues on many of them.

HOPS

1. *Output data*

Average Yield per ha, 1994-98: 29·25 zentners (50 kg); range 26·3 (1998) to 33·3 (1996).

Average Price (per zentner): 1994, £204; 1995, £211;1996, £206 (contract), £165 (spot); 1997, £222 (contract), £119 (spot); 1998, £226 (contract), £109·50 (spot).

Main varieties (73% of total area):

	ha 1998	av. yield 1994-98 (z. per ha)	(contract prices) av. £ per zentner 1996	1997	1998
Target	580	33·8	104	142	113
Golding	485	27·6	282	275	277
Northdown	181	30·0	254	254	257
Challenger	211	29·8	242	245	251
Fuggle	321	24·8	255	258	260

Total area of hops (ha): 1984: 5,091; 1996: 3,112; 1997: 3,067; 1998: 2,447.

EC income aid for 1998 (£ per ha): £362.

2. *Variable Costs per mature hectare* (materials only)

	£
Fertilizers and Manure	150
Washes and Powders	575
Herbicides	125
String	175
Pockets/Bales	50
Drying Fuel	150
Total...	1225

3. *Average Direct Labour Costs per mature hectare*

	£
Growing	700
Picking	700
Drying	175
Total...	1575

N.B. The above costs are the author's approximations for 2000 based on a limited sample of crops for the three years 1996-98.

A new hop garden (erecting the poles, wiring and planting) could cost in the order of £14,250 to £16,500 per hectare (£5,775 to £6,675 per acre).

Acknowledgement: T. W. Smith, Grower Liaison Manager, English Hop Products Limited.

VINEYARDS

There are 386 vineyards in England and Wales, covering 842 cropping hectares. The largest vineyard is over 100 hectares but the average only 2·18 hectares. The South East predominates with 46% of vineyards, 65% of the area, 51% of wine production and 53 (46%) of the 114 wineries. Any vineyard over 0·5 hectare must be registered with the Wine Standards Board, though many of the smaller vineyards are run purely as a hobby.

In 1996 UK wine production reached a record 2·66 million litres. Subsequent crops have been considerably smaller: 0·65 million litres in 1997 and 1·14 in 1998, largely due to late frosts. Around 90% of production is white wine and 10% red, but with the introduction of a red grape variety more suitable to our climate red wine production is increasing. There is also a very significant increase in the production of English sparkling wine using traditional methods.

There is no EU ban on planting vines in the UK and there will not be until production exceeds 2·5 million litres on a five-year average. A Quality Wine Scheme for England and Wales was introduced in 1991 and a Regional Wine Scheme in 1997. In 1997 17% of production was Quality Wine. Hybrid varieties may be planted in the UK but may not currently be made into quality wine. They may be used for quality sparkling wine and regional wine. All wines sold in the UK bear the same VAT and duty, irrespective of origin. UK wine supplies only 0·3% of the home market.

Vineyards need south facing, well-drained and sheltered land, less than 100 metres (330 ft.) above sea level, in the southern half of England and Wales. A high level of management and marketing is essential, as is expert advice. There is no minimum area for profitable production. A small enterprise selling wine at the farm gate and to local hotels and restaurants may be more profitable than one with 10 hectares selling only grapes.

There are two principal growing systems; the intensive Double Guyot, the most common in France and Germany and now 60% of British vineyards, and the more extensive Geneva Double Curtain, 40% of the home crop. The Double Guyot system will yield little until year 3 and be in full production in year 4. Geneva Double Curtain will not have a full yield until year 5 or 6. Investment capital of £12,000 to £15,000/ha (£4,850-£6,075/acre) is typically required for the vineyard. Equipment for a winery costs £50,000-£60,000 and a suitable building is needed.

Yields and quality are very variable, according to the variety of grape and the year. In a reasonable year a yield of 5-6 tonnes/hectare (2-2·5 tonnes/acre) could be expected. One tonne of grapes will produce about 900-950 75cl bottles of wine.

The following costs refer to a *commercial* enterprise on a suitable site. Establishment costs could be double if the site has to be drained and provided with windbreaks and rabbit fencing. Annual growing costs can also be significantly greater.

	Double Guyot per ha	(per acre)	Geneva Double Curtain per ha	(per acre)
Number of Vines	3,450	(1,400)	1,500	(605)
	£		£	
Establishment Costs	15,000	(6,070) over 2 years	12,000	(4,850) over 3 years
Including materials	11,000	(4,450)	6,500	(2,630)
Labour	2,500	(1,010)	2,400	(970)
Subsequent annual costs				
Materials	700	(285)	700	(285)
Labour (growing)	1,200	(485)	1,000	(405)
Harvesting	250	(100)	250	(100)

Prices: Grape prices will vary according to the variety and the vintage. They range from £350 to £750 per tonne delivered to a winery. Transport as well as picking costs has therefore to be deducted. Wine prices vary widely but are likely to be in the range £3·50 to £5·50 a bottle at retail. English sparkling wine may retail at £10 to £15 a bottle but is more costly to produce.

A retail price of at least £4·00 per bottle is necessary to break even for most enterprises.
e.g. £4·00 less 17·5% vat and £1·085 duty = £2·32*
Less own winery costs (materials and labour) £1 per bottle** = £1·32.
At 5 tonne per ha and 950 bottles per tonne = £6,270 per ha (£2,540/acre).
*An allowance may also have to be made for a retail mark up of 25%.
**Having wine made under contract costs about £1·75 a bottle.

Acknowledgements:
Stephen Skelton, Chairman, United Kingdom Vineyards Association (UKVA).
Chris Foss, School of Wine Studies, Plumpton College, near Lewes, East Sussex.
Researcher: Angela Edwards.

FRUIT

Established crops: per hectare (per acre in brackets)

Note: The *wide range* of yields, prices and costs, both from farm to farm and season to season, has to be stressed. Thus these figures (which are deliberately rounded) can only be considered to be broad guidelines, *i.e.* yields and prices in any particular year may differ markedly. Similarly, labour requirements, both regular and casual, vary considerably. *Prices* are net of marketing, handling and transport and assume sales in the open market unless otherwise stated and exclude pick-your-own crops. **Yields refer to *marketed* yields only, of established crops.** The figures relate to *average* levels; "high" outputs may be about 50 per cent above those shown; naturally the top producers will achieve still better results, especially in good years.

	Dessert Apples	Culinary Apples	Pears	Plums
Yield: tonnes/ha (tons/acre)	14 (5·6)	20 (8)	11 (4·4)	9 (3·6)
Net Price (£/tonne)	420	275	460	1600
	£	£	£	£
OUTPUT	5900 (2380)	5500 (2225)	5050 (2050)	14400 (5825)
Variable Costs: [1]				
Fertilizer...	50 (20)	50 (20)	50 (20)	50 (20)
Sprays	400 (162)	400 (162)	300 (121)	325 (132)
Packaging	650 (263)	750 (304)	525 (212)	1425 (576)
Casual Labour (picking)	975 (395)	825 (334)	725 (292)	1750 (707)
TOTAL VARIABLE COSTS[1]	2075 (840)	2025 (820)	1600 (645)	3550 (1435)
GROSS MARGIN	3825 (1540)	3475 (1405)	3450 (1405)	10850 (4390)
Regular Labour (hours) ...	185 (75)	185 (75)	185 (75)	135 (55)

	Strawberries	Raspberries	Blackcurrants
Yield: tonnes/ha (tons/acre)	9 (3·6)	5 (2)	7·5 (3)
Net Price (£/tonne)	1500	2850	625
	£	£	£
OUTPUT	13500 (5465)	14250 (5765)	4690 (1900)
Variable Costs: [1]			
Fertilizer	50 (20)	75 (30)	100 (40)
Sprays	550 (223)	325 (132)	325 (132)
Packaging	2875 (1163)	1625 (657)	— —
Casual Labour... ...	3750 (1516)	3250 (1313)	350 (142)
Other	500 (203)	500 (203)	300 (121)
TOTAL VARIABLE COSTS [1] ...	7725 (3125)	5775 (2335)	1075 (435)
GROSS MARGIN	5775 (2340)	8475 (3430)	3615 (1465)
Regular Labour (hours) ...	200 (80)	300 (120)	125 (50)

(1) Excluding establishment, storage and transport.

Sources: In particular, for yields and prices, the annual "Economic Results from Horticulture", by Alan Renwick and Will Staunton, Rural Business Unit, Department of Land Economy, University of Cambridge. Supplemented by updated data based on periodic small-scale surveys, mainly in Kent.

FRUIT ESTABLISHMENT

It is important to appreciate that the figures on page 41 refer only to established crops. In previous years establishment costs have to be borne, with no (or, later, low) returns.

Apples and Pears. Trees, stake, etc., approximately £4·75/tree. Total establishment costs £3,500-£17,500/ha depending especially on planting density, which varies from 750 to 3,500/ha.

First picking: apples — commonly year 3, 30% of full crop.

pears — commonly year 4, 20% of full crop.

Full picking: apples — generally year 6 to 9; pears — year 7 to 12.

Orchard duration: traditional, apples 20 years, pears 30 years plus; denser bed systems 15 years.

Strawberries. Costs in establishment year approximately £4,750/ha for traditional system, £11,000/ha for intensive systems; 60% of the cost is for plants. 35% pick in year 1 in intensive systems, none in traditional systems, full pick in year 2; generally 3 years cropping.

Raspberries. Establishment costs approximately £3,000/ha, including wirework. 50% pick in year 2, full pick in year 3; 10 years cropping.

Blackcurrants. Establishment costs approximately £6,000/ha using bushes, £3,000/ha using cuttings. Takes 1½ years to establish from 1 year old bushes (*i.e.* planting November 1995 gives first crop in July 1997), 2½ years from cuttings. Approximately one-third of full crop in first picking year, 75% in second, peak in third, levelling out at slightly lower yield thereafter; 8 or 9 years cropping.

Researcher: Angela Edwards (who assisted further with revising the established fruit and vegetables data). Acknowledgements: Farm Advisory Services Team Ltd. and SmithKline Beecham. Figures updated by author.

FIELD-SCALE VEGETABLES

Per hectare (per acre in brackets)

Note: The same comments regarding variability apply as to fruit (page 41). The same main source has been used, for most of the crops, plus the annual "Report on Farming", from the same department. The "other" variable cost figures are intended only as a general indication of their level; survey data on many of these crops is rarely available and, when it is, particularly variable between farms and seasons.

	Carrots	Dry Bulb Onions	Dwarf Beans (for Processing)
Yield: tonnes/ha (tons/acre)	20 (8)	35 (14)	7 (2·8)
Price (£/tonne)	100	100	220
	£	£	£
OUTPUT	2000 (810)	3500 (1415)	1550 (630)
Variable Costs: [1]			
Seed	400 (162)	325 (132)	275 (112)
Fertilizer	150 (61)	125 (51)	75 (30)
Sprays	350 (142)	375 (152)	100 (41)
Other*	100 (40)	400 (160)	325 (132)
TOTAL VARIABLE COSTS [1] ...	1000 (405)	1225 (495)	775 (315)
GROSS MARGIN	1000 (405)	2275 (920)	775 (315)
Regular Labour (hours) ...	50-150	40-60	N.A.

42

	Brussels Sprouts	Cabbage	Spring Greens
Yield: tonnes/ha (tons/acre)	14 (5·5)	35 (14)	20 (8)
Price (£/tonne)	320	175	250
	£	£	£
OUTPUT	4475 (1810)	6125 (2480)	5000 (2025)
Variable Costs: [1]			
Seeds/Plants	500 (202)	625 (253)	370 (150)
Fertilizer	110 (44)	140 (57)	140 (57)
Sprays	265 (107)	210 (85)	240 (97)
Other*	500 (202)	1975 (800)	2525 (1021)
TOTAL VARIABLE COSTS [1]	1375 (555)	2950 (1195)	3275 (1325)
GROSS MARGIN	3100 (1255)	3175 (1285)	1725 (700)
Regular Labour (hours)	75 (30)	75 (30)	60 (24)

* Other = Casual Labour, Packaging, etc.

	Cauliflower	Broccoli	Calabrese	Sweetcorn
Yield: tonnes/ha (tons/acre)	15 (6)	15 (6)	9 (3·6)	12·5 (5)
Price (£/tonne)	250	250	750	120
	£	£	£	£
OUTPUT	3750 (1520)	3750 (1515)	6750 (2730)	1500 (605)
Variable Costs: [1]				
Seed/Plants	750 (305)	725 (293)	750 (304)	125 (50)
Fertilizer	140 (57)	125 (50)	125 (50)	100 (40)
Sprays	160 (65)	150 (61)	250 (101)	50 (20)
Other*	1725 (698)	1300 (526)	2000 (810)	250 (100)
TOTAL VARIABLE COSTS ...	2775 (1125)	2300 (930)	3125 (1265)	525 (210)
GROSS MARGIN	975 (395)	1450 (585)	3625 (1465)	975 (395)

	Lettuce (Outdoor)	Parsnips	Leeks	Rhubarb
Yield: tonnes/ha (tons/acre)	30 (12)	25 (10)	21 (8·4)	37·5 (15)
Price (£/tonne)	450	210	500	700
OUTPUT	13500 (5465)	5250 (2125)	10500 (4250)	26250 (10625)
Variable Costs:				
Seed/Plants	1225 (494)	135 (54)	675 (273)	145 (59)
Fertilizer	140 (57)	80 (32)	125 (50)	65 (26)
Sprays	285 (114)	335 (136)	400 (162)	75 (30)
Other*	6300 (2550)	1800 (730)	6450 (2610)	N/A
TOTAL VARIABLE COSTS ...	7950 (3215)	2350 (950)	7650 (3095)	N/A
GROSS MARGIN	5550 (2250)	2900 (1175)	2850 (1155)	N/A

* Other = Casual Labour, Packaging, etc.

HORTICULTURE — WHOLE FARM DATA

Comparative whole farm data is less generally available for horticultural holdings than for various types of farm in different regions of the country (see sources of reports listed on page 5). Data from across a wide area of England is presented below. Because the results vary so much from year to year two-year averages are presented: for 1995/96 and 1996/97. The data are collected by eight College/University centres: Askham Bryan, Cambridge, Exeter, Manchester, Newcastle, Nottingham, Reading and Wye.

All financial figures are *per hectare*. The averages cover a wide range.

| Type of Holding | Specialist Glass | | Specialist | Market |
	Mainly edible crops	Flowers & nursery stock	Fruit	Gardens
No. of Farms in Sample	48	51	38	53
Average Size (ha [acres])	1·21 (3·0)	1·03 (2·55)	62 (153)	20 (50)
	£	£	£	
Gross Output...	245,890	425,700	4,885	40,540
Less:				
Bought Seed and Plants ...	21,515	68,100	60	10,375
Market Charges	12,780	7,090	440	1,115
Packing Materials	12,715	22,380	410	1,615
Net Output	198,880	328,130	3,975	27,435
Other Costs:				
Labour (inc. Unpaid Manual)	75,090	141,385	2,085	13,535
Glasshouse Fuel	29,995	14,445	—	145
Manures	7,820	18,510	50	1,520
Sprays and Fumigants ...	3,425	5,075	330	480
Horticultural Sundries ...	11,840	21,650	305	1,460
Power and Machinery ...	21,275	30,765	740	2,905
Land Rent, Glass Deprecn.	19,675	23,535	255	1,215
Other Fixed Costs	19,600	33,920	465	3,650
Total Other Costs	188,720	289,285	4,230	24,910
Management and Inv. Inc. ...	10,160	38,845	−255	2,525
Grower and Spouse Labour(+)	24,595	30,715	375	3,955
Net Income	34,755	69,560	120	6,480
Tenant's Valuation	171,560	314,455	4,415	35,210

Source: Horticultural Business Data, compiled by R. L. Vaughan and R. T. Crane, Department of Agricultural and Food Economics, The University of Reading, 1998.

Glasshouse Crop Outputs (approx. 5-year UK averages, 1993-97):

	Yield T/ha (t/acre)	Price £/tonne	Output £/ha (acre)
Tomatoes, heated	370 (147)	620	230,000 (93,000)
Tomatoes, cold	120 (48)	445	53,500 (21,650)
Cucumbers	440 (175)	625	275,000 (111,250)
Lettuce	35 (14)	865	30,275 (12,250)

MUSHROOMS

	Per sq. metre bed area per year	Per tonne of compost
Yield	92kg	170kg
	£	£
Value (£1·70/kg net)	156·0	290·0
Spent compost	1·0	2·0
TOTAL OUTPUT	157·0	292·0
Variable Costs:		
Spawn (including levy)...	3·8	7·0
Compost (raw materials)	11·3	21·0
Casing (peat and lime)	5·4	10·0
Heating and electricity	6·5	12·0
Packaging (14p/kg)	13·0	24·0
Pesticides and disinfectant	2·2	4·0
Miscellaneous	1·1	2·0
TOTAL VARIABLE COSTS	43·3	80·0
GROSS MARGIN	113·7	212·0

Notes:

1. Length of cropping period determines·
   (i) number of crops grown per year;
   (ii) volume (and cost) of compost, casing and spawn used per unit area;
   (iii) the weight of mushrooms produced per tonne of compost.
   Assumptions: 5 crops/year (more are possible); 170 kg mushrooms/tonne compost spawned; 108 kg compost/m²/crop (22 lb/ft²/crop).

2. *Price:* £1·70 kg net. The average annual wholesale price 1986-1997 rose from £1,370 to £1,600/tonne, most of the improvement taking place since 1993. Prices in 1999 were under pressure from imports. UK annual production was around 106,000 tonnes in 1997. There is a trend for more of the crop to be sold direct to retail concerns and processors and less through wholesale markets and agents. In 1998 64% of GB sales went direct to supermarkets and 3·5% to processors. The share of imports in total home sales rose from 18% in 1986 to 43% in 1997.

3. *Labour:* Total £60-70/m²/year: about 40% composting and growing, 60% picking and packing. These figures are reduced if compost is purchased (see below).

4. *Capital investment:* Composting machinery £30-40,000. Typical building (50m² per tier of trays) £10-12,000 including heating/cooling system. Trays £15-20 per sq. metre, life 5-10 years (depending on handling). Buildings for composting, peak heating, spawn running, packhouse and coolstore may also be required.

5. Above figures based on tray/movable shelf system (approx. 42% of UK crop) using mainly home made compost; other systems include mechanised shelf (37% of crop), bags (11%) and block (9%). Phase I compost can be purchased at £24/tonne plus delivery, Phase II (pasteurised plus spawn) at £85-90, Phase III (spawn run) in bulk £114/tonne and in blocks £130/tonne. 66% of compost used is Phase I, 23% Phase II and 11% Phase III, with Phase III share increasing. Yields may be higher if Phase II or III compost is used; variable costs will be greater but fixed costs, (labour, machinery and buildings), will be lower.

6. Note: mushroom growing is not recommended as a casual enterprise. It is a highly specialised business requiring production and marketing expertise.
   For further details of systems, costs and returns see "Economics of Mushroom Production, Crop Year 1997", Special Studies in Agricultural Economics, Report No. 43, School of Economic Studies, University of Manchester.

Researcher: Angela Edwards.

ORGANIC FARMING

Towards the end of 1998 the area of organic farming in the UK was estimated to be about 70,000 ha (175,000 acres), with about a third as much again in conversion. While this is below 1% of UK farmland the rate of increase has been rising rapidly in 1999, for a number of reasons: poor prices for conventionally produced crops and livestock, good premium price levels, increasing demand — owing largely to health concerns (*e.g.* BSE/CJD and the introduction of genetically modified crops) and the introduction and augmentation of the aid scheme covering the required conversion period (see next page). The market potential is shown by the fact that 60 to 70% of UK consumption of organic produce is imported. The percentage of agricultural land organically farmed is nearly 2% in the EU as a whole and is approximately 10% in Austria.

The benefits to the nation claimed are as follows:

(i)   lower yields = less surpluses = less national and EU expenditure on storage and disposal; additionally, less need for set-aside;

(ii)   environmental (including wildlife and water pollution) benefits of non-use of inorganic fertilizers and agrochemical sprays;

(iii)   reduction in use of fossil energy;

(iv)   increasing concern over health means a rising demand and thus an expanding market (as noted above).

(v)   a saving in imported produce (again as noted above).

Against these points critics argue that:

(i)   it is unproven that inorganic fertilizers and (tested and approved) agrochemicals harm the environment;

(ii)   it is unproven that organically produced foods are more nutritious, healthier or tastier;

(iii)   there is insufficient land available to feed the present population adequately if all farming were organic;

(iv)   since organic farming requires more land than conventional farming to produce a given amount of food, less land would be available for environmental purposes, recreation and woodland;

(v)   if organic production became widespread in the UK compared with other countries our competitive position in terms of production costs per tonne would become increasingly eroded.

The economics to the farmer (though this is of secondary interest to many organic farmers) depend *primarily* upon:

(i)   relative yield compared with conventional farming;

(ii)   the price premium compared with conventional farming.

In the case of cereals both research and experience suggests that yields of organic crops are typically between 60% and two-thirds of those of conventionally produced crops, but the premium has easily compensated for this to date and there is also the obvious saving in fertilizer and spray costs. Hence the gross margin is normally much higher. However, there are also the wider whole farm effects to be considered, *e.g.*, unless the farm already has a substantial percentage of its area down to leys this will probably have to be increased in order to maintain yields and this extra grass has to be utilised profitably — which is far from easy, and the extra capital requirements could be heavy.

Furthermore, there is a two year "conversion period" to undergo before full price premiums can be claimed; (though note the aid scheme, next page). Also, in the case of vegetable crops, quality (in the sense of appearance) can be badly affected by pests and diseases.

As regards relative cultivation costs, in one ADAS monitored study these were reported to be 15 per cent higher on the organically grown wheat (approximately £17·50 more per ha (£7 per acre) at present costs). However no spraying is required. Survey data have indicated overall labour requirements to be 10-30% higher than on conventional farms, with machinery costs generally similar.

In the case of livestock, present premiums are highly attractive, *e.g.* around 11p per litre (some 60% over conventional) in the case of milk. This particularly benefits the larger farm, especially on land that favours grass rather than cash crops, where the reduction in stocking rate caused by the lack of nitrogen fertilizer is less important. Concentrate feed costs per tonne are much higher.

As already stated, *the big questions are the relative yields and the price difference.* Future price premiums will depend on how much the consumption of organic produce increases compared with increases in supply.

An *Organic Farming Scheme* for England to encourage new organic producers (but providing nothing for existing producers), with extra help for the conversion period, was introduced in 1999, to replace the Organic Aid Scheme. The uptake has been considerable. Participants must register their proposed land for conversion with one of the organic sector bodies or with the United Kingdom Register of Organic Food Standards and provide a conversion plan. There is a minimum eligible size of 1 ha; there is no maximum limit. The rates of aid (£/ha) are:

Year:	1	2	3	4	5	Total
AAPS eligible land and land in						
permanent crops	225	135	50	20	20	450
Other improved land	175	105	40	15	15	350
Unimproved land	25	10	5	5	5	50

Participants would also receive a lump sum of £300 in the first year, £200 in the second and £100 in the third. This sum would only be payable once for any one organic unit; existing organic units should not be eligible. A separate scheme operates in Scotland.

No gross margin data for organic enterprises are included in this section because a specialist publication is available on the subject: the "1999 Organic Farm Management Handbook", by Nic Lampkin and Mark Measures (tel. 01970 622248 or 01488 658279): £10 including postage.

Addresses:

United Kingdom Register of Organic Food Standards (UKROFS), c/o MAFF, Room G43, Nobel House, 17 Smith Square, London SW1P 3JR. (Telephone: 0171-238 6348).

Organic Farmers and Growers Limited, Churchgate House, 50 High Street, Soham, Ely, Cambridgeshire CB7 5HF. (Telephone: 01353 720289).

Soil Association/British Organic Farmers, Bristol House, 40-56 Victoria Street, Bristol, BS1 6BY. (Telephone: 0117 929 0661).

Elm Farm Research Centre, Organic Advisory Service, Hamstead Marshall, Newbury, Berkshire RG15 0HR. (Telephone: 01488 658279).

Bio-Dynamic Agricultural Association, Netherfield Farm, Beeswing, Dumfries DG2 8JE. (Telephone: 01387 730217).

Organic Food Federation, The Tithe House, Peaseland Green, Elsing, East Dereham, Norfolk NR20 3DY. (Telephone: 01362 637314).

Centre for Organic Agriculture, University of Aberdeen, Regent Walk, Aberdeen AB24 3FX. (Telephone: 01224 273856).

TURF

The market for turf appeared steady in 1999 after some overproduction in the previous year or so, largely due to new entrants into cultivated turf production, many thought to be farmers looking for a new enterprise. Within the turf sector the share of seed sown turf or "turfgrass" continues to grow at the expense of pasture turf. There is less good pasture available and it can now be cheaper to grow cultivated turf than treat and prepare existing pasture for cutting. Special seed mixtures and cultivation techniques produce a range of types of turfgrass that can be matched to particular sites and uses. The Turfgrass Growers Association (TGA) has introduced quality standards and buyers are increasingly specifying the precise type of turf they require. It is estimated that there are 5,000-6,000 ha (12,500-15,000 acres) of turfgrass grown in the UK. Although several turfgrass companies were originally set up by farmers, the business has moved away from mainstream farming.

Farms and farmers may be involved however in the following ways:

1. Selling existing pasture turf to a turf company

This is the traditional option but its share of the turf market is declining. The approach may be by the farmer to the company or vice-versa. Minimum 5-6 year ley/pasture generally needed for spring or autumn lifting, 8-10 year grass better for summer cutting.

Important features: good root structure, number and type of weeds, level, well-drained, stone-free land; good access; timing (farmer wants lifting completed in time to drill next crop).

Payment varies between £750-1500/hectare (£300-600/acre), but mainly £900-1200/ha (£360-480/acre). Usually initial payment plus further payments as turf is lifted. There may be a penalty clause if lifting delays prevent subsequent timely drilling. Lifting can take from two months to even a year. It can be done at any time of year except when there is snow on the ground. The turf company usually sprays against broadleaved weeds, fertilizes and mows before lifting; the farmer may do these tasks, for payment. He may graze the land, for a rent, if lifting is delayed.

Apparently the effect on the land is not detrimental; some say there are benefits (removal of accumulated pests, etc. in the top inch of grass, roots and topsoil).

Some local authorities require planning consent for turf stripping. In some instances it has been refused on the grounds that pasture turf is not an agricultural crop. Cultivated turf, however, *is* deemed to be an agricultural crop.

2. Farmer cutting, lifting and selling pasture turf himself

Not usual. The turf must be treated, as in option 1. A small turf cutting machine can be hired for about £50 a day. This slices off the turf which must then be cut into lengths and picked up by hand. Two or three workers are required. It is slow going even in good conditions. The wastage figure is commonly 10 to 20% of the area, perhaps more.

Turf has a short life once cut and stacked—3 days in summer, 7 days in winter, preferably less. Thus transport and outlets must be well organized: probably to a very local market; may soon be over-supplied.

3. Renting land to a turf company for production of special turf

Turf companies rent land for turfgrass production in addition to using their own land. As before, well-drained, stone-free land with good access is required. Typically the land is rented on a per crop basis and one or two crops grown. A turf crop usually takes 15 to 18 months from preparation to harvest but autumn sown crops may be harvested within 9 months. Rent levels depend on the quality of the land and the profitability of competing agricultural enterprises. Currently rents are £850-1200/ha/crop (£350-500/acre) or approximately £550-800/ha/yr (£220-325/acre/yr).

4. Specialist turf production

On their own land turf producers can grow turf continuously, taking a crop every 18 months to two years on average. On rented land (as in option 3), they take one or two crops and move on. Usually they produce a quick growing type of turf which sells quickly on rented land and cultivate more specialist and slower growing turf on their own land. A high level of agronomic expertise and considerable investment in machinery are needed and labour requirements are heavy. As the business is very competitive a high degree of marketing expertise is essential. While the bulk of the trade goes into general landscaping or garden centres there is an increase in the number of contracts where the quality and type of turf is specified. It is estimated that a turf farm would need to be 60 hectares (150 acres) or more in size to be viable — in order to justify the machinery necessary and to produce a succession of turf for the market. It is very unlikely that a farmer will grow turfgrass either for a company or "on spec".

Costs and Returns
Variable Costs plus Rent per crop

Domestic/general contract turfgrass

	£/ha	(£/acre)
Seed	275-500	(110-200)
Fertilizer	125-250	(50-100)
Herbicide...	25-100	(10-40)
Fungicide...	0-100	(0-40)
Rent (for 18 months) ...	850-1,100	(350-450)
Total	1,275-2,050	(520-830)

It may be necessary to irrigate and on occasions use netting to grow the grass through for certain sites.

Labour

Special seed bed preparation (including subsoiling and stone burying), regular mowing (twice a week May/June), picking up clippings, harvesting (2 men on harvester plus one loading lorry) between 0·2-0·4 ha/day (0·5-1·0 acre).

Total costs of order of £4,250-6,250/ha (£1,725-2,525/acre), approximately 47-70p/sq.m. (39-57p/sq.yd.)

The cost of *specialist machinery* for turf production can be up to £150,000.

Value of Turf (on the field)

	per sq. metre	per sq. yd.	per ha*	per acre*
Pasture turf	45-50p	38-43p	£4,050- 4,500	£1,650-1,875
Hardwearing, domestic general contract	80-90p	68-77p	£7,200- 8,000	£3,000-3,300
Football, hockey, prestige landscape	100-110p	85-94p	£9,000-10,000	£3,700-4,100
High quality/specialist**	150-200p	125-170p	£13,500-18,000	£5,450-7,400

* assuming 90% recovery, but some producers work on 85%.
** for some contracts the price may be higher.
Delivery charges average 35p/sq.m. Delivered turf is subject to VAT.
N.B. On tenanted land landlord's permission is necessary to cut pasture turf.

References.

Turfgrass Growers Association, Nutwood, 2 Ivy Close, Worlingworth, Woodbridge, Suffolk IP13 7PF. (Telephone: 01728 628422).

Sports Turf Research Institute, Bingley, West Yorkshire BD16 lAU. (Telephone: 01274 565131).

Researcher: Angela Edwards.

GOLF

A survey by the Royal and Ancient in the late 1980s suggested that, with golf the fastest growing sport in the world, there would be a shortfall of some 700 golf courses in the UK by the millennium. The early 1990s saw a boom in golf course construction with close to 100 a year being built. By the middle of the decade the bubble had burst and many of the courses were at financial risk or in receivership and were put onto the market to be sold at a fraction of their initial development cost. Buyers were often multi-site specialist golf concerns. During 1998 only 10 new courses were built in Great Britain. Currently, although overall supply exceeds demand, a new course can be profitable in the right location.

There are five important requirements for a golf course: location within about 20 minutes' drive of a substantial centre of population (200,000 at least), a good distance from other similar courses, good road access, an attractive free-draining site and good staff and management. Driving ranges and Golf Courts may need to be located even closer to centres of population to be successful. Planning consent may be a problem.

There are a number of options open to a farmer:

Type of facility

- 18-hole course: 45-60 ha (110-150 acres) with Clubhouse and Pro Shop (600 sq. metres), parking, proper access and maintenance buildings. It takes between 1 and 2 years to construct.
- 9-hole course: 20 ha (50 acres).
- 9-hole Par 3 course: 5 ha (12 acres).
- Driving range: 4 ha (10 acres).
- Pitch and putt course: 1·5 ha (4 acres).
- Golf Court: 2·5-8·0 ha (6-20 acres). This is a new concept which allows 18-hole golf to be played on a relatively small area using a cleverly designed combination of 4 greens and 6 to 8 tees. Played by the hour.

Type of business organisation

- To sell land with planning permission. Could have twice the agricultural value, possibly much more if it is near London and with hotel or housing consent.
- To let land to a developer/operator. Assuming the latter pays for constructing the course, a long lease will be required. This can be at a premium with a nominal rent or an annual rental of two to five times the agricultural value, with reviews.
- To form a joint company with a developer/operator. This obviously means the farmer shares in the success or failure. The land would be all or part of the farmer's equity. A well constructed agreement is essential.
- To develop and operate the course himself. Not recommended; the farmer needs good knowledge of golf and exceptional management ability besides access to substantial capital.

Construction methods and cost

- Specialist golf course constructor.

  18-hole course (45 ha): £650,000-£1,200,000 according to drainage, earthmoving and irrigation, but excluding green keepers building and machinery.

  9-hole course (20 ha): £400,000-550,000.

  9-hole par 3 course (5 ha): £180,000-£250,000.

Driving range (4 ha): £150,000-£200,000, to include offices, storage, equipment, fencing and floodlighting.

Golf Court (2·5-8 ha): £300,000.

Green keepers building: £100,000.

Full inventory of new machinery for 18-hole course: £300,000.

Clubhouse (600 sq. metres): from £600,000 fitted out.

* Direct labour may reduce costs by a third.

* Using own farm labour it is possible to reduce costs but it is very risky in terms of resultant course quality.

A golf course architect should be employed. Professional advice is available for investment appraisal and feasibility studies as well as golf course design and management.

Returns

A well-run golf business should achieve more than a 15% return on capital employed by the fourth year after a gradual build up: year 1 loss, year 2 break even, year 3 a small profit (5-8%). Thus an 18-hole course could produce £300,000 annually if it is successful.

Acknowledgement

PGA Golf Management, Bush House, 72 Prince Street, Bristol BS1 4HU.

Researcher

Angela Edwards.

FORESTRY
(Estimated for 2000)
A. Establishment Costs (before grant)
1. *Unit cost of operations*

Year/s	Operation	Estimated Cost (£)	
1.	Trees for planting		
	(i) Bare rooted:		
	Conifers	80-150 per 1,000	
	Broadleaves	270-340 per 1,000	
	(ii) Rooted in small peat blocks:		
	Conifers	140-180 per 1,000	
	Broadleaves	270-340 per 1,000	
1.	Tree Protection		
	(i) Fencing (materials and erection)		
	Rabbit	1·50-2·50 per metre	
	Stock	2·00-2·75 per metre	
	Deer	3·50-6·00 per metre	
	Split post and rail ...	5·50-6·50 per metre	
	(ii) Tree guards/shelters		
	Plastic spiral (600-750 mm)	18-22 per 100	
	Plastic tubes (1200 mm)	70-80 per 100	
	Stakes	30 per 100	
1.	Planting at approximately 2 m spacing		
	Conifers	130-160 per ha	
	Broadleaves*	450-650 per ha	
2-3.	Replacing dead trees**		
	Operation	30-40 per ha	
	Plant supply	35-45 per ha	

Costs specific to location		*Upland*	*Lowland*
1. Ground Preparation:	ploughing ...	90-110/ha	40- 60/ha
	mounding ...	250-300/ha	250-300/ha
1. Drainage		40- 60/ha	—
1. Fertilizing...		90-190/ha	—
1.4 Weeding per operation***			
Hand weeding		120-150	180-200/ha weeded
Herbicide		70-80/ha weeded	70-90/ha weeded

   * Includes cost of erecting guards/shelters.

  ** Replacing dead trees (beating up) may be necessary, once in the second year and again in the third year. Costs depend on number of trees.

*** Up to 2 weeding operations may be necessary in each of the first 4 years in extreme situations. Costs are inclusive of materials.

Access roads may need to be constructed and can typically cost between £6,000 and £22,000 per kilometre (£9,600 to £35,000 per mile) depending on availability of roadstone and the number of culverts and bridges required.

2. *Total Establishment Costs up to Year 3.*
(i) *Conifer—Lowland Sites*

On a fairly typical lowland site, requiring little or no clearing or draining, the approximate cost before grant of establishing a conifer plantation would be in the range £1,200-£1,800 per hectare. Up to 8 separate weeding operations may be required.

(ii) *Conifer—Upland Sites*

Establishing a similar conifer plantation on an upland site could cost £1,100 to £1,500 per hectare. Normally some form of site preparation and drainage is required but only one weeding operation may be necessary. Overall costs tend to be £100-£200 per ha less than on lowland sites.

(iii) *Hardwoods*

Costs of establishing hardwood plantations are highly dependent on the fencing and/or tree protection required. If tubes are needed the overall costs will be influenced by the number of plants per hectare. Costs could be in the range £1,600-£2,400 per ha. Site conditions normally mean that hardwoods being grown for timber production are restricted to lowland sites.

(iv) *Farm Woodlands*

Establishment costs for farm woodlands may be lower than those indicated for hardwoods in (iii) above if lower planting densities are used. Initial establishment costs in the first year of the order of £1,600 per ha for woods under 3 ha and £1,500 per ha for woods of 3 to 10 ha would be typical.

(v) *Size Factor*

Savings in fencing and other economies of scale may reduce average costs per ha by 10 to 20% where large plantations are being established; conversely costs for small woods may easily be 25% higher per ha established.

(vi) *Method of Establishment*

A range of organisations and individuals undertake forestry contracting work and competitive tendering can help to control costs.

B. Maintenance Costs

Once trees have been established they will normally require some maintenance and management work each year. For trees being grown primarily for timber production on a large scale, operations required may include ride maintenance, fence maintenance, pest control, fire protection, management fee and insurance charges. Costs will normally fall within the range £10-£50 per ha per annum depending upon the size of the plantation and the complexity of management. One or more fertilizing operations may be needed in the first 20 years in the life of a tree depending on the quality of the site. Estimated cost £90-£150 per ha, depending on elements applied. For trees being grown for sporting and amenity purposes, annual maintenance costs are likely to be less and may range up to about £10 per ha.

A brashing operation which involves removing branches up to two metres may be required for access reasons as the crop matures. Opening up inspection racks over 5-10% of the crop may cost £30-£50 per ha. Brashing 40-50% of the crop could cost £150-£300 per ha.

C. Production

Production is usually measured in terms of cubic metres (m^3) of marketable timber per hectare and will vary according to the quality of the site, species planted and thinning policy. Sites in lowland Britain planted to conifers typically produce an average of 12 to 18 m^3 of timber per ha per year over the rotation as a whole and would accordingly be assessed as falling in yield classes 12 to 18. Under traditional management systems thinning begins 18 to 25 years after planting and is repeated at intervals of approximately 5 years until the wood is clearfelled at between 40 and 60 years. Approximately 40-45% of total production will be from thinnings. Broadleaves typically produce an average of between 4 and 8 m^3 of timber per hectare per year and fall in yield classes 4 to 8.

Prior to a thinning sale the trees normally have to be marked and measured at an estimated cost of 35p per m^3, which is equivalent to £100-£125 per hectare depending on species, crop density and age. For a clearfelling sale the cost can range from £250 to £350 per ha, or about £1 per m^3 where a full tariff applies, *i.e.* where each tree is measured individually.

53

D. Prices

Prices for standing timber are extremely variable, depending on tree size and quality, ease of extraction from site, geographical location (nearness to end user), quantity being sold, world market prices and effectiveness of marketing method used.

Conifers

Average prices paid for standing coniferous timber sold from Forest Enterprise areas in the year to 31st March, 1999, were:

Harvesting stage	Average tree size (m^3)	England	Price (£ per m^3) Wales	Scotland
1st Thinning	Up to 0·074 ...	2·16	5·24	3·28
	0·075-0·124 ...	5·54	3·32	1·81
Subsequent	0·125-0·174 ...	9·62	6·46	3·23
Thinnings	0·175-0·224 ...	10·60	6·13	7·34
	0·225-0·274 ...	9·41	10·83	6·64
	0·275-0·424 ...	13·04	10·15	8·05
	0·425-0·499 ...	13·47	9·26	11·34
Clearfelling	0·500-0·599 ...	14·44	14·08	8·77
	0·600-0·699 ...	18·01	13·35	11·58
	0·700-0·799 ...	15·99	15·33	13·50
	0·800-0·899 ...	15·60	16·53	11·29
	0·900-0·999 ...	17·26	20·23	9·37
	1·000 and over...	20·21	16·91	4·09

Hardwoods

The hardwood trade is very complex. Merchants normally assess and value all but the smaller trees on a stem by stem basis. Actual prices fetched can show considerable variation depending on species, size, form, quality and marketing expertise of the seller. Felling usually takes place in the winter months.

Some indicative prices for hardwoods are given below, but it is important to note that actual prices fetched can vary quite widely. Wood quality is particularly important in determining prices.

Harvesting stage	Tree size Range (m^3)	Price range £ per m^3	Possible use
First thinnings	<0·13	1-12	Firewood, board products and pulp wood. Poles for refineries and turnery.
Subsequent thinnings...	0·13-0·3	5- 20	Smaller sizes and lower
	0·3 -0·6	8- 22	quality material may go
	0·6 -1·0	10- 40	for fencing or for use in the mining industry. Trees
Clearfellings	1·0 -2·0	15- 80	over 30 cm in diameter
	2+	25-150	and of better quality may go for planking, furniture or joinery.
			High quality material may go for veneers and can fetch between £150 and £300/m^3 depending on species and specifications.

Prices for Oak, Ash, Sycamore, Cherry and Elm tend to be significantly higher than for Beech, which seldom exceeds about £45/m^3 standing even for stands containing significant volumes of first quality planking.

E. Timber Marketing

In-house marketing by the owner or agent can be cost effective but only if they have detailed, up-to-date knowledge of timber buyers in the market place. The alternative is marketing through a forestry manager or management company, but this can be expensive and is not guaranteed to test the open market fully.

Nationwide electronic sales of timber by auction and tender are now available for all types and quantities of timber. This cost effective (1·5 to 2·3% sales commission) method offers full exposure to the trade and should realise the correct market value. (Beacon Forestry, Edinburgh). For small, unusual or low value timber parcels free advertising is available in the Forestry Commission's bi-monthly timber marketing magazine, "Woodlots".

F. Market Value of Established Plantations and Woods

The value of woods depends on many factors, such as location, access, species, age and soil type. The following table gives an indication of the range of current (1999) market values of commercial woodlands of different ages, based on recent market sales.

Market Value of Commercial Sitka spruce Woodlands

Age of Commercial Woods and Plantations	Price Range for crop and land £/ha	£/acre
0-5 years	250-1000	(100- 400)
6-10 years...	750-1375	(300- 550)
11-15 years...	1000-1875	(400- 750)
16-20 years...	1500-2750	(600-1100)
21-25 years...	1500-3500	(600-1400)

From years 20 to 25 onwards prices of commercial woods will also be increasingly influenced by the quantity of merchantable timber they contain. Depending on the time of clearfelling, the timber may be worth between £1,900 to £6,000 per hectare (£750 to £2,500 per acre).

Woods with high amenity or Ancient Woodland status can often command a premium over prices fetched for commercial woodlands and also those which are freehold including minerals and sporting rights.

The value of woods containing mature hardwoods will depend on the quality and value of the timber they contain and the quality of access.

G. Grants

(a) *Woodland Grant Scheme (WGS)*

The WGS is administered by the Forestry Commission. The grants available are as follows:

Establishment grants are determined by the type of wood (conifer or broad-leaved) and whether new planting or restocking is being undertaken. Levels of payment in £ per hectare are as follows:

New planting: conifers   £700 (for any size of wood)
                broadleaves   £1350 for woods less than 10 hectares
                               £1050 for woods 10 hectares or more
Payment is 70% after planting and 30% in year 5, but the plantation must be maintained to a standard acceptable to the Forestry Authority for 10 years after planting. A stocking density of 2250 trees per hectare is required unless the woods are native woodlands or small (3 ha or less) amenity woodlands.

Restocking (including natural regeneration):

conifers	£325
broadleaves	£525

Payment is 100% after planting (or once establishment has been achieved through natural regeneration). A stocking density of 2250 trees per hectare is required for conifers and 1100 for broadleaves. In certain woodlands a discretionary payment of up to 50% of the agreed costs of work to encourage natural regeneration may also be made.

New planting of short rotation coppice:

Set-aside land	£400
Non set-aside land	£600

A special *locational supplement* was announced in mid-1998 increasing the above rates to £1,000 ha to encourage production of short-rotation coppice willow for Europe's first commercial wood-burning electricity generating plant being built in North Yorkshire; 2,000 ha required within a 50 mile radius. The supplement is only available to March 2001.

More generally a *"location supplement"* of £600 per hectare is available if planting either conifers or broadleaves in one of the 13 Community Forests in Britain. No more than 10 hectares per landholding will qualify for the supplement.

A *'better land supplement'* of £600 per hectare is payable for new woodland (excluding short rotation coppice) plantings on arable or improved grassland.

A *community woodland supplement'* of £950 per hectare is available to encourage the creation of new woodlands close to towns and cities which will be of value for informal public recreation. The new woodlands must be within 5 miles of the edge of a town or city and be where there are few other woodlands that can be used by the local community for recreation. To be eligible for this supplement there must be free access to the woods for the public and appropriate car parking facilities must be close at hand or to be constructed.

Management grants, of £35 per hectare per year, are available for any age of woodland which has special environmental potential requiring additional management input and/or where public access to woodlands will be created, enhanced or maintained.

Woodland Improvement Grants are available on a discretionary basis, based on 50% of the agreed costs of capital payments for work in existing woodlands which will enhance their value for conservation, landscape or recreation. Applicants in selected areas may submit bids for *Challenge Funds* where they are considering either: (a) undertaking work to bring unmanaged woods back into management; or (b) managing their woods in a way that will enhance biodiversity. Applications are competitive and whilst the Forestry Commission will not fund 100% of the costs it is expected that Challenge Funding will result in a contribution in excess of 50% of costs.

Challenge Funds are also available on a competitive basis to assist in meeting the costs of new planting to expand the area of woodland in selected locations. These include the following areas:

National Parks in England and Wales,
South West Forest,
Bracken land in Wales,
Central Scotland Forest,
Grampian Forest.

Forestry Commission Conservancy offices can supply details of projects running in their areas.

Livestock Exclusion Annual Premia of £80 per hectare per year for up to 10 years are available for certain types of woodland in Less Favoured Areas where protection or regeneration is a high priority. This supplement will be reviewed in September 1999.

(b) *Farm Woodland Premium Scheme (FWPS)*

This scheme was introduced in April 1992 as a successor to the Farm Woodland Scheme. It is administered by The Forestry Authority and offers annual payments to compensate farmers for loss of income from farming where woodlands are established on agricultural land. To qualify for entry to the FWPS the proposed woods must attract establishment grants under the Woodland Grant Scheme (WGS).

The magnitude of annual payments depends on the type of land and its location:

	Annual Payment (£ per ha)		
	Arable Land	Other Improved Land	Unimproved Land
Outside Less Favoured Areas (LFAs)	300	260	Ineligible
Disadvantaged Areas of LFAs	230	200	60
Severely Disadvantaged Areas of LFAs	160	140	60

For the above purposes arable land is land eligible for Arable Area Payments. To qualify as improved grassland outside the LFAs (Less Favoured Areas) over half the sward must comprise, either singly or in mixture, ryegrass, cocksfoot, timothy or white clover. Within the LFAs, to qualify as improved grassland, over one third must comprise the above species *or* alternatively the land must have been "improved" by management practices such as liming and top-dressing provided there is no significant presence of sensitive plants indicative of native unimproved grassland.

Arable land and improved grassland will be eligible for the better land supplement under the WGS.

Unimproved land is land other than arable or improved grassland which has been in agricultural use for at least three years prior to the date of the application for the FWPS. Only unimproved land which is in LFAs can be entered in the FWPS.

Annual payments continue for 15 years for woodland containing more than 50 per cent by area of broadleaved trees and 10 years for woodland containing less than 50 per cent broadleaved trees or fast growing broadleaves that will be felled in less than 30 years (*e.g.* poplars). Woodlands planted for the purpose of agroforestry, Christmas trees or coppicing are not eligible for annual payments under the FWPS (unless coppicing is for conservation purposes, in which case prior approval will be required).

There is a minimum area requirement of 1 hectare to enter the FWPS but no restriction on the minimum size of individual woods created, providing WGS criteria are met. Not more than 200 hectares of an agricultural business can be entered into the FWPS (and not more than 40 hectares of unimproved land in the LFAs).

H. *Woodland and Set-aside*

Farm woodland planted under the Woodland Grant Scheme and the Farm Woodland Premium Scheme on arable land meeting the eligibility requirements for arable area payments will count towards a farmer's set-aside obligations. Farmers will receive the Woodland Grant and Farm Woodland Premium Scheme payments, not set-aside payments. The exception is short-rotation coppice planted on set-aside land, which is not eligible for entry into the Farm Woodland Premium Scheme and will receive set-aside payments.

I. Taxation

Income from commercial woodlands is no longer subject to income tax, and tax relief cannot be claimed for the cost of establishing new woodlands.

In general Woodland Grant Scheme grants are tax free but annual payments under the Farm Woodland Premium Scheme and Livestock Exclusion Annual Premia are regarded as compensation for agricultural income forgone and are liable to income tax.

The sale of timber does not attract Capital Gains Tax, although the disposal of the underlying land may give rise to an assessment.

Woodlands which are managed commercially or which are ancillary to a farming business may be eligible for either Business Property Relief or Agricultural Relief for Inheritance Tax purposes.

Acknowledgement. The above estimates are based in part on information supplied by John Clegg & Co.

A magazine, "Forestry and British Timber", is published monthly (Miller Freeman, telephone 01732-377651).

SHORT-ROTATION COPPICE

The UK government has a legal commitment to reduce emissions of six greenhouse gasses by 12½% from 1990 levels by 2008-2012; and it made promises in its manifesto to reduce carbon dioxide emissions by 20% and generate 10% of electricity from renewable resources by 2010. It also has a target 1500 MW of electricity to be generated from renewable resources by 2000. A number of power stations are planned which will use renewable energy resources of which short rotation coppice (SRC) will form a valuable part. (MAFF calculated that to generate 10% of electricity from renewable resources by 2010 would require 110,000-150,000 of SRC planted by 2007, to be in production by 2010).

In the summer of 1999 the first of these power stations, in Yorkshire, is nearing completion (another in Carlisle has been granted planning permission). Farmers within a 40-mile radius of the station are being offered contracts to grow up to 2,000 ha of SRC, which will eventually supply 75% of the raw material (forest residues will make up the balance). The project is supported by MAFF and qualifies for the Locational Supplement to the Woodland Grant. The crop can be grown on set-aside land and qualify for the annual area payment. At present there are around 520 ha of SRC in the UK, most of it in the catchment area, and another 750 ha are expected in 2000 and 2001.

ARBRE, the company concerned with the first power station, offers a 16-year contract to farmers for growing SRC. The minimum area per farm is 5 ha at present but in 2000 will be 10 ha. The farmer is required to provide a sterile seedbed ready for spring sowing and to roll after planting. ARBRE provides and erects rabbit fencing, provides and plants cuttings at about 15,000/ha and provides post-planting weed and pest control if necessary. After the first winter the crop is usually cut back to encourage coppicing. After another three years the crop is harvested and then harvested every three years thereafter. The farmer helps to transport the bundled crop to a storage site on the farm. At some point during the following 12 months the crop is chipped on site into wagons and transported to the power station. The farmer has little input other than maintaining the rabbit fencing and providing some transport and storage, but fertilizer can be applied to increase yield (Yorkshire Water, part of the consortium, will provide sewage sludge free or for transport cost alone). After 16 years ARBRE can be contracted for further cycles or will reinstate the land to its original use or the farmer can use the crop for other markets. (Border Biofuels, another similar company, will be largely following the ARBRE model.)

The farmer receives a payment based on yield, currently £20 per oven dried tonne (ODT), index linked for the contract term. Yields should average 30 ODT/ha for the first harvest, probably increasing for subsequent ones. Interim payments are paid between harvest years. Of the £1000/ha of Woodland Grant Locational Supplement £367/ha is passed to the farmer, who also receives the set-aside payment for the land, though this payment cannot be guaranteed for more than five years.

ARBRE has begun planning for the next generation of power stations, three times the size of the first and therefore each requiring 5-6,000 ha of SRC.

On Arable land: in addition to the prescribed level of "compulsory" set-aside, up to 100% voluntary set-aside is at present permitted for energy crops. Although there is no guarantee that this will continue the expectation is that it will for energy crops. On arable land EU member states can pay up to 50% of establishment costs for perennial energy crops. MAFF has set this at £2,000/ha; hence the grant will be £1,000/ha linked with the ARBRE power station project. British Biogen hopes that this will apply nationally in future where a farmer can prove he has a market outlet for his energy crop or a genuine on-site use.

On Grassland: there is a new EU Rural Development Regulation which allows support for planting costs for perennial crops on grassland (no percentage yet quoted) but not annual payments. British Biogen hopes that MAFF will negotiate something equivalent to arable land, *i.e.* 50% of establishment costs plus an annual payment equivalent to other land uses. This might be related to headage payments or a farmer might possibly trade in headage payments for area support.

Contracts for SCR for subsequent power stations may differ from the current one to some degree. In the future it is possible that growers could establish the crop themselves and provide wood chip at the power plant gate. A price for this would have to be set to reflect the fact that the grower had borne all the costs of production and management himself.

Costs and Returns with an ARBRE contract:

Establishment Costs	£/ha
Cuttings (15,000 at 7p)	1,050
Weed and pest control	140
Rabbit frncing	350
Cultivations	100
Planting	200
Total	1,840

Returns (£per hectare)

Year	1	2	3	4	5
Production (OD tonnes)					30
Price (£ per OD tonne)	20				22·5
Sale Value					675
Interim payment	110	113	117	120	-460
Woodland Grant	367				
Set-aside payment (approx.)*	240	240	240	240	240
Total Returns/Gross Margin	644**	353	357	360	455

* Set-aside cannot be guaranteed after five years.

** Gross returns less £73 spray costs for seedbed preparation.

After year 5 sales would occur in years 8, 11 etc.

Researcher: Angela Edwards.

SET-ASIDE

The Provisions

The set-aside scheme must be complied with in order to obtain the area payments introduced under the 1992 and 1999 CAP Reform programmes to compensate for reduced market price support.

Using the assumptions described on page 8, giving a euro value of 70p, including agrimonetary compensation, the following would be the payments per hectare (acre) in year 2000, to the nearest £1:

England	Scotland non LFA	Scotland LFA	Wales non LFA	Wales LFA	N. Ireland non LFA	N. Ireland LFA
242 (98)	233 (94)	214 (87)	212 (86)	207 (84)	214 (87)	207 (84)

A simplified scheme with no set-aside commitment is available for those claiming payments on a standardised area that would produce 92 tonnes of grain at average grain yields for the area; this is 15·62 ha (38·6 acres) in England. However, only the cereals aid rate per ha is then paid, even on land used to grow oilseeds or protein crops. To claim the higher aid rates for these crops it is necessary to join the general scheme and set aside land. Those growing more than the 15·62 ha may opt out of set-aside and claim the cereal aid rate on just the 15·62 ha, but over 20 ha (50 acres) or so the penalty of doing so in terms of the area payments forgone is prohibitive, particularly when the set-aside percentage requirement is low.

Two previous eligibility requirements for set-aside land no longer apply, namely that it must have been cultivated with a view to harvest or have been in a set-aside scheme the previous year and that it had to have been farmed by the claimant for at least two years (with certain exemptions). Rules were further relaxed in December 1998, allowing the exchange of ineligible for eligible land (thus helping to free up rotations) and giving more flexibility when sowing a crop coming out of set-aside for the next year harvest.

A number of different set-aside options are available:

1. *Obligatory set-aside*

    Prior to 1996 there was a choice between rotational set-aside and three different options of so-called "flexible" set-aside, with the required set-aside percentages higher for the latter than the former. In 1996 the distinction between the two was abolished and there is now complete flexibility of choice. The percentage was 5% in 1997 and 1998 and 10% in 1999 and 2000. These percentages are percentages of the total area of claimed land plus the set-aside area. The eligible crops consist primarily of cereals, oilseed rape (with specified requirements), linseed, field beans, dried peas and maize. These crops are eligible for aid whether grown for grain, seed or fodder — except in the latter case for any crop(s) grown on land counting towards the forage area under the beef regime (stocking rate restriction). A change made in 1998 was that land from which "multi-annual" crops, such as blackcurrants, have been harvested in the previous year is now eligible for set aside; also, member states may allow producers to set aside an area in excess of the area under aided crops, provided this is used for multi-annual crops for biomass production.

2. *Voluntary set-aside*

    This is open to all those receiving area aid under the main scheme. However, there has been a limit: the extra set-aside area, together with the obligatory set-aside area, could not exceed the total cropped area on which area aid is claimed, plus any penalty set-aside (now abolished, see 5 below). Under the Agenda 2000 agreements member states are able to set a maximum area, which cannot be less than 10% and may be up to 100%; the UK decision is awaited.

3. *Additional Voluntary set-aside*

Where land was set-aside under the *old 5-year scheme,* the limit described overleaf for voluntary set-aside could be exceeded right up to 100%, but it had to remain in set-aside for a further five years. All land claimed as additional voluntary set-aside must have been five-year set-aside claimed for in 1997. The set-aside payment is reduced on that area which exceeds the cropped area: this is at 70% of the full rate.

4. *Guaranteed set-aside*

Where the farmer undertakes that the same plots will be set aside for five years the prevailing set-aside payment (in ecus/hectare) will not be reduced for five years, though it may be increased. This only applies up to the percentage limit for non-rotational set-aside or on any ex-5 year scheme set-aside land. If any of the latter exceeds the cropped area on which arable area payments are claimed the lower additional voluntary set-aside rate is paid. One may opt out of the agreement to enter a scheme under a forestry or agri-environment action programme, or if compulsorily purchased; a penalty is imposed if withdrawn for other reasons. Only land down to short rotation coppice with the aid of a Woodland Grant planting grant or entered into the Countryside Access Scheme (see page 63) is now eligible for new guaranteed set-aside agreements.

5. *Penalty set-aside*

This was imposed if a regional base area for eligible crops were exceeded; it received no set-aside payment. However, penalty set-aside has now been abolished.

Transfers of part or all of ones set-aside obligation are no longer allowed.

Land normally ineligible for area payments or set-aside are permanent grass, permanent crops (*e.g.* top fruit), woodland or a non-agricultural use. Land entered into certain agri-environmental and forestry schemes may be counted as set-aside.

Whether it is better to choose rotational or non-rotational set-aside depends on how variable in quality the land is (the more it varies the more this is likely to favour non-rotational) and how much the rotational benefits are valued (possible increases in yield, opportunities for grass weed control, good entry for oilseed rape). Non-rotational entails easier management and probably lower costs and provides greater scope for environmental benefits.

A range of non-food crops may be grown on set-aside land (*e.g.* industrial rape and linseed [see pages 21-22]), under contract and with strict rules, including a few perennial crops such as short rotation coppice. Otherwise no cash crop must be planted, nor must any livestock or non-agricultural animals be grazed upon it. Indeed no lucrative non-agricultural activity is allowed, unless it could equally well be carried out if there were a standing crop; certain small-scale local and/or charitable events may be given permission.

The minimum size of each set-aside block must be 0·3 ha; the minimum width has been 20 metres, but in June 1999 the EU farm council agreed that this could be reduced to 10 metres provided the member state proves an environmental benefit. Given these requirements, field margins may be set aside. The land must be kept in good agricultural condition.

The rotational set-aside period is from 15th January to 31st August, but from 15th July producers may sow crops for harvest the next year. From 1st September to 14th January producers may not sell any green cover remaining on the land, whether for grazing, hay or silage, but they may harvest these crops for their own use or graze their own animals on it during this period. No crop may be sown to harvest or graze before 15th January, *e.g.* stubble turnips.

Rules. *Green cover* is required on set-aside land in England and Wales and Northern Ireland by 15th January, unless a harvest crop is still in the ground on 1st October; natural regeneration is permitted; cover crops must not contain more than 5% legumes. All livestock must be removed from set-aside land by 15th January. *Cutting is* allowed at any time but it is not advised between April and mid-July; if a non-selective herbicide is used cutting is banned between 15th April and 30th June and cultivation banned before 1st July (except for registered organic farmers [1st May]). 25% of each set-aside field may be left uncut, for up to three years, to provide a more varied habitat for wildlife. Non-selective, non-residual *herbicides* are allowed to be used in England and Wales after 15th April (1st May in Scotland). No cultivation of set-aside for weed control is allowed until after 30th June (except for organic producers). If a non-selective herbicide is used between 15th April and 30th June set-aside may not be cut until 1st July (15th July in Scotland). Between 15th July and 15th August green cover must either be cut short at least once and the cuttings left on the ground to rot or be destroyed by 31st August. *Cultivations* are allowed from 15th July for crops to follow set-aside for harvesting the following year (after 15th January). Grazing of the farmers' own animals (or other farmers' animals if no payment is made) and hay and silage making for the farmers' own use are allowed after 1st September. *Fertilizer and manure* applications are not allowed unless the manure or slurry is generated on the same farm and applied on green cover; liming is allowed. Hedging and ditching are allowed. Drainage is permitted after 15th July.

Gains and Losses

On the land that has to be set aside the farmer will lose the crop gross margins forgone less the set-aside payment and fuel and repair costs saved (approximately £85/ha, £35/acre); contractors' charges, where used *e.g.* for harvesting, will also be saved. There will also be some saving in interest on working capital. Adding to the (likely) net loss will be the cost of cover crops, if sown, cutting, etc.

With rotational set-aside there should be some yield benefit. There should also be some timeliness benefit if the same labour and machinery is available as before. Both are difficult to estimate financially.

On some larger farms at least it has been possible to cut fixed costs, primarily regular labour and machinery depreciation/leasing — possibly by enough to compensate. But for many smaller and medium-sized farms this is impossible. However, some savings in casual labour and overtime, and, given time, machinery depreciation, should be possible on many farms.

Any net loss may also have been reduced by crop substitutions: primarily higher for lower gross margin crops. However, unless the farmer had been slack in his choice of crops in the past this possibility was limited and could have led to rotational losses, *e.g.* if more second and third wheats were grown, but it should at least have been possible to put a higher percentage of the land into first wheats.

Inevitably the possibilities and balance of gains and losses are different on every farm.

The Countryside Access Scheme

This voluntary scheme, launched in autumn 1994, offered farmers additional payments on top of the set-aside payments for providing new opportunities for public access to suitable farmland for walking and other forms of quiet recreation. The scheme has now been closed to new applicants (though all existing agreements will continue until the end of their five-year terms), but elements remain available under the Countryside Stewardship and Environmentally Sensitive Area schemes (pages 203-4).

A NOTE ON DIVERSIFICATION

While diversification is to be encouraged, wherever feasible, especially to help maintain incomes when the main farm enterprises are falling in profitability, a number of points need stressing. Most new enterprises require a substantial amount of capital; many need skills (both in production and marketing) which take time, or a particular type of personality, to acquire; the market may be limited; hence there is often a considerable level of risk attached. Nevertheless, there are many ventures to be seen where entrepreneurial skills have achieved notable success.

Some of these "diversification enterprises" have been included above and there are more in the next section. There are many others. Some are as follows:

Christmas Trees	Wild Boar	Tourism:
Herbs	Adventure Games	Bed and Breakfast
Crayfish	Clay Pigeon Shooting	Caravans
Llamas	Barn Conversions	Holiday Cottages
Ostriches	Horses:	"Added Value" enterprises:
Quails	Riding School	Yoghurt, ice cream, etc.
Rabbits	Trekking	
Snails		

2. GRAZING LIVESTOCK

DAIRY COWS

Holstein Friesians (per Cow)

Performance level (yield (1)) ...	Low	Average	High	Very High
Milk Yield per Cow (litres) (2)	5500	6250	7000	7750

	£	£	£	£
Milk Value per Cow (3) ...	1018	1156	1295	1434
PLUS Value of Calves (4) ...	55	55	55	55
PLUS Value of Cull Cows (5) ...	77	77	77	77
LESS Cost or Market Value of Replacements (6, 7)	187	187	187	187
OUTPUT ...	963	1101	1240	1379
Concentrate Costs (8) ...	158	194	233	276
Miscellaneous Variable Costs (10) ,,,	123	127	131	135
GROSS MARGIN before deducting Forage Variable Costs (inc. Bought Fodder)* ...	682	780	876	968
(Margin of Milk Value over Concentrates [9]) ...	860	962	1062	1158

*No deduction has been made for annual value of leased or purchased milk quota, which will vary considerably between farms.

Gross Margins per Cow and per Hectare (Acre) at 4 different stocking rates (11) are:

Performance level ...	Low	Average	High	Very High
1. At 1·75 cows per forage hectare (low):				
(0·57 forage hectares (1·4 acres) per cow)				
Forage Var. Costs & Bulk Feeds per Cow (11)...	65	65	65	65
GROSS MARGIN per Cow ...	617	715	811	903
GROSS MARGIN per Forage Hectare ...	1080	1250	1420	1580
GROSS MARGIN per Forage Acre ...	437	506	575	639
2. At 2 cows per forage hectare (average):				
(0·5 forage hectares (1·25 acres) per cow)				
Forage Var. Costs & Bulk Feeds per Cow (11)...	**80**	**80**	**80**	**80**
GROSS MARGIN per Cow ...	**602**	**700**	**796**	**888**
GROSS MARGIN per Forage Hectare ...	**1205**	**1400**	**1590**	**1775**
GROSS MARGIN per Forage Acre ...	**488**	**567**	**643**	**718**
3. At 2·25 cows per forage hectare (high): ...				
(0·45 forage hectares (1·1 acres) per cow)				
Forage Var. Costs & Bulk Feeds per Cow (11)...	95	95	95	95
GROSS MARGIN per Cow ...	587	685	781	873
GROSS MARGIN per Forage Hectare ...	1320	1540	1755	1965
GROSS MARGIN per Forage Acre ...	534	623	710	795
4. At 2·5 cows per forage hectare (very high):				
(0·4 forage hectares (1 acre) per cow)				
Forage Var. Costs & Bulk Feeds per Cow (11)...	110	110	110	110
GROSS MARGIN per Cow ...	572	670	766	858
GROSS MARGIN per Forage Hectare ...	1430	1675	1915	2145
GROSS MARGIN per Forage Acre ...	579	678	775	868

1. Performance level refers primarily to milk yield, although increases in this are usually (though not *necessarily*) associated with higher gross margins. Some increase in concentrate feeding (kg/litre) has been assumed as yield rises: see further note 8, page 67.

2. *Yield.* The yield referred to is litres produced during a year divided by the average number of cows and calved heifers in the herd. The average yield given (6,250 litres) is an estimated national figure for sizeable herds of black and white cows in 2000. Note the *average* yields in 1998/99 for *costed herds* (*e.g.* Axient Milkminder, ADAS Milk Cheque, Dalgety, Bibby) are invariably well above national averages and are likely to exceed 6,750 litres in 2000. Average yields in the national Milk Recording Scheme are similarly high.

3. *Milk Price.* This is assumed (as an average for the 2000 calendar year) to be 18·5p per litre, after deducting transport costs. It incorporates all adjustments: for milk composition, hygiene and seasonality. This is an average for all milk marketing groups, after bonuses etc., assuming an average-sized herd. Variable transport charges according to the amount collected mean that smaller herds will achieve a lower average price.

The average price received by individual producers depends on seasonality of production and compositional quality. Output and Gross Margin per cow are changed approximately as follows by each 0·25p per litre difference in price at each performance level:

Low	Average	High	Very High
±£13·5	±£16·5	±£17·5	±£19·5

Seasonality Price Adjustments (Milk Marque and most of the major dairy companies, p per litre):

	April	May	June	July	Aug.	Sept.	Oct.-Mar.
1999/2000	−1·5	−2·2	−1·1	+2·6	+2·2	+0·4	0

There is a level delivery option: no seasonal adjustments if supplies in a calendar month are within 10% of an agreed daily volume.

Compositional Quality Payments

Constituent values vary widely between buyers and months. As an example, Milk Marque's were, in June 1999:

Butterfat: 1·78p per litre per 1 per cent.
Protein: 2·99p per litre per 1 per cent.

The *standard litre* is 4·15% butterfat and 3·35% protein.

Breeds and average milk composition by breed are as follows (England and Wales, MMB recorded herds, 2-year averages, 1995/6 and 1996/7):

		% Cows 1988/9*	2000**	Butterfat %	Protein %
Holstein Friesian	...	94·1	95·5	4·055	3·26
Ayrshire		1·9	1·5	4·06	3·32
Dairy Shorthorn	... ...	0·6	0·3	3·87	3·275
Jersey		1·7	1·5	5·535	3·87
Guernsey		1·4	1·2	4·805	3·555
All Breeds	... ...			4·085	3·27

*No later data traced. **Author's guesstimate.*

Within Breed Quality Variation. For Friesians only, the upper and lower deciles in the 1986/87 Milkminder (MMB) sample were as follows:

Upper: Butterfat 4·11%; Protein 3·32%.
Lower: Butterfat 3·75%; Protein 3·17%.

The difference in milk value between these two levels is approx. 1·2p per litre (6·3% of the average price).

Hygiene Price Adjustments (Milk Marque, from October 1999, p per litre):
Note: these adjustments vary widely between the different dairy companies.

A. Bactoscan (bacteria measure)

Band	Bactoscan Reading	Price Adjustment (ppl)
A+	0- 65,000	+0·3
A	66-115,000	nil
B	116-250,000	- 0·5
C1*	Over 250,000	- 6
C2**	Over 250,000	-10

*1st month. **2nd and any subsequent months.

B. Somatic Cell Count (Mastitis) (from April 1999).

Band	Count	Price Adjustment (ppl)
1+	0-150,000	+3
1	151-250,000	nil
2	251-400,000	- 0·5
3*	Over 400,000	- 6
4**	Over 400,000	-10

*1st month. **2nd and any subsequent months.

C. *Antibiotics.* The price of all milk in a consignment that fails an antibiotics test is 1p/litre.

Organic milk: 29·5p per litre expected for 1999/2000 (Organic Milk Suppliers Co-operative). Milk Marque's organic premium was 11·1 ppl in June 1999.

4. *Value of Calves.* Average annual value per cow of purebred and beef cross heifer and bull calves of all qualities, at 10-20 days old, allowing for mortality and average calving index of 385 days. The Calf Processing Aid Scheme has ended.

5. *Value of Cull Cows.* £280, allowing for casualties; 27·5% per annum replacement rate.

6. *Cost of Replacements.* £680 per down-calving heifer (purchase price or market value (mainly home-reared)); 27·5% per annum replacement rate.

7. *Herd Depreciation:* thus averages (approximately) £110 per cow per year, *i.e.,* 27·5 per cent of £400 *(i.e.,* £680-£280).
   Net Replacement Cost = £55 per cow per year, *i.e.,* herd depreciation (£110) less value of calves (£55).
   Bull. AI is assumed in the tables; bull depreciation would be approx. £360 a year (£2,500 purchase price less £700 cull value, 5-year herd life); tight calving pattern: 60 cows per bull, well spread calving pattern: 100; 10 to 20 tonnes silage, 0·75 tonnes concentrates a year.

8. *Concentrate Costs.*

Amounts: Performance level:	Low	Average	High	Very High
kg/litre (approx.) :	·25	·27	·29	·31
tonnes/cow :	1·375	1·69	2·03	2·4

Price: taken (for 2000) as £115 per tonne, which is an average of home-mixed rations and purchased compounds of varying nutritive value, averaged throughout the year.
   A difference of £10 per tonne has approximately the following effect on margin over concentrates and gross margin per cow, on the assumptions made regarding the quantity fed at each performance level:

Low	Average	High	Very High
±£14·5	±£17·5	±£21	±£25

67

Seasonality. Typically, specialist spring calving herds (60% or more calvings between January and May), compared with autumn calving herds (60% or more calvings between August and December), use 0·09 kg per litre/550 kg (£63) per cow per year less concentrates. See further note 12 below.

Typical Monthly Variation in Concentrate Feeding (kg per litre)

Winter			Summer		
October	...	...	0·31	April	...	...	0·26
November	...	...	0·33	May	...	...	0·16
December	...	...	0·33	June	...	...	0·16
January	...	...	0·33	July	...	...	0·21
February	...	...	0·32	August	...	...	0·25
March	...	...	0·30	September	...	...	0·28

Average winter: 0·32   Average summer: 0·22

Average whole year: 0·27

The actual distribution on any individual farm will obviously vary according to such factors as seasonality of calving, level of milk yield, grazing productivity during the summer, and the quantity and quality of bulk feeds in the winter. The March figure in particular will be affected by type of soil and seasonal rainfall.

Yield with no concentrates and good quality silage: approximately 4000 litres (autumn calvers; 4,500 claimed in New Zealand).

9. *Margin over Concentrates and Concentrates per litre*

The emphasis in the initial tables should be laid on the differences between the margin of milk value over concentrates per cow; the same large variation can occur with widely differing combinations of milk yield and quantity of concentrates fed.

In the following table, at each yield level figures are given for (a) *margin of milk value over concentrates* per cow (£) and (b) *concentrates per litre* (kg) at five levels of concentrate feeding.

Yield level Milk Yield per cow (litres)	Low 5,500		Average 6,250		High 7,000		Very High 7,750	
	(a)	(b)	(a)	(b)	(a)	(b)	(a)	(b)
	£	kg	£	kg	£	kg	£	kg
1·00 tonne (£115) concs. per cow	903	·18	1041	·16	1180	·14	—	—
1·50 tonne (£172) concs. per cow	846	·27	984	·24	1123	·21	1262	·19
2·00 tonne (£230) concs. per cow	788	·36	926	·32	1065	·29	1204	·26
2·50 tonne (£287) concs. per cow	—	—	869	·40	1008	·36	1147	·32
3·00 tonne (£345) concs. per cow	—	—	—	—	—	—	1089	·39

On the same assumptions re the other items of output and variable costs as in the tables on page 65 a very high *margin over concentrates of £1,200 per cow* (in 2000) would give the following results (£):

Stocking rate	Average	High	Very High
Gross Margin per Cow	988	969	950
Gross Margin per Forage Hectare	1975	2180	2375
Gross Margin per Forage Acre	800	880	960

This level of margin over concentrates (£1,200) can be achieved by a range of combinations of yield and concentrate feeding. With the price of milk (18·5p/l) and concentrates (£115/tonne) assumed the following are examples: 7,500 litres, 1·63 tonnes/cow, ·22 kg/l; 8,000, 2·43, ·30; 8,500, 3·24, ·38.

10. *Miscellaneous Variable Costs* (average)

	£
Bedding*	17
Vet. and Med.	39
A.I. and Recording/Consultancy Fees	42
Consumable dairy stores, etc.	29
Total	127

* *Straw* can vary from 0·4 to 1·5 tonne per cow and from £10 to £30 per tonne (or even more in some areas in exceptional years).

11. *Stocking Rate and Forage Costs.* **The stocking rates given assume that nearly all requirements of bulk foods — both winter and summer — are obtained from the forage area,** *i.e.* little is bought in. On average about 55 per cent of the forage area (or production) is grazed and 45 per cent conserved. It will be observed that as the stocking density increases, gross margin *per cow* falls, but gross margin *per hectare* rises.

The levels of nitrogen are assumed to be as follows: 1·75 cows per forage hectare, 160 kg (128 units/acre), 2·0, 220 (176); 2·25, 275 (220); 2·5, 360 (288). An increase in potash application is also assumed. Seed costs clearly depend on the percentage of permanent pasture, if any, the length of leys, etc. **The following forage costs per hectare (fertilizer, seed and sprays) have been assumed for grassland:** 1·75 cows per forage hectare, £75 (£30/acre); 2·0, £100 (40); 2·25, £130 (53); 2·5, £160 (65). Forage maize costs are higher, averaging £210/ha (£85/acre).

A small amount of purchased bulk fodder is assumed, increasing with the stocking rate as follows (per cow): low £10, average £15, high £20, very high £25.

An increase in stocking density can be obtained not only by intensifying grassland production, as above, but also by buying in winter bulk fodder (assuming the same level of concentrate feeding in both cases). This will cause the gross margin *per cow* to fall still further, but will usually result in a higher gross margin *per hectare* than where all forage is conserved on the farm — at any given level of grassland management.

In the table below four examples are given: two policies at two different stocking rates. (A) and (B) assume the land is used for grazing only, i.e. all winter bulk fodder is purchased. (C) and (D) assume the land provides grazing and half the winter bulk fodder, the other half being bought in. (A) and (C) assume a stocking rate equivalent to 2 cows per hectare where the land provides both grazing and all the winter bulk fodder, which is an average level of stocking. (B) and (D) assume the equivalent of 2·5 cows per hectare where all bulk food is provided both summer and winter, which is a very high level of stocking. It is assumed that the full winter fodder requirement is 2 tonnes of hay (or other equivalent foods), costing £130 per cow if it is all purchased. (Prices vary widely according to the season and part of the country.) Forage variable costs per hectare (acre) are £110 (45) and £185 (75) at the average and high levels of stocking respectively.

		Margin of Milk Value over Concentrates			
		Low	Average	High	Very High
		Gross Margin per Forage Hectare (Acre)			
		£	£	£	£
(A)	All winter fodder purchased; average stocking rate... ...	1905 (770)	2265 (915)	2615 (1060)	2945 (1190)
(B)	All winter fodder purchased; very high stocking rate ...	2350 (950)	2795 (1130)	3230 (1305)	3650 (1475)
(C)	½ winter fodder purchased; average stocking rate... ...	1490 (605)	1745 (705)	1995 (805)	2230 (900)
(D)	½ winter fodder purchased; very high stocking rate ...	1830 (740)	2145 (870)	2455 (995)	2755 (1115)

69

It must obviously not be forgotten that "fixed" costs per hectare, *e.g.* labour and depreciation on buildings, can increase considerably if an increase in stocking density is achieved by keeping more cows, at least when cow numbers outstrip the capacity of existing buildings and labour. Furthermore, husbandry problems such as poaching will multiply, unless zero-grazing is practised — with its further additions to fixed costs and management difficulties. Obviously, too, there is the cost of additional quota to consider.

12. *Seasonality.* Price and concentrate feeding differences according to the seasonality of production have already been outlined in notes 3 and 8.
   Typically, autumn calving herds tend to average 6 or 7% (300-400 litres) above spring calving herds but feed 80% (0·6-0·7 tonnes) more concentrates cow/year; spring calving herds should normally only be feeding about 0·15 kg/litre (for the whole year). The average milk price would be expected to be higher for autumn calving herds, but the difference is less than might be supposed and has been reduced in recent years with better prices being paid for summer milk.

13. *Quota.* For many years the price of unused quota averaged around 35p a litre and leasing 5p to 5·5p, with levels in Scotland significantly higher. However, values have been higher and very variable since late 1993, rising to peaks of 80p and 20p respectively in late 1994/early 1995. Values are particularly dependent on the levels of farmgate milk prices and milk production v. quota. Between mid-1998 and mid-1999 unused 4% butterfat quota ranged between 33p and 40p a litre to buy and between 6·5 and 8·5p a litre to lease, dropping to approximately 30p and 5·9p respectively in mid-August 1999.

14. *Labour:* see page 135.

15. *Building Costs:* see page 171.

16. *Costs per litre (Holstein Friesians)*

	Average (pence)		"Premium" (pence)	
Concentrates	3·36		2·65	
Forage and Bought Bulk Feed	1·28		0·95	
Vet. & Med.	0·63		0·45	
Miscellaneous Variable Costs	1·41		1·00	
Total Variable Costs		6·68		5·05
Labour: direct (milking etc.)	3·74		3·05	
: field/farm work	1·45		1·00	
Power and Machinery	2·75		1·90	
Rent/Rental Value	1·75		1·20	
General Overheads	1·35		0·85	
Total Fixed Costs		11·04		8·00
Net Replacement Cost		0·80		0·30
Total (excl. Quota Leasing/Purchase)		18·52		13·35

Notes on the above
With regard to the average costs the variable costs per litre are derived from the data (and therefore the assumptions made) in the main per cow cost table on page 65. The labour cost is as on page 135. The average fixed costs are as for the medium-sized farm data on page 158, with adjustments made to allow for the greater use of resources by dairy cows compared with followers (and possibly cereals). The "premium" figures are as estimated for the average of the most profitable 20% of herds.
Labour includes farmer and any unpaid family labour.
Power and machinery cover all machinery and equipment costs, including the use of farm vehicles, etc.
General overheads similarly relate to the whole farm, including property repairs.

Where the dairy is part of a farm with other enterprises on a significant scale most of the fixed costs per cow and therefore per litre are difficult to determine.

The net replacement cost is herd depreciation less the value of calves.

As said in the table, the cost of additional quota, whether leasing charges or the annual cost of purchased quota, is not included.

Note too that neither interest on capital nor any management charge have been included.

If leasing or buying extra quota is being considered it is of course not the average but the marginal cost of producing the extra milk that needs to be considered. This will depend largely on whether the extra milk is being obtained through increasing yield per cow or by keeping more cows (or a combination of the two).

Channel Island Breeds

	Low	Average	High	Very High
Performance level (yield)	Low	Average	High	Very High
Milk Yield per Cow (litres)	3825	4350	4875	5400
	£	£	£	
Milk Value per Cow	880	1000	1120	1240
Concentrate Costs per Cow	145	178	214	253
Margin of Milk Value over Concentrates per Cow	735	822	906	987
Herd Depreciation less Value of Calves ...	44	44	44	44
Miscellaneous Variable Costs	123	127	131	135
GROSS MARGIN per Cow before deducting Forage Variable Costs	568	651	731	808
Forage Variable Costs/Bought Fodder ...	68	68	68	68
GROSS MARGIN per Cow	500	583	663	740
GROSS MARGIN per Forage Hectare (2·35 cows per hectare: 0·425 hectares/cow) ...	1175	1370	1560	1740
GROSS MARGIN per Forage Acre (1·05 acres/cow)	476	554	631	704

Notes

1. *Yield.* Average of Jerseys and Guernseys. See Note 2 for Holstein Friesians (page 66). Guernseys average some 200 litres more than Jerseys (*i.e.* approximately 4250 for Jerseys, 4450 for Guernseys) but the latter achieve a higher average price of around 3p per litre. Note that the average for Channel Island *costed herds* should not be compared with the average national (Pocketbook) figure for Holstein Friesians; costed herd yield averages are invariably well above national averages; (*i.e.* they are likely to be close to 4,750 litres for CI costed herds in 2000).

2. *Milk Price.* This has been assumed to be 23p per litre (average of Jerseys and Guernseys), *i.e.* 4·5p above Holstein Friesian milk; (24·25p Jersey milk, 21·75p Guernsey). Milk Marque's Channel Island premium (*i.e.* additional to compositional quality benefit) was 0·8 ppl in June 1999.

3. *Concentrate Costs.*

Amounts: Performance level:	Low	Average	High	Very High
kg/litre :	·315	·34	·365	·39
tonnes/cow :	1·205	1·48	1·78	2·105

Price: taken (for 2000) as £120 per tonne.

The following table shows for each production level (a) the margin of milk value over concentrates per cow (£) and (b) concentrates per litre (kg) at three levels of concentrate feeding.

Performance level	Low		Average		High		Very High	
Milk Yield per cow (litres) ...	3825		4350		4875		5400	
	(a)	(b)	(a)	(b)	(a)	(b)	(a)	(b)
	£	kg	£	kg	£	kg	£	kg
1·0 tonnes (£120) concs. per cow	760	·26	880	·23	1000	·21	—	—
1·5 tonnes (£180) concs. per cow	700	·39	820	·34	940	·31	1060	·28
2·0 tonnes (£240) concs. per cow	—	—	760	·46	880	·41	1000	·37
2·5 tonnes (£300) concs. per cow	—	—	—	—	—	—	940	·46

4. *Net Annual Replacement Value.* (*i.e.* Value of Calves less Herd Depreciation) were calculated as follows:

	£ per cow in herd
Cost of replacements: 27·5 per cent of herd per year @ £375...	103
LESS Value of culls: 27·5 per cent of herd per year @ £160 (allowing for casualties)*	44
Herd Depreciation	59
Annual Value of Calves**	15
Net Annual Replacement Cost	44

   * Cull cow prices for Guernseys are about £50 higher than for Jerseys.

** Allowing for calving index of 390 days and calf mortality; mixture of pure bred calves and beef crosses. Guernsey calves, especially crosses, fetch more than Jersey calves, averaging perhaps £10 more per head — but a lot more for some Guernsey beef crosses.

5. *Miscellaneous Variable Costs.* See Note 10 for Holstein Friesians (page 69).

6. *Stocking Rate.* See, in general, Note 11 for Holstein Friesians (page 69). The effect of varying the stocking rate on gross margin per forage hectare is as follows:

		GM/Cow before deducting Forage V.Cs.				
	Forage	Low	Average	High	Very High	Forage V.Cs.
Cows per	Hectares	£568	£651	£731	£808	per Cow
Forage	(Acres)					(inc. Bought
Hectare	per Cow					Fodder)
		Gross Margin per Forage Ha (Acre) (£)				£
2·1	0·48 (1·18)	1075 (435)	1250 (506)	1420 (575)	1580 (639)	55
2·4	**0·42 (1·03)**	**1200 (486)**	**1400 (567)**	**1590 (643)**	**1775 (718)**	**68**
2·7	0·37 (0·92)	1315 (532)	1540 (623)	1755 (710)	1965 (795)	81
3·0	0·33 (0·82)	1420 (575)	1670 (676)	1910 (773)	2140 (866)	94

A small amount of purchased bulk fodder is assumed, increasing with the stocking rate as follows (per cow): low £8, average £12, high £16, very high £20.

At the average stocking rate given above for combined Channel Island breeds (2·4 cows per forage ha) the average figure for Jerseys would be approximately 2·55 and that for Guernseys 2·25.

Ayrshires

Performance level (yield)	Low	Average	High	Very High
Milk Yield per Cow (litres)...	4850	5500	6150	6800
	£	£	£	
Milk Value per Cow ...	907	1028	1150	1272
Concentrate Costs per Cow...	139	171	205	243
Margin of Milk Value over Concentrates per Cow ...	768	857	945	1029
Herd Depreciation less Value of Calves ...	60	60	60	60
Miscellaneous Variable Costs ...	123	127	131	135
GROSS MARGIN per Cow before deducting Forage Variable Costs ...	585	670	754	834
Forage Variable Costs/Bought Fodder ...	76	76	76	76
GROSS MARGIN per Cow ...	509	604	678	758
GROSS MARGIN per Forage Hectare (2·1 cows per hectare: 0·475 hectares/cow)...	1070	1270	1425	1590
GROSS MARGIN per Forage Acre (1·175 acres/cow) ...	433	514	577	643

Notes

1. *Yield.* See Note 2 for Holstein Friesians (page 66).
2. *Milk Price.* See in general, note 3 for Holstein Friesians (page 66). The price assumed in the above table is 18·7p per litre. The compositional quality of milk from Ayrshires is higher than for the black and white breeds.
3. *Concentrate Costs.* See notes 8 and 9 for Holstein Friesians (pages 67-68). In the above table, the levels of feeding per kg (and tonnes per cow) are as follows: low ·25 (1·21 tonne), average ·27 (1·485), high ·29 (1·785), very high ·31 (2·11); price £115 per tonne.

   The following table shows, for each production level, (a) the margin of milk value over concentrates (£) and (b) concentrates per litre (kg) at three levels of concentrate feeding.

Performance level	Low		Average		High		Very High	
Milk Yield per Cow (litres)...	4850		5500		6150		6800	
	(a)	(b)	(a)	(b)	(a)	(b)	(a)	(b)
	£	kg	£	kg	£	kg	£	kg
1·00 tonnes (£115) concs. per cow	792	·21	913	·18	1035	·16	1157	·15
1·50 tonnes (£172) concs. per cow	735	·31	856	·27	978	·24	1100	·22
2·00 tonnes (£230) concs. per cow	677	·41	798	·36	920	·32	1042	·29
2·50 tonnes (£287) concs. per cow	—	—	741	·46	863	·41	985	·37

4. *Net Annual Replacement Value.* (*i.e.* Value of Calves less Herd Depreciation) were calculated as follows:

	£ per cow in herd
Cost of replacements: 27·5 per cent of herd per year @ £550...	151
LESS Value of culls: 27·5 per cent of herd per year @ £240 (allowing for casualties) ...	66
Herd Depreciation ...	85
Annual Value of Calves* ...	25
Net Annual Replacement Cost ...	60

* Allowing for calving index of 385 days and calf mortality; mixture of pure bred calves and beef crosses.

5. *Miscellaneous Variable Costs.* See Note 10 for Holstein Friesians (page 69).
6. *Stocking Rate.* See, in general, Note 11 for Holstein Friesians (page 69).

Shorthorns. The above data could be used for Shorthorns, although one would expect their cull and calf prices to be higher and the stocking rate is likely to be slightly lower: similar to Holstein Friesians.

DAIRY FOLLOWERS *(per Heifer reared)*

A. Holstein Friesians

Performance Level	Low £	Average £	High £
Value of heifer (allowing for culls) (1)...	640	640	640
LESS Value of calf (allowing for mortality) ...	68	68	68
OUTPUT	572	572	572
Variable Costs:			
Concentrate Costs (2) ...	134	119	104
Miscellaneous Variable Costs (3) ...	64	67	70
TOTAL VARIABLE COSTS (excluding Forage) ...	198	186	174
GROSS MARGIN per Heifer, before deducting Forage Variable Costs ...	374	386	398
Forage Variable Costs (fert. and seed) ...	44	51	55
GROSS MARGIN per Heifer...	330	335	343
Forage Hectares (Acres) per Heifer reared (4)...	0·95 (2·3)	0·725 (1·8)	0·575 (1·4)
GROSS MARGIN per Forage Hectare (5) ...	347	462	597
GROSS MARGIN per Forage Acre ...	140	187	242

B. Channel Island Breeds

Performance Level	Low £	Average £	High £
Value of heifer (allowing for culls) (1)...	355	355	355
LESS Value of calf (allowing for mortality) ...	15	15	15
OUTPUT	340	340	340
Variable Costs:			
Concentrate Costs (2) ...	110	100	90
Miscellaneous Variable Costs (3) ...	59	62	65
TOTAL VARIABLE COSTS (excluding Forage)	169	162	155
GROSS MARGIN per Heifer, before deducting Forage Variable Costs ...	171	178	185
Forage Variable Costs (fert. and seed) ...	35	40	43
GROSS MARGIN per Heifer...	136	138	142
Forage Hectares (Acres) per Heifer reared (4)...	0·75 (1·85)	0·575 (1·4)	0·45 (1·1)
GROSS MARGIN per Forage Hectare (5) ...	181	240	316
GROSS MARGIN per Forage Acre ...	73	97	128

N.B. On average, Channel Island heifers calve about three months younger than Holstein Friesians.

C. Ayrshires

Performance Level	Low £	Average £	High £
Value of heifer (allowing for culls) (1)...	520	520	520
LESS Value of calf (allowing for mortality) ...	35	35	35
OUTPUT	485	485	485
Variable Costs:			
Concentrates (2)...	125	113	100
Miscellaneous Variable Costs (3) ...	64	67	70
TOTAL VARIABLE COSTS (excluding Forage)	189	180	170
GROSS MARGIN per Heifer, before deducting Forage Variable Costs ...	296	305	315
Forage Variable Costs (fert. and seed) ...	44	50	54
GROSS MARTIN per Heifer ...	252	255	261
Forage Hectares (Acres) per Heifer reared (4) ...	0·9 (2·2)	0·7 (1·75)	0·55 (1·35)
GROSS MARGIN per Forage Hectare (5) ...	280	364	475
GROSS MARGIN per Forage Acre ...	113	147	192

Notes

1. The heifer values are based on the purchase price of down-calving heifers, allowing for culls. Most heifers are home-reared. If heifers are reared for sale, the price of whole batches are likely to be lower than the values given in the tables, by perhaps 10 or 15 per cent. On the other hand the purchaser will often take the batch a few months before the average expected calving date, thus reducing feed and area requirements for the rearer.

2. The lower levels of concentrate costs are the combined result of more economical feeding and a lower average calving age. (Other things being equal, however, including the overall level of management, a lower calving age requires higher levels of feeding.) Average (Holstein Friesians) = £39 to 3 months (see page 77) plus 250 kg calf concentrates @ £120/tonne and 500 kg @ £100/tonne.

3. Miscellaneous variable costs exclude straw. Straw requirements average approx. 1 tonne per heifer reared, but are variable, depending on time of year and age when calved, as well as system of housing and extent of outwintering. Vet. and med. approximately £35 per heifer reared.

4. The lower levels of area per heifer reared are the combined result of a higher stocking density and a lower average calving age.

   With an average calving age of 2 years 4 months, a "replacement unit" (*i.e.* calf + yearling + heifer) equals about 1·25 livestock units. The three stocking rates given above are equivalent to approximately 0·67, 0·58 and 0·5 forage hectares (1·65,1·45,1·25 acres) respectively per Holstein Friesian cow. The low figure assumes an average calving age of 2 years 6 months (1·4 livestock units) and the high figure one of 2 years 2 months (1·15 livestock units).

5. Much higher gross margin figures per hectare can be combined by intensive grazing methods, particularly if combined with winter feeding systems which involve little dependence on home-produced hay or silage (cf. Note 11, last three paragraphs, page 69).

6. *Contract Rearing:* see page 93.

7. *Labour:* see page 136.

Self-Contained Dairy Herd: Cows and Followers

At average annual replacement rates (27·5 per cent of the milking herd), nearly one-third of a replacement unit is required for each cow in the herd, *i.e.* roughly one calf, yearling and heifer for every three cows (including calved heifers) — with a few extra calves reared to allow for culling. At average stocking rates for both this means nearly 1 hectare devoted to followers for every 2 hectares for cows. Since surplus youngstock are often reared and frequently the stocking rate is less intensive the ratio is often well over 1:2 in practice. 1: 2·5 is about the minimum where all replacement heifers are reared, unless their winter feeding is based largely on straw and purchased supplements, or unless there is a combination of long average herd life and early calving, *i.e.* at 2 years old or just over.

Gross Margin per Forage Hectare (Acre) (£) for the Whole Herd (i.e., Cows and Followers Combined); (at four levels of performance, including four commensurate levels of stocking rate, for the dairy cows; and three levels of performance, including different stocking rates, for the followers) are as follows, *assuming a 2:1 land use ratio* (dairy cow area: followers area); (Holstein Friesians only):

| | | G.M. per Forage Hectare (Acre) Dairy Cows | | | |
		Low £	Average £	High £	Very High £
		1080 (437)	1400 (567)	1755 (710)	2145 (868)
G.M. per Forage	Low	347 (140)	835 (338)	1050 (425)	1285 (520)	1545 (625)
Hectare (Acre),	Average	462 (187)	875 (354)	**1085 (439)**	1325 (536)	1585 (641)
Followers	High	597 (242)	920 (372)	1130 (457)	1370 (554)	1630 (660)

As an example, the above table indicates that at the average level of performance and stocking rate for both cows and followers, the whole dairy gross margin per hectare (acre) figure falls to £1085 (439) compared with £1400 (567) for the dairy cows alone, a reduction of 22·5 per cent. If more than the assumed (minimum) number of dairy followers are kept and the ratio is 1·5:1 (*i.e.* 40% of the dairy herd forage area is devoted to followers rather than a third) the whole forage area figure (on the assumption again of average performance) falls to £1025 (415), which is a reduction of 27 per cent compared with cows only. However, the requirements per hectare for labour, machinery and buildings are of course less for heifer rearing than for dairy cows. The higher the value of replacement dairy heifers and cows the less the discrepancy between the gross margins of dairy cows alone and the self-contained herd.

Note that *for a combined, self-contained enterprise budget for the dairy herd and followers* there are the following differences:

Fewer calves for sale (as the required number of heifer calves are retained).

No replacement heifers/cows are purchased. (Thus high prices for replacement heifers reduces the gross margin of the milking herd and raises that of the dairy followers, but they have no effect on the gross margin of the combined, fully self-contained dairy herd breeding all its own replacements [assuming no surplus stock are reared]).

Value of any culled or surplus heifers are included.

Variable costs of replacements are added to those for the cows (on the basis of approximately one in-calf heifer entering the herd each year for every three cows [which allows for mortality and culling]).

BEEF

Finished Cattle Prices

During the first half of 1999 finished cattle prices for medium steers were fairly steady at between 90 and 92·5 p/kg lw, having fallen to nearly 75p in an autumn trough the previous year.

The prices assumed in the subsequent tables relate either to the *2000 calendar year* or *2000/2001* as appropriate (*e.g.* the latter is used for winter finished beef). They assume a spring (March/April) peak of 97·5p and an autumn (October) trough of 92·5p for steers; heifer prices are assumed to be 10% lower.

Premiums

These have been substantially changed by the Agenda 2000 agreements. See pages 9-11 and page 92 for additional details. Briefly the following payments have been assumed for the year 2000:

Suckler Cow Premium. £114/head.

Beef Special Premium. Steers £85, young bulls £112.

Slaughter Premium (new). Adult cattle £27, calves £17.

Extensification Premium (substantially altered). 1·6 to 2·0 LU per forage ha £23, below 1·6 £46.

For the Hill Livestock Compensatory Payments see pages 91/92.

Calf prices

Highly variable. It is the balance between three (or four) factors: calf (or store) prices, finished cattle prices and feedingstuff prices (and in some cases stocking rate), that will mainly determine the levels of the gross margin and profit for the different beef systems included in the following pages. Small differences in each factor can cause large differences in the margins. The values assumed for 2000 below relate to *all qualities*, in *all* markets, *at 7 to 10 days old*. (Prices for poorer quality calves fell to very low levels following the cessation of the Calf Processing Aid Scheme at the end of July 1999 but recovery is anticipated).

	Bulls	Heifers
Holstein Friesians	60	—
Hereford × Holstein Friesians	85	40
Limousin × Holstein Friesians	105	50
Simmental × Holstein Friesians	125	60
Charolais × Holstein Friesians	135	65

Note. Results from the Meat and Livestock Commission's Beefplan recording and costing service have been widely used in estimating many of the figures in this section.

Early Weaning—Bucket Rearing (per calf)

	3 months	6 months
Value of Calf	155	245
Less Calf (1)	62	62
Output	93	183
Variable Costs:		
Milk Substitute and Concentrates (2)	39	77
Miscellaneous Variable Costs (3)	24	36
Hay (4)	—	6
Total Variable Costs	63	119
Gross Margin per Calf reared	30	64

1. £60 per calf (Holstein Friesian bull calves, 1 week old, average of all qualities except the poorest); 4 per cent mortality assumed, mainly in first 3 weeks.
2. Milk substitute: 15 kg @ £1200/tonne = £18. Calf concentrates: to 3 months, 160 kg @ £130/tonne = £20·75; to 6 months, additional 300kg @ £125/tonne = £37·50. Calves fed less well, *i.e.* with lower concentrate costs, will fetch proportionally lower market prices, probably resulting in a lower gross margin.
3. Misc. Variable Costs include vet. and med.: 9 (3 months), 13 (6 months); bedding: 4 (3 months), 8 (6 months); passports, ear tags etc.
4. Hay: 7 kg to 3 months, 200 kg to 6 months. Variable costs assume made on farm; double the cost if purchased.
5. Weights: at start, 50 kg; at 3 months, 115 kg; at 6 months, 200 kg. *Contract rearing charge* (both 0 to 3 months and 0 to 6 months): £8 per week. Direct labour cost: approximately £17 per head to 3 months, £30 per head to 6 months. **Labour requirements** (all beef systems): see page 136.

BEEF
Single Suckling (per cow): Lowland

System	Spring Calving		Autumn Calving	
Performance Level (1)	Average	High	Average	High
	£	£	£	£
Value of Calf (2)	261	283	314	341
Calf Sales/Valn. per Cow (3) ...	235	263	283	317
Headage Payment (4)	114	114	114	114
Less Cow and Bull Depreciation and Calf Purchases (5)... ...	59	58	67	66
Output	290	319	330	365
Variable Costs:				
Concentrate Costs (cow and calf)	25	20	35	32
Miscellaneous Variable Costs (6)	52	43	57	48
Total Variable Costs (excluding forage)	77	63	92	80
Gross Margin per cow, before deducting Forage Variable Costs	213	256	238	285
Forage Variable Costs	34	30	40	34
Purchased Bulk Feed	21	16	20	14
Gross Margin per Cow	158	210	178	237
Cows per ha (7)	2·0	2·4	1·7	2·0
Forage Ha (Acres) per Cow ...	·5	·42	·59	·5
	(1·24)	(1·04)	(1·45)	(1·24)
Gross Margin per Forage Hectare	315	505	303	475
Gross Margin per Forage Acre...	127	204	123	192

1. Performance level relates to variations in two factors: weaner calf weight and stocking rate. "High" refers to the average levels likely to be achieved by the better fifty per cent of producers. It is clearly possible to set still higher "targets".
2. Weight of calves (kg) at sale/transfer: spring calving: average 275 (at approximately 7 months old), high 290 (slightly older); autumn calving: average 330 (at approximately 11 months old), high 350 (same age). Price (per live kg): average 95, high 97·50p. These prices are averages for bull and heifer calves; on average the former fetch 15p/live kg more than the latter.
3. Calves reared per 100 cows mated: average 90, high 93.
4. Headage payments: see page 92. Numbers are assumed to be within available quota. At the stocking rates assumed the stocking density limit (2 LU/ha) is exceeded for spring calving herds and the payments would be scaled down accordingly; however, the limit may not be exceeded when *all* the grazing livestock on the farm are considered and this is what is assumed in the table. No extensification premiums have been included. No allowance has been made for any overshooting of regional reference herd limits. An addition to the premium from the "national envelope" is possible, but the level is at present unclear (July 1999).
5. Assumptions. Herd life: spring calving, 7 years; autumn calving, 6 years. Purchase price £600, average cull value £290. Calves purchased: average, 4 per 100 cows mated, premium 3, at £80. Bull: purchase price £2,250, cull value £575; (one bull per 35 cows on average; 4-year herd life).
6. Vet. and med. £24; bedding: spring calving £17, autumn £22; miscellaneous £11. Where yarded in winter, straw requirements average 0·5-0·75 tonne per cow for spring calvers and around 0·75 tonne for autumn calvers.
7. The forage area includes both grazing and conserved grass (silage and hay) plus any other forage crops, such as kale. The higher stocking density implies better use of grassland. Higher stocking rates can also be achieved by buying in more of the winter bulk fodder requirements, or by winter feeding largely on arable by-products, including straw. Purchased bulk fodder and/or straw balancer concentrates will reduce gross margin per cow but increase gross margin per hectare.

Suckler Cow "quotas" (premium rights) are tradeable: their value varies widely from year to year. In the second half of 1998 they were in the range £140-£160 to buy, £40-£70 to lease, both in the lowlands and the LFAs, but the sale value rose beyond £250 in mid-1999.

BEEF
Single Suckling (per cow): Upland and Hill

System	Upland Spring Calving		Upland Autumn Calving		Hill	
Performance Level (1)	Average	High	Average	High	Average	High
	£	£	£	£	£	£
Value of Calf (2)	282	315	338	366	292	325
Calf Sales/Valn. per Cow (3) ...	257	296	308	344	260	299
Headage Payments (4)	174	174	174	174	233	233
LESS Cow and Bull Depreciation and Calf Purchases (5)... ...	59	58	67	66	67	66
OUTPUT	372	412	415	452	426	466
Variable Costs:						
Concentrate Costs (cow and calf)	20	20	40	40	35	32
Miscellaneous Variable Costs (6)	54	49	65	60	50	45
TOTAL VARIABLE COSTS (excluding forage)	74	69	105	100	85	77
GROSS MARGIN per cow, before deducting Forage Variable Costs	298	343	310	352	341	389
Forage Variable Costs	34	30	45	40	40	35
Purchased Bulk Feed	22	10	12	5	22	10
GROSS MARGIN per Cow	242	303	253	307	279	344
Cows per Forage ha (7, 8) ...	1·6	1·9	1·2	1·5	1·0	1·2
Forage Ha (Acres) per Cow ...	·62	·53	·83	·67	1·0	·83
	(1·53)	(1·31)	(2·05)	(1·66)	(2·5)	(2·06)
GROSS MARGIN per Forage Hectare	385	575	305	460	280	415
GROSS MARGIN per Forage Acre...	156	233	123	186	113	168

1. Performance level relates to variations in two factors: weaner calf weight and stocking rate. "High" refers to the average levels likely to be achieved by the better fifty per cent of producers. It is clearly possible to set still higher "targets".
2. Weight of calves (kg) at sale/transfer: upland spring calving: average 275 (at approximately 7·5 months old), high 300 (same age); upland autumn calving: average 365 (at approximately 11·5 months old), high 385 (same age); hill: average 300, high 325. Price (per live kg): upland spring calving: average 102·5p, high 105p; upland autumn calving: average 92·5p, high 95p; hill: average 97·5p, high 100p. These prices are averages for bull and heifer calves; on average the former fetch 5p/live kg more than the latter.
3. Calves reared per 100 cows mated: upland average 91, high 94; hill: average 89, high 91
4. Suckler cow premium and hill compensatory allowances: see page 92. Numbers are assumed to be within available quota. Extensification payments are included at the lower rate for upland herds and the lower rate for hill herds. No allowance has been made for any overshooting of regional reference herd limits. The HLCAs for 2000 are assumed to continue at the 1999 levels; they are to be changed to an area basis, but probably not before 2001.
5. Assumptions. Herd life: spring calving, 7 years; autumn calving and hill, 6 years. Purchase price £600, average cull value £290. Calves purchased: upland average, 4 per 100 cows mated, premium 3, at £80; hill: average 3, premium 2. Bull: purchase price £2,250, cull value £575.
6. Vet. and med: spring calving £26, autumn £30, hill £24; bedding: spring calving £15, autumn £18, hill £12; miscellaneous: spring calving £13, autumn £17, hill £14. Where yarded in winter, requirements average 0·5-0·75 tonne per cow for spring calvers and around 0·75 tonne for autumn calvers.
7. The forage area includes both grazing and conserved grass (silage and hay) plus any other forage crops, such as kale. The higher stocking density implies better use of grassland. Higher stocking rates can also be achieved by buying in more of the winter bulk fodder requirements, or by winter feeding largely on arable by-products, including straw. Purchased bulk fodder and/or straw balancer concentrates reduce gross margin per cow but increase gross margin per hectare.
8. Forage Hectares (Acres) per cow and Gross Margin per Forage Hectare (Acre) relate to "in-bye equivalent" (3 hectares of rough grazing are taken as being equal to 1 hectare of in-bye land).

Suckler Cow "quotas" (premium rights): see foot of page 78.

BEEF

Double and Multiple Suckling (per cow)

	Output level (1)			
	Double Suckling	Multiple Suckling		
No. of calves reared per cow	1·9	2·5	3·5	4·5
	£	£	£	£
Value of Calf...	250	245	240	235
Calf Sales per Cow	475	612	840	1058
Headage Payments (2)	114	114	114	114
Calf Costs (including Replacement)				
LESS Calves (3)	84	132	220	309
Cow Depreciation	55	55	60	65
OUTPUT (3)	450	539	674	798
Variable Costs:				
Concentrates	55	70	85	100
Miscellaneous Variable Costs (4) ...	60	70	85	100
TOTAL VARIABLE COSTS (excluding forage)	115	140	170	200
GROSS MARGIN per cow, before deducting				
Forage Variable Costs	335	399	504	598
Forage Variable Costs	40	45	55	60
Purchased Bulk Feed	25	30	35	40
GROSS MARGIN per Cow	270	324	414	498
Cows per ha	1·9	1·85	1·8	1·75
Forage Hectares (Acres) per Cow... ...	·525	·54	·56	·57
	(1·3)	(1·34)	(1·38)	(1·41)
GROSS MARGIN per Forage Hectare ...	515	600	745	870
GROSS MARGIN per Forage Acre ...	210	245	300	350

Notes

1. The different levels of output refer only to different numbers of calves reared per cow. The standards are averages at each level of output. There are wide variations in prices obtained and paid per calf and in concentrate costs: together they can make a very large difference to the gross margin.

2. Headage payment: see page 91. "National envelope" supplement may be added. No extensification premium included.

3. Calf cost assumed: £80 (average steers and heifers, 1 week old). Calf mortality assumed: 5 per cent (double suckling) to 8 per cent (4·5 calves per cow).

4. Miscellaneous variable costs include straw: approximately 1 tonne per cow.

N.B. There is very little survey data available for these enterprises, since multiple suckling in particular is not widely practised. Hence these estimates must be treated with caution.

BEEF

Finishing/Rearing on Suckler-Bred Stores (per head)

	Winter Finishing Average £	Winter Finishing High £	Grass Finishing Average £	Grass Finishing High £	Overwintering and Grass Finishing Average £	Overwintering and Grass Finishing High £	Grazing and Yard Finishing Average £	Grazing and Yard Finishing High £	Overwintering and Selling as Stores Average £	Overwintering and Selling as Stores High £
Sales	504	525	418	427	437	461	490	540	400	434
LESS Store (1)	314	310	332	314	272	269	282	265	269	266
OUTPUT*	190	215	96	113	165	192	208	275	131	168
Variable Costs:										
Concentrates (2)	78	67	4	3	54	45	51	37	46	40
Miscellaneous (3)	33	30	22	20	36	34	37	34	33	31
TOTAL VARIABLE COSTS (excl. Forage)	111	97	26	23	90	79	88	71	79	71
GROSS MARGIN per head before deducting Forage Variable Costs	79	118	70	90	75	113	120	204	52	97
Forage Variable Costs	21	23	19	19	33	33	31	31	20	21
Purchased Bulk Feed	12	14	—	—	16	16	10	6	10	5
GROSS MARGIN per head*	46	81	51	71	26	64	79	167	22	71
No. per ha	9	10	4	5	3·75	4·50	4	5	11	13
No. per acre	3·6	4	1·6	2	1·5	1·8	1·6	2	4·5	5·3
GROSS MARGIN per Forage Ha*	415	810	205	355	100	290	315	835	240	925
GROSS MARGIN per Forage Acre*	170	330	85	145	40	115	125	340	95	375
Weight at start (kg)	330	330	335	320	280	280	285	270	280	280
Weight at end (kg)	520	530	445	445	470	485	500	540	400	425
Purchase Price (p per kg LW)	95	94	99	98	97	96	99	98	96	95
Sale Price (p per kg LW)	97	93	94	96	93	95	98	100	100	102
Concentrates per head (kg)	675	625	40	25	475	425	450	350	400	375
Silage per head (tonnes)	3·25	3·75	—	—	3·6	3·5	2·1	2·3	2·3	2·7

*The output and gross margin figures exclude the beef special premium, as this will depend, per head, on the overall stocking rate on the farm. Where the above beef enterprises represent the only livestock on the farm the full payment per head (see page 92) is likely to be obtained for the centre three systems but not for the first and last. It is assumed that extensification premiums are unlikely to be applicable. Neither has the recently introduced slaughter premium (approx. £19/head) been added; part of this is likely to be absorbed by a higher price for the store.

All-System Assumptions:
(1) Allowing for mortality at 1 per cent.
(2) Concentrate costs per tonne: winter: average £115, high £107.50; summer: average £105, high £97.50.
(3) Including vet. and mec. and bedding.

Additional Note: The gross margin per ha figures must be treated with considerable caution, especially with regard to winter fattening/rearing systems: small variations in land requirements and margins per head cause wide variations in the per ha figures, and capital requirements are considerable. Differences in buying and selling prices per kg can be critical. Very little recent survey data is available on several of these systems.

BEEF

Finishing/Rearing on Dairy-Bred Stores (per head)

	Winter Finishing		Grass Finishing		Overwintering and Grass Finishing		Grazing and Yard Finishing		Overwintering and Selling as Stores	
	Average £	High £	Average £	High £	Average £	High £	Average £	High £	Average £	High £
Sales	494	519	437	465	446	470	480	539	387	420
Less Store (1)	312	281	340	336	285	282	223	230	259	256
Output*	172	238	97	129	161	188	257	309	128	164
Variable Costs:										
Concentrates (2)	66	63	5	4	48	40	69	48	46	40
Miscellaneous (3)	33	30	21	20	46	42	38	34	33	31
Total Variable Costs (excl. Forage)	99	93	26	24	94	82	107	82	79	71
Gross Margin per head before deducting Forage Variable Costs	73	145	71	105	67	106	150	227	49	93
Forage Variable Costs	21	23	19	19	32	32	31	32	19	21
Purchased Bulk Feed	14	12	—	—	16	16	10	6	10	5
Gross Margin per head*	38	110	52	86	19	58	109	189	20	67
No. per ha	7·5	9	4	5	3·5	4·25	3·5	4·5	11	13
No. per acre	3	3·6	1·6	2	1·4	1·7	1·4	1·8	4·5	5·3
Gross Margin per Forage Ha*	285	990	210	430	65	245	380	850	220	870
Gross Margin per Forage Acre*	115	400	85	175	25	100	155	345	90	350
Weight at start (kg)	335	305	350	350	300	300	230	240	275	275
Weight at end (kg)	520	535	475	495	490	505	500	550	395	420
Purchase Price (p per kg LW)	93	92	97	96	95	94	97	96	94	93
Sale Price (p per kg LW)	95	97	92	94	91	93	96	98	98	100
Concentrates per head (kg)	575	575	50	40	425	375	600	450	400	375
Silage per head (tonnes)	3·4	3·4	—	—	3·6	3·6	3·5	4·5	2·6	3·0

*The output and gross margin figures exclude the beef special premium, as this will depend, per head, on the overall stocking rate on the farm. Where the above beef enterprises represent the only livestock on the farm the full payment per head (see page 92) is likely to be obtained for the centre three systems but not for the first and last. It is assumed that extensification premiums are unlikely to be applicable. Neither has the recently introduced slaughter premium been added; part of this is likely to be absorbed by a higher price for the store.

All-System Assumptions:
(1) Allowing for mortality at 1 per cent.
(2) Concentrate costs per tonne: winter: average £115, high £107·50; summer: average £105, high £97·50.
(3) Including vet. and med. and bedding.

Additional Note: The gross margin per ha figures must be treated with considerable caution, especially with regard to winter fattening/rearing systems: small variations in land requirements and margins per head cause wide variations in the per ha figures, and capital requirements are considerable. Differences in buying

BEEF

Traditional Finishing of Strong Store Cattle (per head) (1)

	Summer Finishing	Winter Finishing
	£	£
Sales	481 (2)	507 (3)
LESS Purchased Store	390 (4)	389 (4)
OUTPUT*	91	118
Variable Costs:		
Concentrates	4	44 (6)
Miscellaneous Variable Costs	20	32 (7)
TOTAL VARIABLE COSTS (excluding Forage)	24	76
GROSS MARGIN per Head before deducting Forage		
Variable Costs	67	42
Forage Variable Costs	16	12
GROSS MARGIN per Head*	51	30
No. per ha (acre)	4 (1·6)	9 (3·65)
Forage Hectares (Acres) per Head...	·25 (·62)	·11 (·275)
GROSS MARGIN per Forage Hectare*	205	270
GROSS MARGIN per Forage Acre*	83	109

*No headage payment (beef special premium) has been included; although the animal is eligible at 21 months old (if on the farm at that age of course) the stocking rate assumed would limit the numbers eligible per farm for summer finishing and especially for winter finishing; even where available, the payment is likely to be largely cancelled out under these systems by a higher sum paid for the store. Neither has any extensification premium or the new slaughter premium (approx. £19 in 2000) been added; again the latter is likely to be partly absorbed by a higher price paid for the store.

Notes

1. The financial results of this enterprise are highly dependent on the market margin, *i.e.* the difference between the price per kg paid for the store and the price per kg obtained for the finished animal. Other important factors are the stocking rate and the degree of dependence on cash-crop by-products and the quality of conserved grass (and hence the quantity of concentrates required in relation to the liveweight gain) in the case of winter finishing.
2. 520 kg @ 92·50p.
3. 520 kg @ 97·50p.
4. 400 kg @ 97·50p.
5. 420 kg @ 92·50p.
6. 400 kg @ £110/tonne.
7. Including straw: average 0·75 tonne per head.

BEEF

Cereal Beef (per Head)

	Calves reared on farm		Reared calves purchased	
	Average	High	Average	High
	£	£	£	£
Sales (1)	500	527	500	527
Slaughter premium	19	19	19	19
LESS Calf (2)	62	61	158	157
OUTPUT (3)	457	493	361	389
Variable Costs:				
Concentrates (4)...	252	238	212	198
Other Feed	2	2	2	2
Miscellaneous (5)	48	40	40	36
TOTAL VARIABLE COSTS ...	302	280	254	236
GROSS MARGIN per Head ...	155	213	107	153

Notes

1. Weight at slaughter (kg): average 525, high 540. Price: average 95p per live kg, high 97·5p. All year round production is assumed. Days (on farm) to slaughter: calves reared on farm: 420; reared calves purchased: 330.

2. £60 per Hereford Friesian bull calf (1 week old average of all qualities except the poorest) + mortality (average 4, high 2 per cent). Reared calves purchased at about 3 months old at £155; average mortality 2, high 1 per cent.

3. No headage payment (Beef Special Premium) is included, because of the stocking rate constraint in the regulations. However, in some farm circumstances it may be available for a limited number. The (new) slaughter premium is as estimated for 2000.

4. £39 calf rearing (to 12 weeks: see p. 77) + finishing ration + £4 food to losses. Finishing ration: 17 parts barley @ £68 per tonne (estimated average price, 2000 calendar year), 3 parts concentrate supplement @ £190 per tonne; plus milling and mixing. Total, £100 per tonne.

   Quantity (kg from 12 weeks (115 kg) to slaughter; FCR average 5·1, high 4·6): average 2090, high 1955.

   A difference of £5 per tonne in the cost of barley changes the feed cost by approximately £8·50 per head.

5. Calves reared on farm: vet. and med. 10, bedding 20, other 18; reared calves purchased: 8, 19, 13 respectively.

Note: Interest on Capital

As examples of the need to be aware of interest paid or forgone on capital invested in beef production, interest on the cost of the calf and variable costs alone, at 7·5%, are likely to be £15 to £20 a head for cereal beef and £25 a head for 18-month beef (page 85).

BEEF

18 Month Beef and Silage Beef (per Head)

| | 18 month Beef | | Silage Beef | |
	Average £	High £	Average £	High £
Sales	502	535	513	541
Less Calf	99	97	158	157
Plus Headage Payments*	104	104	62	53
Output	507	542	417	437
Variable Costs:				
Concentrates	124	113	129	105
Other Feed	5	8	4	3
Miscellaneous	68	66	48	40
Total Variable Costs (excl. Forage) ...	197	187	181	148
Gross Margin per Head before deducting				
Forage Variable Costs	310	355	236	289
Forage Variable Costs	35	35	25	25
Gross Margin per Head	275	320	211	264
No. per ha (acre)	3·25 (1·3)	3·6 (1·45)	7 (2·8)	9 (3·6)
Forage Hectares (Acres) per Head... ...	·31 (·76)	·28 (·69)	0·14 (·35)	0·12 (·27)
Gross Margin per Forage Ha (per year) ...	895	1150	1475	2375
Gross Margin per Forage Acre (per year) ...	360	465	600	960

Notes

18 Month Beef

Autumn-born dairy-bred calves, beef crosses.

Slaughter weights (kg): average 515, high 535. Sale price per live kg: average 97·5p, high 100p

Calf price/value £95 (1 week old bulls); mortality: average 4, high 2 per cent.

Concentrates (kg; average with high performance in brackets): milk subst. 14; other: first winter 360 (335), at grass 115 (110), second winter 500 (490). Price of concentrates per tonne: first winter (inc. calf rearing) £115 (£107·50), summer £105 (£97·50); second winter, £107·50 (£100). Silage: 4·5 tonnes (average and high): 0·75 tonne first winter, 3·75 tonnes second.

Miscellaneous (average): vet. and med. £22, bedding £24, other £22.

Intensive grazing of fresh leys and good quality silage are needed — especially to achieve the high performance levels.

*Headage Payment. The full beef special premium (page 92) is only available for all the stock (up to 90 head) if the overall stocking rate on the farm is below 2 livestock units per hectare. Male cattle 6 to 18 months old are counted as 0·6 LU and those under 6 months are excluded. The full (estimated) payment is therefore included, although the high stocking rate would exceed the limit if there were no other livestock on the farm. The actual payment will vary from farm to farm and be reduced if regional limits are exceeded. The new slaughter premium is added.

Silage Beef

Three months old dairy-bred calves fed indoors on grass silage and concentrates, for slaughter at 14 to 17 months old. (Where week-old calves are bucket reared on the farm, add as on page 77). Good quality silage is the key to high performance per herd (otherwise concentrates per head rise and/or daily liveweight gain falls). High yields of silage per ha raise gross margins per ha.

Slaughter weights (kg): average 540, high 555. Sale price per live kg: average 95p, high 97·5p.

Calf price (3 months old): £155. Concentrates per head (kg): average, with high performance in brackets: 1200 (1050); price per tonne £107·50 (£100). Silage required: approximately 5·5 tonnes per head.

Miscellaneous (average): vet. and med. £9, bedding £20, other £19.

*Headage Payment: see above for 18 month beef. Because of the very high stocking rate with this system only a crude allowance has been included: 50% of the full rate for average, 40% for high. The new slaughter premium is added.

Note that the gross margin per hectare figures must be interpreted with considerable caution: small differences in silage yields can have a large effect and, more important, the working capital and building requirements per hectare are extremely high: well above even the high needs of 18 month beef.

BEEF

24 Month Beef from Bucket Reared Calves (per Head)

	Autumn-born calf £	Spring-born calf £
Sales (1)	486	512
Less Calf	99	88
Headage Payments*	189	189
Output	576	613
Variable Costs:		
Concentrates	100	115
Miscellaneous	80	85
Forage	50	40
Total Variable Costs	230	240
Gross Margin per Head...	346	373
No. per ha (acre)...	2 (·8)	2·25 (·9)
Forage Hectares (Acres) per Head	0·5 (1·25)	0·45 (1·1)
Gross Margin per Forage Hectare	690	840
Gross Margin per Forage Acre...	280	340

Notes
(1) 525 kg. Autumn-born: 92·5p per kg; spring-born: 97·5p. Beef cross calves.
  *Beef special premiums: 2 payments, at 9 and 21 months old, plus estimated slaughter premium in 2000.

VEAL

General points. Veal consumption is very low in the UK: approximately 0·06 kg (2 oz) per head per year compared with 2·2 kg (5 lb) in France; UK consumption is only about 0.6% of EU production, yet only about 20% of total UK consumption is home produced. Continental demand is mainly for white veal, produced in individual veal crates, a system that is illegal in the UK, where the less economic "welfare system" of groups kept in straw pens is required, producing "pink veal" at heavier weights. Imported "white veal" is 30-40% cheaper.

As little veal is now produced in the UK validated economic data is rarely seen. A wide variety of breeds are used: beef cross heifer calves are perhaps the most suitable and hence most common. Some farmers produce "light veal" at 75-100 kg dw in 4 months, some "heavy veal" at 125-135 kg dw in 6 months and some heavier still — but the new calf slaughter premium is only available at up to 7 months of age and 160 kg dw; (there is also a regional UK ceiling, of 24,000 calves).

The following figures could be broadly typical of present UK production, though as a true average they can only be tentative.

							£
Sale value (115 kg dcw) (1)	...	...	...	...	...	...	402
LESS Calf (2)	...	...	...	...	...	...	52
Slaughter premium (2000)	...	...	...	...	...	...	12
OUTPUT	...	...	...	...	...	...	362
Variable Costs:							
Milk powder (325 kg) (3)	...	...	...	...	...	...	268
Miscellaneous (4)	...	...	...	...	...	...	30
TOTAL VARIABLE COSTS	...	...	...	...	...	...	298
GROSS MARGIN per Head (5)	...	...	...	...	...	...	64

Notes

1. Sold at 5-6 months old at 200-230 kg liveweight (bought at 45-55 kg), 105-125 kg dressed carcass weight; weeks to slaughter 16-20. Killing out percentage, 52-55 per cent. Price assumed: £3·50 per kg dcw (£1·875 per kg liveweight).

2. £50 per calf (beef cross heifer, average 2 weeks old); 4 per cent mortality assumed, mainly in first three weeks.

3. Milk powder: £825 per tonne. Conversion rate 1·95-2 kg of food per kg liveweight gain = 300-350 kg total.

4. Miscellaneous: vet and med. 12, straw 10, other 8.

5. The gross margin is obviously highly dependent on calf price, the market price of veal, and feed efficiency.

SHEEP

A. Lowland Spring Lambing (per Ewe)

(Selling lambs off grass)

Performance level	Low	Average	High
Lambs reared per ewe (1)	1·3	1·45	1·6
Average price per lamb (£) (2)	34·50	35·50	36·50

	£	£	£
Lamb sales	44·9	51·5	58·4
Ewe Premium (2)	15·0	15·0	15·0
Wool (3)	1·8	1·8	1·8
Cull ewes and rams	5·3	5·3	5·3

Sub-total	67·0	73·6	80·5
LESS Ewe and ram replacements	16·5	16·5	16·5

OUTPUT...	50·5	57·1	64·0

Variable Costs:			
Concentrates (52 kg ewes, 12 kg lambs)		7·5	
Vet. and Med.		4·5	
Miscellaneous and Transport		5·0	

TOTAL VARIABLE COSTS (excluding			
Forage)		17·0	

GROSS MARGIN per Ewe before deducting			
Forage Variable Costs	33·5	40·1	47·0
Forage Variable Costs (inc. bought forage			
and keep)	7·0	7·5	8·0

GROSS MARGIN per Ewe	26·5	32·6	39·0
Stocking Rate (Ewes, with lambs, per			
forage hectare (acre))	8 (3·25)	11 (4·45)	14(5·65)
GROSS MARGIN per Forage Hectare ...	210	360	545
GROSS MARGIN per Forage Acre	85	145	220

Notes

1. *Lambs reared per ewe* (× 100 = lambing percentage) is derived as follows *(average figures* only):

   Lambs born per 100 ewes lambing = 173

   Lambs born per 100 ewes put to ram = 161

   (93% of ewes put to ram bear lambs: 1·5% deaths, 5·5% barren)

   Lamb mortality: 10% (inc. half dead at birth or before seen)

   Lambs reared per 100 ewes lambing = 156

   Lambs reared per 100 ewes put to ram = 145

2. *Lamb Prices/Ewe Premium.* The price assumed for lambs sold for slaughter *for the 2000 mid-season lamb crop* assumes that most of the lambs are sold between mid-June and the end of October. Prices are normally highest in March-May and lowest in August-October. Prices were exceptionally low in the last four months of 1998 and are again very low in 1999; it is assumed that this will not be repeated in 2000, but still a lowish level is taken: an average market price of 92·5p/kg lw, giving £36 per finished lamb (39 kglw). However, the average price given in the

above table allows for a proportion (12·5%) sold or retained in the autumn as *store* lambs. Low performance is £1 a lamb less, high £1 more.

A difference in price of £2 per lamb (*i.e.* a difference of approximately 5·15p per kglw for a 39 kglw lamb) causes a difference of £21, £32 and £45 (8, 13, 18) to the low, average and high gross margins per hectare (acre) respectively. Prices of exported lambs are normally above domestic prices.

The *Sheep Annual Premium* payment per ewe is calculated from the shortfall between the basic price set and the average EU market price for lamb marketed at 12 kg or above. Recent levels have been: 1996, £13·66; 1997, £11·61; 1998, £17.36; 1999 (forecast) £17·15. Eligible sheep in LFAs received a supplement of £5·14/ewe in 1998.

The premiums are tradable, with restrictions; the prices of *quotas* (premium rights) have varied widely, especially for lowland quota. In the past, typical ranges per unit have been as follows. Lowland: £15 to £25 to buy and £6 to £8 to lease; LFAs: £30 to £42·50 to buy, £8 to £15 to lease. However, prices were lower than these levels in 1998 but higher than them in early 1999.

3. *Wool.* Prices were low in 1998 and still lower in 1999. 3kg/head at 60p has been assumed for 2000.

4. *Breed will* obviously have a large effect on lambing percentage, rate of liveweight gain (reflected in price per lamb), and amount of wool per ewe.

5. *Stocking Density.* The stocking rates assumed are based on land requirements *throughout the year.* With a given level of management one would expect higher stocking rates to be associated with a lower gross margin per ewe. The assumption made in the initial table, however, is that management performance is affecting both factors together.

N.B. The forage variable costs include purchased forage and keep (where appropriate) (£1·3, £1·7 and £2·0 per ewe at the three performance levels respectively).

The top one-third gross margin per hectare herds recorded by the Meat and Livestock Commission often achieve stocking rates exceeding 15 ewes per hectare. Often such high stocking rates are achieved by substantial use of by-products (*e.g.* autumn or spring grazing of grass grown primarily for seed) and catch crops (*e.g.* rape). Otherwise a stocking rate of 15 per hectare (just over 6 per acre) requires a stocking rate of about 24 ewes (with lambs) per hectare in the spring and early summer.

In an average season for prices and weather, the top few per cent of flocks in the country can achieve gross margins exceeding £750 per hectare (£300 per acre) by a combination of high lambing percentage, high average lamb price and, especially, very high stocking rates.

Where there are no grazing livestock other than sheep on the farm, some ewes, at the higher stocking rates, are often either agisted (away-wintered) or housed indoors, thus reducing the margin. Agistment costs around 35p per week plus transport, *i.e.* approx. £8 per year. Depreciation and Interest on new Housing (1·2 sq. m per ewe) is approximately £5·25 per ewe per year (10-year life); straw, extra hay and perhaps concentrates will also be required for indoor housing.

On the other hand, with only 7 or 8 ewes per hectare (2·75 to 3·25/acre) on a lowland farm of reasonable quality with no other grazing livestock, there should be surplus grass available in the late spring or early summer; this could be cut for hay or used for seed production.

6. *Flock Depreciation.* (*i.e.* Market price of replacements less value of culls). It is assumed above that 20 per cent of the ewe flock is culled each year @ £25 each and that, allowing for 4 per cent mortality, 24 per cent are purchased or home-reared at £60 each. Rams: 1 per 40 to 45 ewes, 3-year life, purchased @ £275, sold @ £35. The net cost is £12 per ewe per year. N.B. Cull ewe prices are approximately £5 per head higher for heavy breeds and £5 lower for light breeds. Cull values have fallen to very low levels in midsummer 1999, but some recovery is assumed.

No other changes in flock valuation are assumed.

7. *Miscellaneous Costs* include lambing and shearing bonus. Contract shearing is approximately 95p per head, including rolling (but can be around £1·15 for small flocks); approximately 60p/ewe for shearing only in upland flocks. Sheepdogs average around £500.

8. *Prices of Specialised Equipment:*

Troughs (2·75 m)	£55 to £65
Racks (2½ to 3 m)	£190 to £210
Foot Baths (3 m)	£90 to £115
Shearer (electric)	£625 to £925
Lamb Creep and Shelter, skids	£575
Netting	75p to £1·25 per metre

9. *Fencing:* approximately £1·55 per metre + 75p labour.

10. *Home-reared tegs* (shearlings). Output: value £57·50 (allowing for culling and mortality) less £32 for the lamb, plus £1·50 for wool = £27. Variable costs (including forage) = £12. Gross margin per head = £15, per forage hectare £255 (£105 per acre).

   If the figures for home-reared replacement tegs are included in the figures per ewe, the latter are increased approximately as follows: output by £6·50, gross margin (per ewe) by £4. The stocking rate in terms of ewes per hectare devoted to sheep will be about 15 per cent less and the overall sheep gross margin per hectare will be slightly reduced.

11. Labour: see page 137.

B. Other Sheep Systems (average performance level only)

System	Early Lambing per ewe	Winter Finishing of Store Lambs per head	Upland Flocks per ewe	Hill Flocks per ewe
Lambs reared per ewe	1·375	—	1·325	1·0
	£	£	£	£
Average price per lamb sold	46·0	46·0	35·0	32·00
Lamb sales	63·3	—	46·4	24·0
Ewe premium	15·0	—	20·0*	20·0*
Wool	1·8	—	1·6	1·3
Subsidy/Hill Livestock	—	—	4·1*	8·9*
Sub-total	80·1	44	72·1	54·2
LESS Livestock Purchases (net of cull sales) ...	10·8	33	11·9	(+) 3·0
OUTPUT	69·3	11	60.2	57·2
Variable Costs:				
Concentrates	17·0	1·5	6·0	3·6
	(140 kg)	(12·5 kg)	(50 kg)	(30 kg)
Vet. and Med.	4·6	0·3	4·0	3·2
Miscellaneous and Transport	6·0	1·7	4·7	2·2
Total Variable Costs (excl. Forage) ...	27·6	3·5	14·7	9·0
GROSS MARGIN per ewe (or head) before deducting Forage Variable Costs ...	41·7	7·5	45·5	48·2
Forage Variable Costs (inc. bought forage)	6·5	1·5	6·0	3·5
GROSS MARGIN per ewe (or head)	35·2	6·0	39·5	44·7
Stocking Rate (No. per Forage Ha [Acre])	14·25	40	9	—
	(5·75)		(3·65)	
GROSS MARGIN per Forage Hectare	500	240	355	—
GROSS MARGIN per Forage Acre	202	97	144	—

* *The LFA ewe premium supplement was £5.14/ewe in 1998; the same is assumed for 2000; hardy breed ewes are assumed for the hill flocks. The 1999 Hill Livestock Compensatory Allowances are assumed to be repeated in 2000 (see page 92); these headage payments are to be replaced by area payments, but probably not until 2001.*

Early Lambing. In this system, 60 per cent of the lambs are sold before the end of May, and the remainder before the end of August. This may be compared with *Mid-Season* lamb production (see table on page 90), in which about 80 per cent of the lambs are sold between early June and mid-September, and *Late* lamb production, in which only two-thirds or so of the lambs are sold for slaughter by the end of the normal grazing season, 60 per cent of total lambs being sold for slaughter or as stores in October/November, or the stores are retained on the farm for winter finishing. The gross margin per ewe tends to be slightly higher with the latter system compared with Mid-Season production, provided the proportion of stores is not too high — but more grass is utilised per ewe, making per hectare results similar.

Winter Finishing of Store Lambs. The gross margin per head is particularly variable, being very dependent on the difference between the purchase and sale price of the lambs. Some of the forage variable costs consist of bulk feed and agistment.

Hill Sheep. The flock is assumed to be self-maintained; thus only about 0·75 lambs are sold per ewe per annum and the fleece of the yearling ewes are included in wool sales. Only the rams are purchased, costing approximately £1·50 per ewe per year. Results obviously vary according to the height of the hill and severity of the winter.

Note. The figures for early lambing, upland and hill sheep are largely based on the relative figures for these systems as compared with the lowland spring lambing results obtained from the Meat and Livestock Commission's Flockplan recording and costing service.

GRANTS FOR BEEF AND SHEEP

Note. 1999 payments (excluding HLCAs) were as for 1998, at the same "frozen" ecu rate (£0·775745). 2000 payments are problematical (in July 1999) and will depend on the euro value during December 1999, agrimonetary compensation and other matters as yet undetermined (see further page 7).

Beef Cows. The *Suckler Cow Premium* was £112·41 (144·9 ecu) per cow in 1999. Eligibility is confined to pure beef or beef cross dairy cows or in-calf heifers producing calves for meat. Limited to the number on the farm in the 1992 base year (but the "quotas") (premium rights) are tradeable (for values see page 78); otherwise there is no upper limit to the number eligible or number kept per farm eligible for the premium. The producer must undertake not to deliver any milk or milk products from any of his production units, except that milk producers with less than 120,000 kg (116,500 litres) of quota may apply for the subsidy. The full premium is subject to a maximum stocking rate: 2 livestock units/ha. In 2000 the premium will be 163 euros/head and is expected to be approximately £114. However, a "national envelope" payment is thought likely to be added: amount at present unknown.

Finished Male Cattle. Beef Special Premium: the full rate was £84·32 (108·7 ecu) per head in 1999 (£104·73 [135 ecu] for bulls), but these are reduced if regional herd size limits are exceeded. Payment is limited to 90 animals per producer per year. There are no quality criteria. It is payable on male animals only, at 9 and 21 months of age (claimable from 7 and 19 months), at the point of slaughter and at the point of sale for slaughter (auction markets). The producer must have kept the cattle on his holding for at least the preceding two months. The maximum carcass weight for intervention is 340 kg. As with the Suckler Cow Premium the full premium is subject to a maximum stocking rate: 2 livestock units/ha. For the (approximate) 2000 rates see page 10.

Extensification Premium. This is an addition to both the Suckler Cow and Beef Special Premiums if the stocking rate is less than 1·4 livestock units/ha; the premium is higher if this is below 1·0 LU/ha. The rates in 1999 were £27·93 (36 ecu) and £40·34 (52 ecu) respectively. These rates are reduced if regional herd size limits are exceeded, as for the Beef Special Premium. For 2000 changes see pages 10-11 (the two-tier system is assumed).

Hill Livestock Compensatory Allowances:

(a) Cows. In 1998, £47·50 per head on eligible cows and in-calf heifers maintained in regular breeding herds on hill land (severely disadvantaged areas) and £23·75 per head on upland (disadvantaged areas) for the purposes of breeding store cattle. In 1999 these rates were raised to £73·39 and £36·69 respectively. Cows kept for selling milk are not eligible.

(b) Sheep. 1998 levels were as follows. Severely disadvantaged areas: for ewes of an approved breed in specially qualified flocks £5·75 per head (restricted to 6 ewes/ha), other eligible ewes in such flocks £3 (also up to 6 ewes/ha). In 1999 these rates were raised to £8·88 and £4·64 respectively. Disadvantaged areas: £2·65 (restricted to 9 ewes/ha) — raised to £4·09 in 1999. A supplement to the ewe premium (see page 89) is paid in all less favoured areas: £5·14 (6·64 ecu) in 1998, £4·72 in 1999 (with a £0·42 supplement anticipated).

(c) Limits. The maximum HLCAs payments per hectare were £88·70 and £60·85 in severely disadvantaged areas and disadvantaged areas respectively in 1998, £102·75 and £60·85 in 1999.

The HLCAs for 2000 are assumed to continue at the 1999 levels; they are to be changed to an area basis, but probably not before 2001.

GRAZING AND REARING CHARGES:
CATTLE AND SHEEP

Grazing charges vary widely according to the quality of the pasture and local supply and demand. The following figures are typical (estimated for 2000):

Summer Grazing (per head per week)
Store Cattle and in-calf heifers over 21 months, dry cows, and fattening bullocks over 18 months...	£4·05
Heifers and Steers, 12-21 months	£3·15
6-12 months Cattle	£2·45
Cattle of mixed ages	£3·20
Ewes	35p-55p

Winter Grazing (per head per week)
"Strong" Cattle...	£2·45-£3·15
Heifers	£1·90-£2·45
Sheep	35p-55p

Note: the above figures assume the farmer whose land the livestock are on does all the fencing and "looking after". Where the owner of the, say, sheep does the fencing, shepherding, etc., the figures may be halved.

Grass Keep (per hectare, per acre in brackets)
Most typically around £160-185 (£65-75), with the best £250-300 (£100-120) and poorish quality £85-£100 (£35-40).

These figures are highly variable, especially between one part of the country and another, and between one season and another. The charge can be very high where the pasture is good, the supply scarce and the demand strong. In an average price year poor quality keep may fetch only £75 (30), top quality (fenced and with mains water) more than £300 (120). For top quality grassland, fertilised, well-fenced and watered, with stock seen daily, prices can be even higher for some lots in the west and north-west in years of grass shortage. The *average* price can exceed £300 (120) in some years in parts of the west and west midlands but can fall below £100 (40) in some eastern and south-eastern counties.

Winter Keep (Cattle) (per head per week)
Grazing + 9 kg hay and some straw	£7·00
Full winter keep in yards	£7·50-£9·75
Calf rearing for beef (0 to 12 weeks or 0 to 6 months)	£8

Heifer Rearing Charges
Points to clarify in any arrangement are: who pays for transport, who pays the vet. and med. expenses, who bears the losses or pays for replacements, how often are payments made (monthly payments save the rearer interest compared with lump sum payments when the heifer is returned)?

Two possible arrangements are:

1. Farmer X sells calf to Rearer at agreed price; the calf is then Rearer's responsibility and he pays for all expenses and bears any losses. Farmer X has first option on heifers, which he buys back two months before calving. Approximate price: £700 above cost of calf for Holstein Friesians. Rearer fetches calf; Farmer X supplies transport for heifer.

2. Farmer X retains ownership of calf. Approximate charges: £30 per month from 10 to 14 days old (£32·50 if two-year old calving), or £27·50 per month from 6 months old (£32 if two-year old calving), (£35 per month from 10 to 14 days to 6 months). As Rearer has no interest on capital to bear, he supplies transport and pays for vet. and medical expenses. In the case of losses by accident/chance, the rearer either refunds payments or replaces calf (this means Farmer X and Rearer share a loss averaging approximately £30 each per heifer reared, assuming 10 per cent losses at average 6 months old). In the case of losses by negligence, the rearer both refunds payments and replaces calf. (The NFU can supply model agreements).

Calf and Heifer Rearing for Shorter Periods
Calf, 10 days to 3 months, £100 (for food, labour and housing) to £110 (all costs, and rearer bearing losses). Heifers, average from 3 months old to steaming up: approximately £14 per month in summer, £40 in winter.

RED DEER

Sales:	Selling at 14-21 months per 100 hinds £	Selling calves per 100 hinds £	Finishing units per 200 calves £
Stag calves	—	3442 (42.5)	—
Hind calves	—	2080 (32.5)	—
Stags, 14-16 months	6732 (42.5)	—	15523
Hinds, 14-16 months	4504 (32.5)	—	13582
Culls (8 hinds, 1 stag)	1000	1000	—
Less purchased stock	—	—	14500
OUTPUT	12236	6522	14605
Variable Costs:			
Supplementary Feed	3905	3100	4095
Forage	1100	700	1000
Vet. and Med	1235	705	600
Miscellaneous	900	600	400
Slaughter/Transport	1000	—	2000
TOTAL VARIABLE COSTS	8140	5105	8095
GROSS MARGIN	4096	1417	6510
GROSS MARGIN per Hind (Stag) ...	41	14.2	32·5
Stocking Rate (No. per ha (acre)) ...	7 (2·85)	8 (3·25)	15 (6)
GROSS MARGIN per hectare	287	113	488
GROSS MARGIN per acre	117	46	195

Numbers of animals sold given in brackets.
Calves housed from September, hinds from November.
Intensive system, on sown pasture. Self-contained herd.
Herd life (years): hinds 12, stags 8. Hinds per stag: 30 approx.
Calves per 100 hinds: 95 reared (to 4 months).
Supplementary feed: hinds: 7 kg silage/head/day over 165 days plus 0·5 kg concs./
head/day for 30 days; calves: 4 kg silage 195 days plus 0.5 kg concs./head/day 30 days;
2 kg silage 45 days plus 1 kg concs./head/day 45 days; 5 kg silage 195 days plus 0·5
kg concs./head/day 45 days. Concentrates £130/tonne; silage £18/tonne.
Sale weights and values:

	Stags		Hinds	
	kg	£/kg	kg	£/kg
Calves	45 lw	1·80 lw	40 lw	1·60 lw
At 14-16 months	48 dw	3·30 dw	42 dw	3·30 dw

Stock: breeding stags £500 plus, hinds £300 plus, yearling hinds £250 plus. Prices reflect
good quality stock sold in UK. Tb accreditation brings premium.

Venison prices reflect projected sales for 1998/99 to wholesale buyers. Farm shop and
local co-operative sales will vary.

Capital costs: perimeter fencing, £4·20/metre; internal fencing, electric £2/metre, mesh
£3·70/metre; handling yard, pens, scales, crush: £6,000—in existing buildings. Total cost
of establishing a 100-hind breeding flock is typically in the order of £40,000, including
breeding stock and £10,000 for fencing, housing and handling facilities. *Labour:* with
an experienced stockman: 400 plus head with additional help when yarding.

Comment: Feed costs are based on exploiting summer compensatory growth and reducing
overwinter feed rates and cost. Veterinary figures are based on successful minimal regime.

In 1994 there were 267 deer farms in England and Wales, 86 in Scotland (MAFF).
In 1995 there were 28,500 farmed deer in England and Wales. Demand has increased
substantially since, largely because of BSE but also because the low fat content of deer
meat is being increasingly recognised. The national herd is consolidating, with fewer,
larger herds, often integrated with other arable or livestock enterprises. Venison and livestock
prices have remained relatively stable, although imports of New Zealand venison are a
recurring threat. Advice is plentiful for newcomers; the "Introduction to Red Deer Farming",
a self-study pack introduced by Barony College, Dumfries (tel. 01387-860251), is a good
source of information.

Acknowledgement: Up to and including the previous edition the above information has
been provided by J. C. Cordery, Sparsholt College Hampshire, for many years, but he
has now had to give up. Russell Marchant of Barony College has kindly revised the
section for this edition.

HORSES: LIVERY

The horse industry is now reported to be the second biggest employer in the rural economy and is also one of the fastest growing.

In detail there are many different forms of livery and the charges, therefore, vary widely also — apart from the effects of local supply and demand. Three fairly standard forms, with typical charges, are as follows:

Grass Livery. Keep at grass, preferably with shelter, water supply and secure area to keep tack and store feed. Some grass livery will provide an exercise arena and off-road riding. Typical charge £12·50 a week (range mainly £10 to £15).

DIY Livery. The owner still has full care of the horse but has the facilities of a stable, grazing and in some cases an all-weather exercise arena. The owner is responsible for mucking out, turning out, grooming, exercising and all vet./med. care and the cost of all feed and bedding. Typical charge £20 a week (range mainly £15 to £25).

DIY Plus Livery. As the above, except that the yard manager is responsible for certain tasks, such as turning out and feeding. Typical charge £27·50 a week (range mainly £25 to £30).

Other Costs:

Grazing. Variable costs will average some £30/horse a year. Average stocking rates are 0·8 ha (2 acres) for the first horse and 0·4 ha (1 acre) for each horse after.

Hay. Average price £2·50 per conventional bale (approximately 20 kg); has to be of good quality. Average consumption is one to two bales per horse per week: less in the summer depending on the grass quality/quantity and the work of the horse. Some horses now have haylage: more expensive, dust free and higher fibre and energy/protein levels; less required per head.

Concentrate Feed. Can range from almost nil to 3 to 4 kg/day depending, amongst other factors, on breed, size and intensity of work. Compound feed averages 25p per kg.

Bedding. Averages around £4-£5 per stabled horse per week, £100-£125 per year. Straw might cost only half as much; however, more expensive, but preferable, alternatives (such as wood shavings, shredded paper and hemp fibre) are now increasingly being used.

Vet. and Med. Averages approximately £150 per horse per year. Some yards include worming of the horse in the livery cost.

Further Notes:

To be successful, a livery enterprise needs higher quality facilities than farm livestock. To the owner the horse can be anything from a highly trained athlete to a family pet. Horses are expensive: even modest quality horses cost between £1500 and £3000. Good customer relations and an effective security system (including burglar and fire alarms) are crucial to success, as is good market research and effective advertising.

A full livery yard will require stables, a secure room to store tack, a vermin-proof hard feed store, storage for hay and bedding and a muck heap. Planning permission is required for the conversion of an existing building to stabling or the erection of new, purpose-built stables. Permission is also required for construction of an all weather arena used for training horses and exercising them in bad weather. Hay and straw should be stored away from the stables and down wind of them to minimise the fire risk. A hard standing area with a water supply and good drainage should be provided for grooming and washing down the horses.

Good ventilation in the stables is crucial as horses are prone to respiratory diseases caused by spores and dust. Provision should be made for owners to soak hay in clean water before feeding it, to reduce respiratory problems.

Fences must be sound and must be free of protruding nails, wire etc. Ideally fields should be fenced using post and rail, but this is expensive. Barbed wire should be avoided wherever possible or should be "protected" with an offset electrified fence. Fields should be divided into smaller paddocks to reduce the possibility of fighting between incompatible horses and to separate mares and geldings. Paddocks may be divided using two or more strands of electrified tape or rope but wire is not advisable as it is not easily visible to the horse.

A good network of safe off-road riding on local bridle paths is a good point. Failing this the farmer should consider providing riding trails around field boundaries.

Construction Costs. The cost of conversion of existing buildings will depend on their quality; prefabricated hardwood and steel internal stable partitions can be purchased from upwards of £700 per stable, depending on size and specification. Free standing timber stables cost between £700 and £1500 (plus base), depending on size and quality. As horses are fairly destructive animals (they both kick and chew) better quality stables will often prove more economic in the long run. All weather arenas (20 metres by 40 metres) cost between £8000 and £15000; construction is a specialist job as good drainage is essential; a badly constructed arena is worthless.

Acknowledgement. Nigel Williams, Miranda Palmer, Liz Deen-Sly; Wye College.

Further financial information on horse enterprises, including riding schools and equestrian centres, is available in "Equine Business Guide", 3rd edition, 1999, by Richard Bacon and Tony O'Regan, Warwickshire College and Welsh Institute of Rural Studies; £16 post free, tel:. 01926 318340.

OSTRICHES

When ostrich farming began in the United Kingdom in 1990 breeding animals, chicks and fertile eggs fetched very high prices and gave rise to unrealistic expectations amongst some producers and investors. It has now settled down. The British Domesticated Ostrich Association has around 120 members, typically with small to medium-sized enterprises.

Ostriches come under the Dangerous Wild Animals Act 1976 and a licence from the Environmental Health Department of the local authority is required; the cost varies from £45 to £360. There is an annual safety and welfare inspection paid for by the producer. The UK has signed the Council of Europe code of recommended welfare practices for ratites kept for farming purposes which, when ratified, will be used as a guideline in any welfare dispute.

Breeding Stock

Adult breeding stock are normally kept in trios of one male and two females, but pairs and colonies are not unusual. A trio will require about 0·2 ha (0·5 acre) for grazing and room in which to exercise — they must be able to run. More land will be required if it is not free draining. A stout hedge or smooth wire fence of a minimum of 1·7 metres (5·5 ft) high should surround the enclosure. Although the adult birds are well adapted to cold weather they need shelter from wind and rain and a dry floor on which to sleep. Although an adult can be dangerous (with a well-aimed kick) the birds are said to be docile and easily handled.

An adult female will start to lay at 2 to 3 years of age and lay 30 to 50 eggs a year (April to October) for 20 to 30 years. An experienced producer will aim to hatch and rear at least half the eggs set, but rearing ostrich chicks is difficult and there may be significant losses in the first few weeks. A 10% replacement rate is anticipated for breeding stock.

Young females that have laid fertile eggs and proven fertile males are worth £400 to £500 each. A trio will therefore cost £1,200 to £1,500.

The birds crop grass and other vegetation, which forms an important part of their diet. They are also fed specially formulated concentrate, barley, silage and vegetable waste. Dry matter and silage must be chopped. The birds must be provided with grit when young and small stones (up to 12 to 15 mm) for adults, oyster shell and perhaps vitamin supplement. A breeding ration fed at 1·5 — 2·0 kg per day for 180 days costs £120 to £150 per tonne.

Fertile eggs are worth £5 to £10 each. (Infertile eggs can be sold for cooking or crafts for about £3 each.) Incubation lasts 42-45 days. Smaller producers can have eggs incubated by a specialist at a charge of £10 to £20 per chick hatched. Chicks are reared indoors with access to heat for two to three months and then given access to outside. They are fed starter crumb and then small pellets costing £250 per tonne. A high level of care and expertise is required.

Day old chicks are sold for £10 to £25 each. It is less usual to buy or sell at 3 to 6 months but the value would be around £40 to £50. Meat birds are grouped according to size rather than age from 12 weeks and kept at 25/ha (10/acre) at 6 months and 18/ha (7·5/acre) when older.

Birds are slaughtered at 12 to 16 months at a live weight of 95 to 110 kg giving 30-35 kg de-boned meat. On-farm slaughtering is permitted under poultry regulations but meat can only be sold locally. The majority of ostriches are processed at one of the relatively few specialist slaughterhouses which must have veterinary and meat hygiene inspections. Charges are in the order of £35 plus VAT/bird if the meat is sold on directly to the wholesaler at £3-£4 5/kg; or £125 plus VAT/bird for slaughter, butchering and returning the meat vacuum packed to the producer. The skin is returned, sold on commission or bought directly by the processing company. Meat sold at retail will fetch from £7-£15/kg. Individual producers can exploit local outlets but no supermarket chain in the UK is now stocking home produced meat due to the difficulty of getting "consistent quality and quantity of meat". It is said, however, that demand is growing significantly, particularly from the catering trade; ostrich meat no longer has the "exotic" tag.

One ostrich meat concern operates a British Farm Assured Ostrich Products scheme in association with the British Domesticated Ostrich Association — producers wishing their meat to come within the scheme must conform to standards respecting origin of stock, husbandry and welfare, feedstuffs, housing and handling and medicines and veterinary treatment.

Ostrich skins can be just as valuable as the meat. The market for hides is recovering after a recent slump in Far Eastern demand but the quality of the hide is all-important and standards are rising. A grade 1 skin (about 40% of total) can fetch £105, Grade 2 (40%), £75-80 and Grade 3 (20%), £40. Sold directly to a wholesaler prices would be about 50% of these. Tanning costs around £30 plus VAT and dying £15 plus VAT.

Feathers are potentially valuable but no market has been established yet.

Gross Margins

Breeding Adults	per hen £	per trio £
Output:		
40 eggs per hen at 75% fertility		
30 fertile eggs @ £8	240	480
10 infertile eggs @ £3	30	60
Assuming 10 year life: culls at £20 each	2	6
less replacements at £500 each	50	150
Output	222	396
Variable costs:		
Feed @ £90 per bird	90	270
Vet and med	3	9
Forage	5	15
Misc. (inc. licence)	3	9
Total variable costs	101	303
Gross Margin	121	93

Meat Birds	per meat bird	per hen
Output:	£	£
Assuming 15 birds produced per hen:		
35 kg of meat each @ £3·5 per kg*	122·5	1,837·5
Skin at £55	55	825
Output	177·5	2,662·5

Variable costs:		
Feed	100	1,500
Vet and med	1	15
Forage	5	75
Egg + incubation	15	225
Slaughter charge**	41	615
Misc. and transport	7	105
Total variable costs	169	2,535
Gross Margin	8·5	127·5

Farmer retailing:		
*35 kg meat at £10/kg	350	5,250
**£125 plus VAT slaughter and butchering charge	147	2,205
Gross margin	130	1,950

N.B. Costs of retailing meat not included

Fixed Costs

Housing £5; fencing £3; labour: adult birds about 25 hours a year and chicks and young birds about 4 hours a year. One stockperson might look after 500 meat birds. Two people are needed at times to handle adult stock.

Contact

British Domesticated Ostrich Association, 33 Eden Grange, Little Corby, Carlisle, CA4 8QU. (Tel.: 01228 562908).

Researcher

Angela Edwards.

SHEEP DAIRYING

				per Ewe	
Performance level (yield)		Low	Average	High
Milk Yield (litres)		175	250	320
		£	£	£
Milk Value (1)		131	187	240
Value of Lambs (2)		10	15	20
Cull Ewes (3)		3	3	3
Ewe Premium (4)		13	13	13
Wool		3	3	3
OUTPUT		160	221	279
Variable Costs:				
Concentrates (5)			54	
Miscellaneous (inc. vet. and med.)...			10	
Forage Variable Costs (6)			11	
TOTAL VARIABLE COSTS			75	
GROSS MARGIN per Ewe...		85	146	204
Ewes (plus replacements) per ha (acre)			11·5 (4·6)	
GROSS MARGIN per Forage Hectare		980	1680	2345
GROSS MARGIN per Forage Acre		395	680	950

Notes
1. *Price.* 75p per litre at farmgate.
2. Lambing % 175 (200 target). Assume a 250 Friesland ewe flock. Retain 100 ewe lambs, of which 65 own replacements; sell 35 at £75/head. Balance sold at 3-5 days old at £3+.
3. Cull ewes: 20% culled at £15/head.
4. Dairy ewes are eligible for 80% of the Annual Ewe Premium; 100% if all lambs are carried on for finishing.
5. *Concentrates.* Milking ewes: 200 days at 1 kg/head/day, 130 days at 0·5 kg/head/day; cost £150/tonne. Ewe lamb replacements: milk powder £24/head, concentrates £11/head.
6. *Forage costs.* Lucerne silage: 1 tonne/milking ewe (hay equivalent one-third of a tonne). Grazing: permanent pasture plus a catch crop of early grass in March/April.

Additional Points
   Fixed Costs per Ewe. Labour £43; power and machinery £20; property £10; other £10; total excluding finance and rent, £83.
   Capital Costs of Equipment. Complete milking unit for 100 ewes (including yokes, bulk tank, dairy equipment, installation): £5,000-£8,000. Simple unit for 50 sheep: £2,000 plus. These are likely to be minimum costs; they do not include freezing capacity or building work.
   Cheesemaking. 5 litres of milk required to make 1 kg of cheese. Wholesale cheese price: approx. £6·50 per kg. Retail price 40 to 60 per cent higher. Cheesemaking equipment £4,000 to £5,000, excluding building (two rooms plus a store). New environmental health regulations have made all processing much more costly. Require separate processing rooms (minimum cost £5,000-£6,000), pasteuriser (£1,000-£4,000), stainless steel or approved plastic utensils (£400-£500), etc.
   Acknowledgement. Data supplied by Anthony Hyde, FRICS, FBIAC. Costings as in "Sheep Dairy News", December 1998.

GOAT DAIRYING

Performance level (yield)	Low	per Goat Average	High
Milk Yield (litres) (1)	500	800	1200
	£	£	£
Milk Value (2)	195	312	468
PLUS Value of Kid(s) (3)	0	0	0
PLUS Value of Culls (4)	4	4	4
LESS Cost of Replacements (4) ...	40	40	40
OUTPUT	159	276	432
Variable Costs:			
Concentrates (5)	30	48	73
Forage (6)	45	72	108
Miscellaneous (7)	44	44	44
TOTAL VARIABLE COSTS	119	164	225
GROSS MARGIN per Goat	40	112	207
Stocking rate: No. per ha(acre) (zero grazed) (8)...	6·5 (2·65)	8 (3·25)	9·5 (3·85)
(Equivalent) Gross Margin per ha (acre)	260 (105)	895 (362)	1965 (795)

Notes

1. *Yield.* Per 300 day lactation, kidding each year. Autumn kidders tend to yield less.

2. *Price.* 39p per litre; seasonal variation from 32p in June to 52p in November. 12·5% solids delivered.

3. *Kid(s).* Prolificacy relates to age, breed, seasonality and feed level. Assumptions: low 140%; average and high 180%. There is now virtually no trade in kids for meat owing to BSE-related carcase inspection and meat dressing regulations.

4. *Culls and Replacements.* 20% replacement at £200/head; culls £20, average life 5 years. Bucks: 1 per 40-50 does. Does normally mate in autumn; gestation 150 days; young goats can be mated from 6 months.

5. *Concentrates.* Average 0·55 kg concentrate per litre, at £110 per tonne.

6. *Forage.* Average 0·9 kg DM forage per litre at £100 per tonne DM (part purchased, part home-grown). Goats can be grazed but are normally storage fed to avoid problems with worms, fencing, milk taints and pneumonia. Farmers able to produce maize silage will have a better forage conversion ratio.

7. *Miscellaneous.* Bedding £10, vet and med. £20 (includes treatment for out-of-season breeding, vaccination against Johnes and humane disposal of unsaleable kids), sundries £14.

8. *Stocking rate.* Based on home-grown forage.

9. *Labour.* 1 full-time person per 100 goats is a guide, but very dependent on technology employed.

10. *Markets.* There is no government support for goat produce and a strong pound makes imported produce cheap. Some successful businesses have been built on producer processing and retailing. Bulk purchasers of goats milk are few and far between. Average herd size is growing rapidly as established producers expand with the market at about 15% average annual growth. Prolificacy and technical improvements allow higher annual growth than the market and there is a cycle in milk and stock cycles.

Organisations. The British Goat Society registers pedigree animals and publishes a monthly newsletter.

Acknowledgements. The above information has been supplied by Dr. T. Mottram, Silsoe Research Institute, Bedford MK45 4HS.

ANGORA GOATS

	Breeding Does (2)	Subsequent Shearing (2)
Yield of Fibre (kg/year) (3)	13·94	5·45
Price of Fibre (£/kg) (3)...	2·90	2·50

	£ per doe	£ per head
Value of Fibre	40·4	13·6
Value of Kids (1·42 per doe mated) (4)	40·5	—
Value of Cull (5)	5·2	11·8
Less Replacements (5)	10·0	12·5
Output	76·1	12·9

Variable Costs:		
Concentrates (6)	24·8	6·4
Vet. and Med	6·0	0·6
Miscellaneous (7)	9·0	2·2
Total Variable Costs (excl. Forage)	39·8	9·2

Gross Margin per Doe/Head before Forage Costs ...	36·3	3·7
Forage Variable Costs	8·0	5·3

Gross Margin per Doe/Head	28·3	-1·6
Stocking Rate (Does (inc. followers) per ha (acre))	10 (4)	15 (6)
Gross Margin per ha (acre)	283 (115)	-24 (-10)

Notes:

The above figures are for a commercial enterprise. Many UK angora flocks are kept on a semi-commercial or hobby basis, in which case different criteria may apply — does retained longer, mortality rates lower, doe/buck ratio different.

1. Angora goats produce mohair; angora rabbits produce angora; cashgora is produced by angora cross feral goats; cashmere is produced by improved feral goats (valuable "down" has to be separated from guard hairs; thus, with cashmere production, "yield of down" must not be confused with "weight of clip" as percentage down is low and can vary widely). Goat meat is called "chevon".

2. The data for Breeding Does include output and inputs for a proportion (4%) of a buck and the doe's progeny. Progeny are sold after 2 clips for breeding or after 3 clips for meat. Stock may be retained for further shearing, but the annual margins shown above under "subsequent shearing" indicate that this is currently unprofitable.

3. Angora goats are usually clipped twice a year. Yield increases over first four clips, but quality decreases. Prices are volatile, being dependent on fashion and on the world market dominated by South Africa and Texas, both currently showing some instability. Demand and prices are more stable for the high quality kid fibre <30 microns in diameter. The following yields and values have been used. Current wholesale values are poor but an allowance has been made for some direct selling of high quality fibre for hand spinning.
   Clip 1: 1·2 kg, £5/kg; clip 2: 2·0 kg, £3·5/kg; clip 3: 2·5 kg, £3/kg; adult doe: 3·0 kg, adult buck 4·0 kg, £2-2·5/kg.

4. 1·5 kids born alive per doe mated; 2% mortality to each clip. Number of doe kids sold for breeding equal to number of replacements (unless the flock size is changing).Value comprises: 0·2 breeders at £50 each, 1·22 kids for meat at £25 each.

5. *Culls.* Breeding stock in commercial flocks are culled after five years on average. Doe: buck ratio averages 25:1. Subsequent shearing stock culled after a further 4 clips. Value of all cull stock: £25 each. Replacement costs: does, £50; bucks, £100. Shearing stock, £25 (as transfer from breeding enterprise). Show quality stock command a premium.

6. *Concentrates.* Price: £160 per tonne. Quantities: Kids—30 kg to clip 2, 15 kg to clip 3; Adults—breeding adults 90 kg per year, shearing 40 kg per year.
7. Veterinary costs can be high. Miscellaneous costs include £1 per shearing per head (it may be more) and bedding materials.
8. Margins are particularly sensitive to the value and number of breeding stock sold, yield and value of fibre, kidding percentage and meat values. When comparing with sheep margins the higher average working capital requirement should be recognised. Fencing requirements similar to sheep, housing a little more.
   Researcher: Angela Edwards.

GRAZING LIVESTOCK UNITS

Dairy cows	1·00	Lowland ewes	0·11
Beef cows (excl. calf) ...	0·75	Upland ewes	0·08
Heifers in calf (rearing) ...	0·80	Hill ewes	0·06
Bulls	0·65	Breeding ewe hoggs,	
		½ to 1 year	0·06
Other cattle (excl. intensive beef):		Other sheep, over 1 year ...	0·08
0-1 year old	0·34	Store lambs, under 1 year	0·04
1-2 years old	0·65	Rams	0.08
2 years old and over ...	0·80		

Source: as advised by MAFF in England and Wales Farm Business Survey

Notes
1. Total livestock units on a farm should be calculated by multiplying the above ratios by the *monthly livestock numbers averaged over the whole year.*
2. The ratios are based on feed requirements. Strictly speaking, when calculating stocking density, allowances should also be made for differences in output (*e.g.* milk yield per cow or liveweight gain per head), breed (*e.g.* Friesians *v.* Jerseys), and quantities of non-forage feed consumed.

OTHER LIVESTOCK UNITS

Breeding sows	0·44	Broilers	0·0017
Gilts in pig	0·20	Other table chicken... ...	0·004
Maiden gilts...	0·18	Turkeys	0·005
Boars	0·35	Ducks, geese, other poultry	0·003
Other pigs	0·17	Horses	0·80
Cocks, hens, pullets in lay...	0·017	Milch goats	0·16
Pullets, 1 week to point of lay	0·003	Other goats	0·11

Source: as advised by MAFF in England and Wales Farm Business Survey

CAP Payments: Stocking Rate for Beef Premiums
Note that the above units are not those to be used for calculating stocking rates for the purpose of determining eligibility for the beef special premium (and, up to and including 1999, extensification premiums). Only dairy cows, beef and sheep animals qualifying for support payments are included in the calculation and the following livestock units are used: dairy and suckler cows (including replacement in-calf heifers) and male cattle over 2 years old, 1; male cattle 6 months-2 years, 0·6; ewes and goats, 0·15. The number of dairy cows used in the calculation are not the actual number on the farm but are based on the farm's milk quota divided by the average yield in the region (5200 kg in England) . The total number of units are divided by the forage area (ha) declared as such (on which no area payments may be claimed) associated with these enterprises to give the stocking rate in units per hectare. A new calculation of stocking rate for use in determining eligibility for the extensification premiums as amended in the Agenda 2000 agreements includes *all* grazing livestock on the farm (including heifers [over six months old]) and the definition of the forage area to be included has also been altered: it will be limited to temporary and permanent pasture and all other forage areas except arable crops; "pasture land" must account for at least 50% of the total forage area declared.

FORAGE VARIABLE COSTS
(£ per hectare (acre) per annum)

	Grass-Dairying (1)	Grass-Other (1)	Forage Maize (2)	Kale	Fodder Beet
Yield: tonnes/ha (tons/acre)	—	—	40 (16) (silage)	40 (16)	65 (26)
Seed	10 (4)	7 (3)	125 (51)	50 (20)	125 (51)
Fertilizer	85 (34)	55 (22)	50 (20)	60 (24)	70 (28)
Sprays	5 (2)	3 (1)	35 (14)	40 (16)	125 (51)
Total	100 (40)	65 (26)	210 (85)	150 (60)	320 (130)

	Rape	Turnips	Rape and Turnips	Stubble Turnips	Swedes
Yield: tonnes/ha (tons/acre)	—	65 (26)	—	—	65 (26)
Seed	15 (6)	20 (8)	30 (12)	25 (10)	25 (10)
Fertilizer	50 (20)	60 (24)	60 (24)	55 (22)	65 (26)
Sprays	—	45 (18)	—	—	40 (16)
Total	65 (26)	125 (50)	90 (36)	80 (32)	130 (52)

(1) These are *average* figures only. Intensively grazed grass may have much higher fertilizer costs in particular — possibly approaching £125 (50) for dairying. The seed costs will vary according to the proportion, if any, of permanent pasture and the length of the leys. Fertilizer inputs are often less on permanent pasture too, but this depends largely on the attitude of the farmer/manager, which will also be reflected in the stocking rates and productive levels per animal achieved. Note that the dairying figure is the average for the grass devoted to the *whole herd, i.e.*, followers as well as cows; the figure for cows alone will usually be higher.

(2) Contract work on maize: drilling £40 (16); harvesting (inc. carting and clamping) 125 (50). For further details on this crop see "Forage Maize", by Q. Straghan and A. Perry, Genus Management, 1993. The area grown in the UK was 103,000 ha in 1998.

An area payment is available for forage maize, provided the area is not included in the stocking rate calculation for beef premiums; the set-aside requirement applies if the payment is claimed except for small farms where the maize is entered under the simplified scheme. Maize has a separate base area; in recent years overshooting has caused the area payment to be cut to only about one third of the full amount in England, *i.e.* to around £90/ha (£36/acre).

Standing maize crops are typically sold for between £400 and £500/ha (£160-200/acre) but can be as high as £1,000/ha (£400/acre) and as low as £125/ha (£50/acre), depending on the potential yield of the crop and local supply and demand.

Labour: grass, pages 130-1; kale, page 132; conservation labour, pages 130-1. Conservation machinery, page 140.

Grass Silage and Hay

Estimated average costs (for 2000) of producing and harvesting, on a full costs basis (*i.e.* including rental value of the land, all labour, share of general overheads, etc.) are:

Hay: £80 per tonne; Silage: £22·50 per tonne.

Approximately half the silage cost is for growing the grass and half for harvesting and storage. The % breakdown of total costs is as follows:

Variable Costs	Fertilizer	Seeds and Sprays	Contract	Sundries	
Silage ...	23	1	10	5	
Hay	18	1	2	2	

Fixed Costs	Rent	Labour	Tractors	Deprec. & Reps.	FYM/Lime
Silage... ...	21	10	16	9	5
Hay	25	16	19	12	5

Sale Value of hay and (far less common because of its bulk) silage vary widely according to the region and type of season (supply/demand situation), quality and time of year. Grass Silage is typically valued at about £25 a tonne (up to £30 when forage is very short in an area, down as low as £15 if it is plentiful), maize silage £18-22 a tonne.

Ensiled whole crop wheat (40 to 50% DM): £30 to £40 per tonne.

Relative Costs of Grazing, Conserved Grass, etc. (1987)

Source. ICI (M. E. Hutchinson, Henley Manor Farm)

	Yield DM tonnes/ha (acre)	Cost per tonne DM (£)	MJ per kg DM	Pence per MJ of ME in DM
Grazed Grass	11·1 (4·5)	38·6	11·8	0·33
Kale (direct drilled)	6·9 (2·8)	42·0	11·0	0·38
Forage Turnips (direct drilled) ...	6·9 (2·8)	38·1	10·2	0·37
Grass Silage	11·1 (4·5)	69·1	10·9	0·63
Big Bale Silage	11·1 (4·5)	74·1	10·9	0·68
Extra Silage...	2·5 (1·0)	7·0	10·9	0·34
Purchased Hay (1)...	—	76·5	8·8	0·87
Brewers' Grains (2)	—	108·5	10·0	1·09
Concentrates (3)	—	155·2	12·8	1·21

(1) At £65/tonne. (2) At £24/tonne. (3)14% CP, delivered in bulk, £133·50/tonne.

Notes
1. In interpreting the above comparative figures for use in planning feed use on the individual farm it is important to remember two points: (a) that own land, labour and capital for equipment are required for home-produced fodder but not for purchased feed, and much more storage is required, and (b) the limitation on the consumption of bulk fodder by ruminant livestock — although this very much depends upon its quality/digestibility.
2. Later data may be obtained from the Kingshay Farming Trust (Tel. 01460 72977).

Relative Value of Feeds

(based on their energy contents fed to dairy cows)

	Weight equivalent (1)	Relative Value (2)		Weight equivalent (1)	Relative Value (2)
Good hay	154	44	Fresh brewers' grains	589	11·5
Medium hay	165	41	Pressed sugar beet pulp	515	13·25
Dried grass	143	47·5	Dried distillers' grains	108	63
Swedes	767	8·75	Molassed dried beet pulp	107	63·5
Potatoes	449	15	Wheat middlings	113	60
Mangolds	857	8	Flaked maize	87	78
Cabbage	1030	6·5	Maize germ meal (14%)	88	77·5
Oats	119	57	Barley straw	218	31
Wheat	98	69·5	Oat straw	228	30
Sorghum	102	66·5	Wheat straw	245	28
Maize	97	70	Pea haulm straw	211	32
			Wheat bran	133	51

(1) equivalent to 100 of barley (2) value (£) compared with feed barley at £68 per tonne.
Source (of Weight Equivalents): ADAS (D. Morgan)
See also Feedingstuffs: Nutritive Values, page 215.

FODDER CROPS, GRASSES AND CLOVERS:
SEED PRICES (1999) AND SEED RATES

Crop	Price	Seed Rate per hectare
Fodder Kale	£8·50 to £12 per kg	5 to 7 kg
Swedes	£25·00 per kg	3·0 to 4·0 kg broadcast
	£45 per kg graded	0·6 to 0·75 kg precision drilled
Turnips	£4·00 to £6·00 per kg	3·0 to 4·0 kg
Stubble Turnips	£3·60 to £4·10 per kg	7·0 kg broadcast
Rape	£1·75 to £2·25 per kg	3·8 kg drilled
		7·5 kg broadcast
Mustard	£1·40 per kg	22 to 28 kg
Rape and Turnips	£30 to £35 per hectare	1·25 kg rape
		3·75 kg turnips
Rape, Kale and Turnips	£50 per hectare	7·5 kg rape, 2·5 kg kale, 1·25 kg turnips
Fodder Turnip	£6·50 to £7·00 per kg	5 kg broadcast
Forage Maize—Silage	£115 to £135 per hectare	110,000 to 120,000 seeds
Forage Maize—zero grazed	£145 to £180 per hectare	130,000 to 160,000 seeds
Arable Silage	£80 per hectare	125 kg oats, 60 kg tares
Tares	£50 per 50 kg	—
Westerwold Ryegrass	£1·90 per kg	35 kg
Italian Ryegrass	£1·65 to £2·00 per kg	33 to 50 kg
Perennial Ryegrass	£1·40 to £2·00 per kg	22 to 33 kg
Hybrid Ryegrass	£1·50 to £2·25 per kg	30 to 40 kg
Cocksfoot	£3·10 per kg	20 to 25 kg
Timothy	£2·60 to £2·70 per kg	7 to 9 kg
Meadow Fescue	£2·75 per kg	11 to 13 kg
Broad Red Clover	£4·75 to 5·50 per kg	18 to 22 kg
Alsike Clover	£3·25 per kg	18 to 22 kg
White Clover	£3·50 to £9·50 per kg	3·5 kg
Kent Wild White Clover	£9·40 per kg	—
Lucerne	£4·90 per kg	18 to 22 kg
Sainfoin	£2·00 to £2·80 per kg	60 to 80 kg
Forage Rye	£19 per 50 kg	175 kg
Rye and Ryegrass	£75 per hectare	125 kg rye
		22 kg Italian Ryegrass
1 year leys	£60 to £70 per hectare	—
2-3 year leys	£55 to £65 per hectare	—
3-5 year leys	£70 to £80 per hectare	—
Permanent Grass	£80 to £90 per hectare	—
White Clover Ley	£90 per hectare	—
Red Clover Ley	£75 to £80 per hectare	—
Wye College mixture	£50 per hectare	—
Horse grazing	£86 per hectare	—
Game Cover mixture	£58 per hectare	—

3. PIGS, POULTRY, TROUT

PIGS

1. Breeding and Rearing (to 30 kg liveweight):
per sow per year and per 30 kg pig reared

Performance Level	Average per sow	Average per pig		High per sow	High per pig
	£	£		£	£
Weaners: 21 (1) @ £32 (3) ...	672	32·00	25 (2) @ £32 (3)	800	32·00
LESS Livestock Depreciation (4)...	30	1·45		35	1·40
OUTPUT	642	30·55		765	30·60
Variable Costs:					
Food (5)	317	15·10		317	12·70
Miscellaneous (6)	55	2·60		60	2·40
TOTAL VARIABLE COSTS	372	17·70		377	15·10
GROSS MARGIN (per year)... ...	270	12·85		388	15·50

Notes

1. Weaners per sow — average: 9·5 reared per litter, 2·2 litters per year = 21 weaners per sow per year.

2. Weaners per sow — high: 10·45 reared per litter, 2·4 litters per year = 25 weaners per sow per year.

3. Price — assumed pig cycle average. (See footnote (N.B.) on p. 107). Prices for average quality 30 kg weaners have varied from £10 (in September 1998) to close to £55 (in April 1996) in recent years.

4. Average livestock depreciation assumes an in-pig gilt purchase price of £160, a cull value per sow of £135 and a 45% replacement rate (*i.e.* approximately 6 litters per sow life). Sow mortality 4·5%. Boars (1 per 20 sows) purchased at £650, sold at £130. "High" compared with "Average": higher gilt and boar purchase prices and slightly fewer sows per boar assumed.

5. Food — 2·15 tonnes per sow: sow 1·25, boar (per sow) 0·05, other feed (per sow) 0·85. Price of feed consumed: £147·50 per tonne; (average of 60% sow (and boar) feed (at £115-125) and 40% piglet and rearing feed (at £180-200), and of home-mixed and purchased compounds). High performance: slightly higher percentage of creep feed but lower feed cost per tonne, as higher proportion home-mixed.

6. Average: vet. and med. £30, transport £5, straw and bedding £10, miscellaneous £10. (Electricity and gas [£12] and water [£4] included in fixed costs below).

7. *Direct Labour Cost* per sow: average £120, good £100; per weaner: average £5·70, good £4·00. See further page 137. *Other Fixed Costs:* approx. £115.

8. *Building Costs:* see pages 172-3.

N.B. *Outdoor Breeding:* see page 109.

PIGS

2. Feeding (from 30 kg liveweight): per pig

A. Average Performance

	Pork £	Cutter £	Bacon £
Sale Value	56·10	65·00	66·25
LESS Weaner Cost*	32·00	32·00	32·00
Mortality charge	0·70	0·85	0·95
OUTPUT	23·40	32·15	33·30
Variable Costs:			
Food	17·60	21·65	23·50
Miscellaneous	2·20	2·60	2·90
TOTAL VARIABLE COSTS	19·80	24·25	26·40
GROSS MARGIN	3·60	7·90	6·90
Liveweight (kg) ,,, ,,, ,,, ,,,	77·5	88·5	92·5
Deadweight (kg)	55	65	69
Killing out (%)	71	73·5	74·5
Price per kg deadweight (p)	102	100	96
Price per kg liveweight (p)	72·4	73·4	71·6
Food Conversion Rate	2·7	2·9	2·95
Food per pig (kg)	128	170	184
Average Cost of Food per tonne	£137·50	£127·50	£126·50
Food Cost per kg Liveweight Gain ...	37·1p	37·0	37·6p
Liveweight Gain per day (kg)	·62	·65	·61
Feeding period (weeks)	11	13	14·5
Mortality (per cent)	2·7	2·9	3·1
Direct Labour Cost per pig	£2·60	£3·30	£3·50
B. High Performance (Food Conversion)			
Food Conversion Rate	2·4	2·55	2·55
Food per pig (kg)	114	149	159
Food Cost per pig (£5/tonne less than average) ...	£15·10	£18·25	£19·30
Food Cost per kg Liveweight Gain	31·8p	31·2p	30·9p
Gross Margin per pig	£6·30	£11·60	£11·50
Direct Labour Cost per pig ...	£2·05	£2·60	£2·80

Notes

* Weaner cost assumes on farm transfer. If purchased (*i.e.*, feeding only) transport and purchasing costs have to be added: these are very variable but average about £1·50 per weaner.

Labour: see page 137. *Building Costs:* see pages 172-3.

Acknowledgement: Main data source: Pig Yearbook (Meat and Livestock Commission), 1999 and previous years, but the pig and feed price assumptions are entirely the author's responsibility. Small differences in the relationship between these can of course cause large differences in margins. Big variations can occur between farms in feed costs per tonne, according to whether the food is purchased as compounds or home-mixed, bought in bulk or in bags, size of unit, etc. The weaner price is crucial as regards the relative margins between breeding and rearing and finishing.

Sensitivity Analysis. The effect on gross margins per pig (£) of changes in important variables (other things being equal) are as follows (per porker, cutter and baconer respectively). Price: 5p per kg dw difference: 2·75, 3·25, 3·45. Food Cost/tonne: £10 difference: 1·28, 1·70, 1·84. FCR: 0·1 difference: 0·65, 0·75, 0·80. The effect of differences in the cost per weaner is obvious.

N.B. No attempt has been made in this section to forecast the actual position of the pig cycle during 2000. The figures represent only what the average trend figures look likely to be in that year, given neither an "up" nor a "down" stage prevailing for much of the year and assuming feed prices stay at the low mid-1998 to mid-1999 levels. The UK Average All Pigs Price (Adjusted Euro Spec. UK average; p/kg dw) has peaked as high as 152p (in July 1996) and fell to the staggeringly low level of 60p in the autumn of 1998 (compared with the previous low during the last 15 years of about 80p). Prices have gradually recovered during the first half of 1999 and this is forecast to continue for the rest of that year. The level assumed above is approximately 100p, which is some way below the five-year average.

3. Combined Breeding, Rearing and Feeding: per pig

	Pork £		Cutter £		Bacon £	
Level of Performance*	Average	High	Average	High	Average	High
Sale Value	56·10	56·10	65·00	65·00	66·25	66·25
Sow/boar deprecn. ...	1·45	1·40	1·45	1·40	1·45	1·40
Mortality charge ...	0·70	0·60	0·85	0·70	0·95	0·75
OUTPUT...	53·95	54·10	62·70	62·90	63·85	64·10
Food	32·70	27·80	36·75	30·95	38·60	32·00
Miscellaneous... ...	4·80	4·50	5·20	4·85	5·50	5·10
TOTAL VARIABLE COSTS	37·50	32·30	41·95	35·80	44·10	37·10
GROSS MARGIN per pig	16·45	21·80	20·75	27·10	19·75	27·00
GROSS MARGIN per sow	345	545	435	675	415	675
Labour per pig ...	7·75	6·05	8·30	6·60	8·50	6·80
Labour per sow ...	163	151	174	165	178	170

* Performance levels refer to breeding and rearing differences as on pages 106-7 and, for feeding, differences in food conversion rate (and labour cost) only.

4. Further Performance Data
(Meat and Livestock Commission Pigplan results, year ended Sept. 1998).

Level of Performance...	Average	Top Third	Top 10%
Breeding			
Sow replacements (%)	42·0	43·7	40·8
Sow sales and deaths (%)	40·9	40·1	40·2
Sow mortality (%)	4·2	3·7	2·7
Litters per sow per year	2·25	2·34	2·41
Pigs reared per litter	9·78	10·21	10·64
Pigs reared per sow per year	22·0	23·9	25·6
Weight of pigs produced (kg)	6·8	6·8	6·8
Average weaning age (days)...	25	24	25
Sow feed per sow per year (tonnes) ...	1·34	1·33	1·37
Feed per pig reared (kg): sow feed... ...	67	61	58
piglet feed ...	0·40	0·15	0·14
Sow feed cost per tonne	£118·4	£117·2	£111·8
Sow feed cost per sow per year	£159·1	£155·8	£153·4
Feed cost per pig reared	£8·07	£7·18	£6·56
Rearing:			
Weight of pigs at start (kg)	6·7	6·7	6·5
Weight of pigs produced (kg)	35·3	39·4	42·5
Mortality (%)	2·4	1·9	2·1
Feed conversion ratio	1·80	1·78	1·61
Daily gain (kg)	·464	·516	·538
Feed cost per tonne	£199·9	£179·8	£184·6
Feed cost per kg gain (p)	35·98	31·96	29·66
Feed cost per pig reared	£10·29	£10·45	£10·68
Feed per pig reared (kg) (1993/4)	51·4	53·6	46·0

Level of Performance...	Average	Top Third	Top 10%
Feeding:			
Weight of pigs at start (kg)	19·4	24·0	31·3
Weight of pigs produced (kg)	89·3	91·3	92·3
Mortality (%)	3·5	2·8	2·9
Feed conversion ratio	2·61	2·55	2·46
Daily gain (kg)...	·603	·658	·669
Feed cost per tonne	£141·2	£126·4	£119·4
Feed cost per kg gain (p)	36·9	32·3	29·4
Feed cost per pig reared	£25·8	£21·7	£17·9
Feed per pig reared (kg) (1993/4)	163	151	141
Carcase weight (kg)	68·1	69·8	70·6

(FCR for rearing and feeding combined, according to sale weight (kg), 2-year averages (1994/5 and 1995/6): 65-75, 2·25 ; 75-85, 2·34 ; 85-100, 2·50).

Source: Pig Yearbook 1999 (MLC).

5. *Outdoor Breeding*

The following comparison between Outdoor and Indoor Breeding Herds is from The MLC's Pig Yearbooks (2-year averages, 1996/7 and 1997/8):

	Outdoor	*Indoor*
Av. no. of sows and gilts	532	224
Sow replacements (%)	44·6	42·5
Sow sales and deaths (%)	41·4	41·6
Sow mortality %)	2·8	5·2
Sows to boar ratio	16	22
Mortality of pigs born alive (%)	10·8	11·4
Average age at weaning (days)	24	25
Live pigs alive born per litter	10 87	11·02
Pigs reared per litter	9·70	9·76
Litters per sow per year	2·24	2·26
Pigs reared per sow per year	21·8	22·1
Sow feed per sow per year (tonnes)	1·43	1·24
Sow feed cost per tonne £	133·3	126·4
Sow feed cost per sow per year (£)	190·7	156·6
Feed per pig reared (kg)	73·5	61·5
Feed cost per pig reared (£)...	10·30	7·90

Comparative data are also available periodically from University of Exeter Pig Production reports, including the following (per sow) from the 1996-97 report:

	£	£
Gross Margin	264	282
Labour	96	157
(Hours)	(16)	(27)
Land Charges	16	1
Buildings Charges	19	48
Other Fixed Costs	57	66
Margin	76	10

Stocking Rate for outdoor pigs is mainly between 12 and 25 per ha (5 and 10 per acre), 20 (8) being the most common. Good drainage is essential. A low rainfall and mild climate are also highly desirable.

One 1994 estimate updated is that the cost of establishing a 200-sow herd indoors is approximately £1,500 a head, compared with around £250 a head outdoors (PIC).

In England and Wales some 30% of breeding sows (and about 4% of rearing/finishing pigs) are now kept outdoors. (Source: "The Structure of Pig Production in England and Wales", University of Exeter's Agricultural Economics Unit, 1998).

EGG PRODUCTION

(brown egg layers, 52 week laying period)

	Cages Average per bird	per doz eggs	Cages High per bird	per doz eggs	Free Range Average per bird	per doz eggs
Performance Level						
	£	p	£	p	£	p
Egg Returns	8·82	36·0	9·45	36·0	16·08	67·0
LESS Livestock Depreciation	2·29	9·3	2·29	8·7	2·48	10·3
OUTPUT (per year)	6·53	26·7	7·16	27·3	13·60	56·7
Variable Costs:						
Food	4·89	20·0	4·89	18·6	5·90	24·6
Miscellaneous	0·98	4·0	0·98	3·7	0·95	4·0
TOTAL VARIABLE COSTS ...	5·87	24·0	5·87	22·3	6·85	28·6
GROSS MARGIN	0·66	2·7	1·29	5·0	6·75	28·1

Notes

Hen-housed data are used throughout, *i.e.* the total costs and returns are divided by the number of birds housed at the commencement of the laying period.

A. Cage Production

1. The yields assumed are:

    Average ... ... 294 (24·5 dozen)

    High ... ... 315 (26·25 dozen)

2. The average price assumed (for 2000), 36p per dozen, includes all quantity and quality bonuses. Farmer to shop and consumer prices are well above packer to producer levels and normally 35p and 65p per dozen premiums respectively are required.

3. Livestock depreciation—the average point of lay pullet is priced at £2·25 (17 weeks old); the cull value is nil and in some cases farmers may have to pay for catching.

4. The food price assumed (for 2000) is £115 per tonne. The feed cost is dependent on breed, housing and environmental conditions, quantity purchased and type of ration. Quantity of feed used = 42·5 kg.

5. *Direct Labour Costs:* average 94p per bird, premium 73p. See page 137.

    Housing Costs: see page 173. Deadstock depreciation averages about £1 per caged bird.

B. Free Range Production

1. Egg yields: 288 (24 dozen).

2. Average price: 67p per dozen.

3. Quantity of feed used = 47·2 kg. Price £125 per tonne.

4. *Direct Labour Costs:* average £3·20 per bird, dependent on automation.

Acknowledgement. See page 113.

REARING PULLETS
(Average per bird reared)

	£
Value of 17 week old bird	2·25
Less Chicks 1·02 (1) @ 50p (including levy)	0·51
Output	1·74
Variable Costs:	
Food: 6·25 kg @ £117 per tonne	0·73
Miscellaneous (2)	0·60
Total Variable Costs	1·33
Gross Margin	0·41

1. Assumes 3 per cent mortality, but 2 per cent allowed in price.
2. Excluding transport (11p), but including full vaccination costs.

Labour 27p; *deadstock depreciation* 30p.

TABLE POULTRY

A. *Broilers* (per bird sold at 43 days)

	p
Returns: 2·30 kg per bird @ 52p per kg lw	119·6
Less Cost of Chick	25·0
Output	94·6
Variable Costs:	
Food: 4·42 kg per bird @ £153 per tonne	67·6
Heat, Light, Miscellaneous	10·8
Total Variable Costs	78·4
Gross Margin	16·2

Capital cost of housing and equipment: £4·90 per broiler space (depreciation cost approximately 3·75p per bird sold).

Labour: 3·6p, excluding catching and cleaning out (3·5p) but includes management; see page 137.

Housing Costs: see page 173.

B. *Christmas Turkeys* (Traditional Farm Fresh)

Size (2)						Light £	Medium £	Heavy £
Returns per bird sold	...	...	...	...	...	12·98	15·34	16·06
Less Cost of Poult	...	...	...	...	...	2·20	2·24	2·04
Output	...	...	...	...	...	10·78	13·10	14·02
Variable Costs:								
Food @ £160 per tonne	...	...	...	...	2·34	3·47	4·77
Miscellaneous ...	...	...	...	...	...	1·67	1·98	2·33
Total Variable Costs	...	...	...	...	...	4·01	5·45	7·10
Gross Margin	...	...	...	...	...	6·77	7·65	6·92
Killing Age (weeks)	...	...	...	...	...	16	20	22
Live weight (kg) ...	...	...	...	...	...	5·4	6·4	11·0
Oven ready weight (kg) ...	...	...	...	...	4·2	5·2	8·8
Food Conversion ...	...	...	...	...	...	2·8	3·5	2·8
Food per bird (kg)	...	...	...	...	...	15·1	22·4	30·8

(1) 6, 8 and 10% mortality allowed for in cost of poult figures for light, medium and heavy weights respectively.

(2) Light and medium = slow growing sexed hens.
     Heavy = stags (as hatched).

(3) Price per kilogram:
     Christmas (fresh, eviscerated): hens 265-325p range; stags 165-200p range.

C. *All Year Round Turkeys* (per bird sold at 20 weeks, sexed stags)

									£
Returns: 12·8 kg @ £1·30 per kg O.R.		...	...	...	...	...	16·64
Less Cost of poult ...	...	...	...	...	...	...	...	1·38
Output	...	...	...	...	...	...	...	...	15·26
Variable costs:									
Food: 45 kg @ £155 per tonne	...	...	...	...	...	6·98
Miscellaneous	...	...	...	...	...	...	...	2·75
Total Variable Costs	...	...	...	...	...	...	9·73
Gross Margin	...	...	...	...	...	...	...	5·53

10% mortality allowed in cost of poult figures.

Note: With both turkey enterprises considerable variations will occur between individual strains and because of different production systems and feeding regimes. The figures should therefore be used only as rough guidelines.

D. *Roasters (Capons)* (per bird sold at 12 weeks; Christmas–males only)

									£
Returns 4·6 kg @ £2·30 per kg O.R.	...	...	...	...	...	10·58
Less Cost of Chick	...	...	...	...	...	...	...	0·53
Output	...	...	...	...	...	...	...	...	10·05
Variable costs:									
Food: 14·2 kg per bird @ £157 per tonne ...	...	...	...	...	2·23
Miscellaneous	...	...	...	...	...	...	...	0·68
Total Variable Costs	...	...	...	...	...	...	2·91
Gross Margin	...	...	...	...	...	...	...	7·14

10% mortality allowed for in cost of chick figures.

E. Ducks (Aylesbury type: per bird sold at 7 weeks)

	£
Returns: 2·7 kg @ £3·30 per kg O.R.	8·91
Less Cost of Duckling	1·38
Output	7·53
Variable Costs:	
Food: 9·5 kg per bird @ £175 per tonne	1·66
Miscellaneous	0·96
Total Variable Costs...	2·62
Gross Margin	4·91

Heavier ducks of the Pekin type can be grown to 15-16 weeks when oven-ready weights of 3·5-4·0 kg can be realised.

Day-old costs allow for 10% mortality.

F. Geese (traditional farm fresh — free range and dry plucked)

	£
Returns: 5·0 kg @ £6·05 per kg O.R.	30·25
Less Cost of Gosling	4·24
Output	26·01
Variable Costs:	
Food: 20·0 kg @ £165 per tonne...	3·30
Miscellaneous	1·25
Total Variable Costs...	4·55
Gross Margin	21·46

Day-old costs allow for 6% mortality.

Acknowledgement: The figures in the whole of the poultry section are provided by Tony Warner, AAW Poultry Consultancy, Lilleshall, Newport, Shropshire.

RAINBOW TROUT
(per tonne of fish)

	£
Sales: 1 tonne of fish @ £1·55 per kg	1,550
LESS 3,440 fingerlings @ 4·8p each	165
OUTPUT	1,385
Variable Costs:	
Food: 1·1 tonnes @ £635/tonne	700
Vet. and med	60
Marketing and transport	110
TOTAL VARIABLE COSTS	870
GROSS MARGIN	515

Notes

Fish growing to 350g from fingerlings at 4·5g.

Prices are expected wholesale, 1999, but most fish farmers sell at least some of their production direct to retailers, caterers and consumers at prices up to £4·20 kg, but with added marketing costs.

Fingerlings price: 4·0 to 5·5p each according to quantity ordered and time of year.

Average feeding period, 10 months. Mortality, from fingerling to market size, 17%. Food conversion ratio, 1·1:1. The price for fish food is for a pigmented high oil expanded pellet.

Current capital costs for construction of earth pond unit approximately £1,000 per tonne of holding capacity, to include buildings, holding systems and installation of water supply and services, but excluding land.

Labour requirement: the basic norm has in the past been 1 man per 50 tonnes of fish produced per annum on a table fish farm, but with mechanisation this can now be as high as 100 tonnes.

Acknowledgement: Data provided by Dr. John Springate, Roche Products Ltd., Heanor.

IV. LABOUR

1. LABOUR COST

1. Statutory Minimum Wage Rates

(from June 6, 1999)

The following minimum weekly rates relate to a 39-hour standard week of normal hours worked on any five days between Monday and Saturday. The rates apply to both men and women.

Normal Hours

Grades I & II Age	Appointment Grade 1		Appointment Grade 2		Craft NVQ3 Grade (2)		Craft Certificate Grade (3)	
	Weekly rate	Overtime per hour	Weekly rate	Overtime per hour	Weekly rate	Overtime per hour	Weekly rate	Overtime per hour
	£	£	£	£	£	£	£	£
19 and over	229·81	8·84	212·79	8·18	200·87	7·73	195·77	7·53

	Full and Part-time Standard Workers			Casual Workers (4)		Night work Supplement	Standby Duty Payments (5)
Age	rate per standard week	rate per hour excluding overtime	overtime rate per hour	rate per hour excluding overtime	overtime rate per hour	rate per hour	rate per day
	£	£	£	£	£	p	£
19 & over	170·23	4·36	6·55	3·69	5·54	87	17·46
18	144·70	3·71	5·57	3·14	4·70	74	14·84
17	119·16	3·06	4·58	2·58	3·87	61	12·22
16	102·14	2·62	3·93	2·21	3·32	52	10·48
15 & under	85·12	2·18	3·27	1·85	2·77	44	8·73

Flexible Working Contracts

19 and over	Number of days on which basic hours worked	Appointment Grade 1 £	Appointment Grade 2 £	Craft NVQ3 Grade (2) £	Craft Certificate Grade (3) £
	4 to 5	241·30	223·43	210·92	205·56
	6	245·90	227·69	214·93	209·47

The above are weekly basic rates; the overtime rates are as for normal hours.

Other Workers

	Number of days on which basic hours worked				
	4-5		6		Overtime
	£/week	£/hour	£/week	£/hour	£/hour
19 and over	178·74	4·58	182·15	4·67	6·55
18	151·93	3·90	154·83	3·97	5·57

Pre-College Students

Age	Basic Pay		Overtime
	£/week	£/hour	£/hour
22 and over	143·91	3·69	5·54
19-21	127·67	3·27	4·91
18	119·93	3·08	4·61
17	89·37	2·29	3·44
16	76·60	1·96	2·95
15 and under	63·84	1·64	2·46

1. For holidays with pay see below.
2. National Vocational Qualification (NVQ) Level 3 craft grade.
3. In 1996 26·7 per cent of the regular whole-time adult (19 years old and over) male labour force in England and Wales were classified as craftsmen (NVQ3) (plus 5·8 per cent as Grade I and 6·75 per cent as Grade II). However, many other workers receive basic wages above the "ordinary" rates.
4. Casual workers: employed on temporary basis by the hour or day; excludes workers continuously employed for more than 13 weeks.
5. Part standby duty days are paid at half these rates.
6. With regards to benefits in kind it is no longer permissible to deduct any sum from the minimum wage for milk, meals, board and lodgings or board alone. A deduction up to a maximum £1·50 a week may be made for a house and up to £19·95 a week for lodgings alone (less if not 7 days a week or not a full-time worker). There are specified provisions for sick pay, paid bereavement leave and paid paternity leave (3 days).

Full details are available from the Agricultural Wages Board (Helpline Telephone: 0845 0000134).

Holiday Pay

Holidays with pay. The number of days holiday that workers are entitled to in a year depends on the number of "qualifying periods" completed during their employment during that year. For those working full-time, 5 days a week, all year this amounts to 4 weeks and a day. There are rules as to timing. Part-time workers working for 1 and 2 days a week are entitled to 4·5 and 8·5 days holiday with pay a year respectively. Casual workers are entitled to holidays with pay when they have been continuously employed for 13 weeks.

For full-time standard, full-time flexible workers and pre-college students the minimum rates are 25% higher than the minimum basic pay rates for a 39 hour week, *i.e.* excluding overtime. For part-time workers holiday rates are the same as basic pay rates based on the average of the total hours worked, including overtime, over the 12 months ending on the last 5th April. For new workers average hours are based on the days worked since 6th April.

2. Estimated Average Earnings, year 2000

Type of Worker	Average Total Earnings		Total Hours
	Annual £	Per Week £	Per Week £
All Hired Men... ...	14,825	285	47·4
Foremen...	17,725	341	47·4
Dairy Herdsmen... ...	17,825	343	52·7
Other Stockmen... ...	14,925	287	46·5
Tractor Drivers... ...	15,750	303	49·4
General Farm Workers...	13,775	265	46·7
Horticultural Workers...	12,425	239	42·4

Government statistics are no longer available for different categories of worker as listed above; the last year such data was available was 1997. The above figure for all hired men is 9% above the 1997 average. The differentials for the listed categories of worker are based on the average differentials for the three years 1995 to 1997 (they differed very little indeed during those years). The same applies to the hours of work.

3. Typical Annual Labour Cost 1999/2000
(regular worker of 19 or more(1): from June 6, 1999 to (approximately) June 5, 2000)

		Average Annual Cost £	Average Weekly Cost £	Average Hourly Cost (2) £
Minimum Wage (non-craftsman rate) (3)		9,030	173·65	5·03
National Insurance Contribution (12·2% of earnings)	1100			
Employer's Liability Insurance (1%)	90	1,190	22·90	
Minimum Cost		10,220	196·55	5·70
Overtime, average 8·3 hours per week @ £6·55 (+ NIC, ELI)		3,200	61·55	
		13,420	258·10	6·03
"Premium" over basic rate, average £34 per week (+ NIC, ELI)		2,000	38·50	
Total Cost (4, 5)		15,420	296·60	6·93

(NIC = National Insurance Contribution; ELI = Employer's Liability Insurance)

1. Assuming not paid craft grade rates (but note the "premium" assumed exceeds the craft grade "premiums").

2. Hours, excluding overtime, based on 46 weeks (of 39 hours) per year, i.e. statutory holidays and an average week and a half's illness have been deducted.

3. Including additional holiday pay.

4. Annual cost (or net value) of cottages, value of perquisites, contribution towards payment of the council tax, etc., would have to be added where appropriate.

5. Total average worker's gross *earnings* on the above assumptions = £13,625 a year, £262 a week, £6·12 an hour.

4. Assessing Annual Labour Requirements

The regular labour staff required for a farm is sometimes assessed by calculating the total number of Standard Man-Days (Man-Work Units), as given on page 216. The number of days supplied by casual labour are first deducted, then 15 per cent is added for general maintenance work; no allowance is made for management, for which 7.5% may be added if required. It is assumed that 275 Standard Man-Days are provided annually per man, including national average hours of overtime and allowing for holidays and illness; allowance needs to be made for any manual labour supplied by the farmer himself. A full-time dairyperson will average 300 SMD a year, again including overtime. (1 SMD = 8 labour hours a year.)

This is a crude calculation in that it makes no allowance for seasonality and the special circumstances of an individual farm, such as soil type, level of mechanization, and condition and layout of the buildings.

The following sections supply the type of data that should be used in assessing labour requirements.

117

2. LABOUR HOURS AVAILABLE FOR FIELD WORK
(per man per month)

	Total Ordinary Hours (1)	Adjusted Ordinary Hours (2)	% Workable	Available Ordinary Hours (3)	Available Overtime Hours (4)	**Total Available Hours**	Total Available "8-hour Days" (5)
January	177	148	50	74	28 (61)	**102** (135)	13 (17)
February	160	134	50	67	33 (55)	**100** (122)	12½ (15)
March	172	149	60	89	69 (82)	**158** (171)	20 (21½)
April	161	139	65	90	86	**176**	22
May	171	151	70	106	110	**216**	27
June	170	150	75	112	112	**224**	28
July	177	157	75	118	113	**231**	29
August	169	150	75	112	104	**216**	27
September	172	152	70	106	82 (69)	**188** (195)	23½ (24½)
October	177	153	65	99	63 (83)	**162** (182)	20 (23)
November	172	144	50	72	26 (59)	**98** (131)	12 (16½)
December	161	135	50	67	25 (65)	**92** (132)	11½ (16½)

(1) 40 hour week, less public holidays. No deductions have been made for other holidays because they may be taken at various times of the year.

(2) After deducting (a) for illness (10 per cent Nov. to Feb., 7½ per cent March, April and Oct., 5 per cent May to Sept.), and (b) for contingencies and non-delayable maintenance (½ hour per day).

(3) Adjusted Ordinary Hours × percentage Workable.

(4) Maximum 4 overtime hours per day summer, 3 hours winter, and 12 to 14 hours' work at weekends, according to season. Same adjustments for illness and percentage workable as for ordinary hours. Figures in brackets indicate hours available if headlights used up to limit of overtime stated. The percentage overtime (without headlights) available from weekend work as opposed to evenings = (January to December respectively): 100, 78, 58, 50, 40, 40, 41, 42, 53, 67, 100, 100.

(5) Total available hours ÷ 8.

Notes

1. *These figures relate to medium land. The percentage workability will be higher with light soils and less with particularly heavy soils.* On heavy soils, of course, the land may be virtually 100 per cent unworkable between late November and early March (or still later, according to the season), particularly if undrained. A rough estimate of variations in workability according to soil type (compared with the figures in the above table) are as follows. Heavy land — March, October, November: one-third less; April: one-fifth less; September: 10 per cent less; May to August: no difference. Light land — October to April: one-sixth more; May and September: 10 per cent more; June to August: no difference.

2. When these figures are used for farm planning, it must be remembered that indoor work, *e.g.* livestock tending or potato riddling, can be continued over the full working-week, *i.e.* the hours available are the Adjusted Ordinary Hours, plus overtime. Also, some handwork in the field has to continue even in rain, *e.g.* sprout picking.

3. To be precise, percentage workability varies according to the particular operation, *e.g.* compare ploughing and drilling.

4. Furthermore, some operations are limited by factors other than soil workability, *e.g.* combine-harvesting by grain moisture content.

5. Factors touched upon briefly above are discussed fully in Duckham's "The Farming Year".

3. SEASONAL LABOUR REQUIREMENTS FOR

CROPS AND GRASS

On the following pages, data on labour requirements for various farm crops and types of livestock are given. Two levels are shown: average and premium. *The average figures relate to the whole range of conditions and farm size. The premium rates do not denote the maximum rates possible,* for instance by the use of especially high-powered tractors under ideal conditions, but relate to rates of work estimated to be obtainable over the whole season, averaging good and bad conditions, with the use of wide implements, largish tractors (75 to 90 kW) (100-120 hp) and high capacity equipment in 8 hectare fields and over, where no time is wasted. **Most farmers with more than 200 hectares (500 acres) of arable land are likely to achieve at least the premium levels shown. Those with over 400 hectares (1,000 acres) will have still bigger machines and therefore faster work rates, and thus require 15 to 25 per cent less labour than even the premium levels given.**

The rates of work include morning preparation, travelling to and from the fields, and allow for minor breakdowns and other stoppages. They relate broadly to medium and medium-heavy land; some jobs, such as ploughing, may be done more quickly on light soils. Operations such as combine harvesting can obviously vary according to many factors to do with the topography and other natural features of the farm.

The usual times of year when each operation takes place are shown; these relate to lowland conditions in the south-eastern half of Britain. They will obviously vary between seasons, soil types, latitude and altitude. In particular, on light land, land can be ploughed over a longer winter period and a high proportion of cultivations for spring crops may be completed in February in many seasons. All such factors must be allowed for in individual farm planning. Conditions in different seasons will also affect, for instance, the number and type of cultivations required in seedbed preparation. Typical monthly breakdowns of requirements are given for various crops.

To illustrate the type of questions that need to be asked for full details of seasonal labour requirements on the individual farm, "Critical Questions affecting Timing" are listed for cereals. Similar questions would, of course, need to be asked for other crops.

Seasonal Labour Requirements

WINTER CEREALS

Operations	Labour-Hours per hectare		Time of Year
	Average	Premium	
Plough (1)	1·4	1·0	July to October (according to previous crop)
Cultivate (often power harrow)	1·0	0·7	September to October (according to previous crop) (half August if ploughed in July)
Drill (often with power harrows), Roll	1·3	0·9	Mid-September to 3rd week October (according to previous crop and soil)
Apply Fertilizer	0·4	0·3	
Spray	0·3	0·2	October-November
Top Dress (three times [2]) ...	1·2	0·9	March and April
Spray (three or four [2]) ...	1·0	0·7	Spring/early summer
Combine, Cart Grain, Barn Work	2·7	2·1	Mid-August to approx. 10th September
Later Barn Work (3)	0·7	0·4	September to June
Total	10·0	7·2	
Straw: Bale	1·3	0·8	Mid-August to end
Cart	3·7	2·8	September

Typical Monthly Breakdown

Month	Average	Premium	Notes
October	2·6	1·9	Approx. 60% of Ploughing,
November ...	—	—	Cults., Drill, Harrow
December ...	—	—	
January	—	—	
February ...	—	—	
March	0·5	0·3	Part Top Dress
April	1·1	0·8	Part Top Dress, Spraying
May	0·3	0·3	Spraying
June	0·3	0·2	Spraying
July	—	—	
August	1·8 (+2·5 Straw)	1·4 (+1·8 Straw)	$2/_3$ of harvesting (4)
September (harvest) ...	0·9 (+2·5 Straw)	0·7 (+1·8 Straw)	$1/_3$ of harvesting (4)
September (prepn. drill)	1·8	1·2	40% of Ploughing, Cults., Drill, Harrow

Notes
1. Some cereal crops are direct drilled or drilled after reduced, or minimal, cultivations, i.e. without traditional ploughing. Direct drilling reduces man-hours per hectare by about 2·5 (average) or 1·8 (premium), and minimal cultivations by about 1·2 (average) and 0·9 (premium).
2. Winter wheat; winter barley will often have one less top dressing and spraying and oats two less.
3. Later barn work excluded from monthly breakdown.
4. Winter wheat (see page 122 for harvest times for winter barley and oats).

SPRING CEREALS

Operations	Labour-Hours per hectare		Time of Year
	Average	Premium	
Plough (1)	1·4	1·0	September-March (according to previous crop and soil type)
Cultivate (often power harrow)	1·0	0·7	March (½ in second half February on light land)
Apply Fertilizer	0·4	0·3	
Drill (often with power harrows), Roll	1·3	0·9	March (¼ at end February on light land)
Top Dress (once, some possibly twice)	0·5	0·3	
Spray (two or three)	0·7	0·5	May
Combine, Cart Grain, Barn Work	2·6	2·0	Last three-quarters of August (affected by variety as well as season)
Later Barn Work (2)	0·6	0·4	September to June
Total	8·5	6·1	
Straw: Bale (unmanned sledge)	1·3	0·8	Mid-August to end
Cart	3·7	2·8	September

Typical Monthly Breakdown

Month		Average	Premium	Notes
October	...	0·4	0·3	Ploughing. How much in
November	...	0·8	0·5	October depends on
December	...	0·2	0·2	area of Winter Wheat, Potatoes, etc.
January	...	—	—	
February	...	—	—	
March	...	2·7	1·9	All Cults. Drilling, Rolling (nearly half in February on light land)
April	... ...	—	—	
May	... ...	1·2	0·8	Spray and top dress
June	... ...	—	—	
July	... ...	—	—	
August (3)	...	2·6 (+2·7 Straw)	2·0 (+1·9 Straw)	
September	...	— (+2·3 Straw)	— (+1·7 Straw)	

Notes
1. See note 1 on page 120.
2. Later barn work excluded.
3. Spring barley; spring wheat and oats partly September (see page 122).

In a *normal* (*i.e.* neither early or late) *season*:

WINTER WHEAT
Drilling mid-September to 3rd week October.
Harvesting mid-August to approx. 10th September.

WINTER BARLEY
As for winter wheat, except that:
Ploughing unlikely to start before cereal harvest, as usually follows a cereal crop.
Harvesting some weeks earlier: mid July to approx. 10th August.

WINTER OATS
As for winter wheat, except that:
Drilling usually first full half of October.
Harvesting earlier (first half of August).

SPRING BARLEY
Drilling end of February to end of March or early April.
Harvesting last half/¾ of August.

SPRING WHEAT
As for spring barley, except that:
Drilling is on average one or two weeks earlier (should be finished in March) — lose more if late than barley.
Harvesting, on average, is two weeks later: last week of August/first half of September (two-thirds in September).

SPRING OATS
As for spring barley, except that:
Drilling is usually a little earlier.
Harvesting is later than spring barley, earlier than spring wheat: end of August/beginning of September.

Critical Questions affecting Timing (Autumn-sown Cereals)

1. Previous crops (affects time available and need for ploughing and cultivations).
2. Will the crop be ploughed traditionally, chisel ploughed, minimally cultivated, or direct drilled?
3. Earliest and latest drilling date, by choice.
4. Effect on yield if drilling is delayed.
5. Autumn weed control?
6. In the spring: (a) whether crop is rolled, and when,

    (b) whether crop is harrowed, and when,

    (c) time of top dressings,

    (d) number of spray applications.
7. (a) Average period for harvesting.

    (b) Earliest dates for starting and finishing harvest, and latest dates for starting and finishing harvest, ignoring extreme seasons (one year in ten).

Critical Questions affecting Timing (Spring-sown Cereals)

1. Previous crops.
2. Will the crop be ploughed traditionally, chisel ploughed, minimally cultivated, or direct drilled?
3. Months when winter ploughing is possible, on average. (Where relevant).
4. Is spring ploughing satisfactory? (Where relevant).
5. Average period of cultivations and drilling.
6. Earliest dates for starting and finishing spring cultivations/ drilling and latest dates for starting and finishing cultivations/ drilling, ignoring extreme seasons (one year in ten).
7. Effect on yield if drilling is delayed.
8. Is the crop rolled (a) within a few days of drilling or (b) later?
9. (a) Average period of harvesting.

    (b) Earliest dates for starting and finishing harvest, and latest dates for starting and finishing harvest, ignoring extreme seasons (one year in ten).

Seasonal Labour Requirements

MAINCROP POTATOES

Operations	Labour-Hours per hectare Average	Premium	Time of Year
Plough	1·4	1·0	September to December
Cultivating, Ridging, Destoning/ Clod sep. (as required) ...	6·5	5·0	March, early April
Plant and Apply Fertilizer (1)	4·5	3·5	Last quarter of March, first
Apply Herbicide	0·3	0·2	three-quarters of April
Spray for Blight (av. 4 times)	1·2	0·9	July, first half August
Burn off Haulm	0·3	0·2	End September, early October
Harvest, Cart, Clamp (2) ...	15·0	10·0	End September, October
Work on Indoor Clamp ...	4·8	3·2	November
Riddle, Bag, Load	40·0	30·0	October to May
TOTAL	74·0	54·0	

(1) Automatic planter. Hand-fed planters: approx. 12 hours plus 8 that could be casual labour.

(2) Mechanical harvester, excluding up to 25 hours for picking off on harvester—usually casual labour. None may be needed on clod- and stone-free soils. Hand harvesting: additional approx. 80 hours of casual labour.

Typical Monthly Breakdown

Month	Average	Premium	Notes
October	12·2	8·2	80% of harvest, ½ burn off
November	5·9	4·0	Clamp work and ¾ plough
December	0·3	0·2	¼ plough
January	—	—	
February	—	—	
March	7·8	6·0	All fertilizer, ½cults., ¼plant
April	3·5	2·7	½ cults., ¾ plant
May	—	—	
June	—	—	
July	0·9	0·7	3 blight sprays
August	0·3	0·2	1 blight spray
September	3·1	2·0	20% harvest, ½ burn off

Note: These figures exclude casual labour and riddling.

Seasonal Labour Requirements

EARLY POTATOES

Operations	Labour-Hours per hectare Average	Premium	Time of Year
Plough	1·4	1·0	September to December
Cultivating, etc.	6·5	5·0	Late February, early March
Plant and Apply Fertilizer ...	4·5	3·5	Late February, early March
Apply Herbicide	0·3	0·2	1st half March (some in February on light land or in early season)
Further Spraying	0·3	0·2	
After-Cultivation/Spray ...	0·3	0·2	April, early May
Harvest, bag, load	30·0(1)	25·0(2)	2nd week June onwards. All June or till mid-July

(1) Excluding 80 hours picking—usually casuals.
(2) Excluding 60 hours picking—usually casuals.

SECOND EARLY POTATOES

Operations	Labour-Hours per hectare Average	Premium	Time of Year
Plough	1·4	1·0	September to December
Cultivating, etc	6·5	5·0	March
Plant and Apply Fertilizer	4·5	3·5	March
Apply Herbicide	0·3	0·2	Half 2nd half March, half 1st half April
Further Spraying	0·9	0·7	End April, May, early June
Harvest	15·0(1)	10·0(2)	Mid-July to end August

(1) Spinner or elevator-digger, excluding picking and riddling—usually casual labour.
(2) Mechanical harvester, excluding picking off on harvester and riddling—usually casual labour.

Seasonal Labour Requirements

SUGAR BEET

Operations	Labour-Hours per hectare		Time of Year
	Average	Premium	
Plough	1·4	1·0	September to December
Seedbed Cults	3·4	2·4	Mainly March (some early April. Some late February
Load, Cart, Apply Fertilizer ...	0·8	0·6	in good seasons)
Drill (and Flat Roll)	2·0	1·3	Between mid-March and mid-April
Spray (herbicide: pre- and post-emergence)	0·6	0·4	Late March/April
Spray (× 2)	0·6	0·4	May/June
Spray (aphis)	0·3	0·2	July
Harvest (machine)	15·0	10·0	End September, October, November
Load	3·4	2·7	End September to early January
TOTAL	27·5	19·0	

Typical Monthly Breakdown

Month	Average	Premium	Notes
October ...	7·7	5·2	45% harvest; + loading
November ...	8·7	5·9	45% harvest; ¾ ploughing; + loading
December ...	1·0	0·8	¼ ploughing; + loading
January ...	0·5	0·4	Loading
February ...	—	—	
March ...	4·1	2·8	Fertilizer, most of cults., some drilling
April	2·7	1·9	Some cults., most of drilling
May	0·3	0·2	Spray
June	0·3	0·2	Spray
July	0·2	0·2	Spray
August	—	—	
September ...	2·0	1·4	10% harvesting; + loading

126

VINING PEAS

Operations	Labour-Hours per hectare		Time of Year
	Average	Premium	
Plough	1·4	1·0	September to December
Cults., Fert. and Drill	2·5	1·8	Mid-Feb. to April
Post Drilling and Spraying ...	1·5	1·0	
Harvesting	20·0	15·0	July and early August

Note
Drilling is staggered in small areas through the season, ranging from early varieties to late varieties.

DRIED PEAS

Month	Labour-Hours per hectare		Operation
	Average	Premium	
October	1·4	1·0 ⎫	
November ...	0·9	0·6 ⎬ Stubble cult., Plough
December ...	0·2	0·2 ⎭	
January	—	—	
February	0·2	0·1	Cult. twice, harrow; drill and fert. (80 per
March	3·4	2·4	cent March); light harrow and roll;
April	0·6	0·4	spray
May	2·5	1·8 ⎫	
June	0.2	0.2 ⎭ Scare pigeons; spray
July	2·2	1·4 ⎫ Possible spray desiccant; combine and
August	2·5	1·6 ⎬ cart, dry
September ...	1·0	0·5 ⎭ Stubble cult.

Assumes direct combining.

FIELD BEANS

A. Winter Beans

Operations	Labour-Hours per hectare		Time of Year
	Average	Premium	
Broadcast Seed	0·6	0·4	
Apply Fertilizer	0·4	0·3	
Plough	1·4	1·0	September/October
Power Harrow	1·0	0·8	
Spray (pre-emergence) ...	0·3	0·2	
Spraying (two or three times)	0·8	0·5	Spring
Combine and cart and barnwork	3·6	3·0	August

B. Spring Beans

Operations	Labour-Hours per hectare		Time of Year
	Average	Premium	
Plough	1·4	1·0	September to December
Cultivate (often power harrow)	1·0	0·7	
Apply Fertilizer...	0·4	0·3	
Drill, Roll	1·3	0·9	End Feb, early March
Spray (two or three times) ...	0·8	0·5	
Combine and cart and barnwork	3·6	3·0	September

OILSEED RAPE

(Autumn Sown)

Month	Labour-Hours per hectare		Operation
	Average	Premium	
October			
November... ...	0·6	0·4	Spray herbicide and insecticide if necessary
December			
January	—	—	
February	—	—	
March			
April	1·0	0·6	Top dress twice
May	—	—	
June	—	—	
July	2·9	2·1	Windrow (1st half July); combine (½ 2nd
August	2·6	1·8	half July; ½ 1st half Aug.); straw, dry
August	2·0	1·3	Cults. (× 2), spray, drill, fert.; harrow, roll,
September ...	3·3	2·1	barn work (0·5)

Seasonal Labour Requirements

HERBAGE SEEDS (first production year)

A. Undersown

Operations	Labour-Hours per hectare Average	Premium	Time of Year
Undersow	0·6	0·4	March, April
Roll	⎰ (0·6	0·4)	Straight after drilling
Load, Cart, Apply Fertilizer	{ 0·4	0·3	September
	⎱ 0.4	0·3	Late February, March
Harvest (by Combine): Mow	1·4	0·9	3 to 4 days before combining
	4·5	3·5	*Ital. Ryegrasses and Early Perennials: late July. Intermed Perennials: late July/ early August.*
Combine and Cart			*Late Perennials/White Clover: mid-August*
	6·0	4·5	Meadow Fescue: early July
	7·0	5·0	Cocksfoot: early July
	10·0	7·0	Timothy: mid-August
			Red Clover: late September

B. Direct Drilled in Autumn

Operations	Labour-Hours per hectare Average	Premium	Time of Year
Plough	1·4	1·0 ⎫	Depends on previous crop—
Seedbed Cults	2·2	1·6 ⎬	Usually July or August
Load, Cart, Apply Fertilizer ...	0·4	0·3 ⎭	
Drill (with harrows behind) ...	0·8	0·6	As early as previous crop allows. This may be up to mid-September for ryegrasses without detriment to the subsequent yield.
Roll (soon after drilling) ...	0·6	0·4	Meadow fescue and cocksfoot are best sown no later than July
Harvest	See above (Undersown)		and it is risky to sow timothy much later than this.

Seasonal Labour Requirements

GRASS

A. Production

Operations	Labour-Hours per hectare Average	Premium	Time of Year
Plough	1·4	1·0	Autumn drilling: may not plough
Seedbed Cults.	2·2	1·6	
Load, Cart, Apply Fertilizer ...	0·4	0·3	
Drill*	0·7	0·5	Mid-March to mid-April (1) or end July to mid-Sept.
Roll	0·6	0·4	Soon after drilling
Load, Cart, Apply Fertiliser*:			
(three lots)	1·2	0·9	March to mid-August (2)
Top*	1·4	0·9	Mid-June to mid-July; if grazed only

Notes

1. Spring drilling may continue to mid-May to enable extra cleaning cultivations or the application of farmyard manure.

2. P. and K. may be applied in September—especially on undersown ley in year sown.

* Only these operations apply where the seeds are undersown in a spring cereal crop soon after drilling. One extra harrowing and rolling are needed if undersown in an autumn-sown cereal crop.

B. Conservation

Operations	Labour-Hours per hectare Average	Premium	Time of Year
Hay (5·5 tonnes per hectare)			
Mow	1·2	0·9	
Turn, etc	2·6	1·9	Two-thirds June, one-third
Bale	1·3	0·9	July
Cart	6·0	4·5	
Total per hectare	11·1	8·2	
Total per tonne	2·0	1·5	
Silage (17 tonnes per hectare)			
Mow	1·2	0·9	
Turn, etc	0·7	0·5	Two-thirds May, one-third
Load	2·3	1·7	June
Cart	3·0	2·3	
Clamp...	2·3	1·7	
Total per hectare	9·5	7·1	
Total per tonne	0·56	0·42	

Specialized Equipment Prices for Grass Conservation: see page 140.

Seasonal Labour Requirements

Typical Monthly Breakdown

A. Production (figures averaged over the life of the ley)

	1-year ley undersown		3-year ley undersown		1-year ley drilled in spring		3-year ley drilled in autumn (1)	
	Av.	Prem.	Av.	Prem.	Av.	Prem.	Av.	Prem.
March	0·9	0·5	0·7	0·5	0·6	0·3	0·6	0·3
April	0·9	0·5	0·7	0·5	0·6	0·3	0·6	0·3
May	0·6	0·3	0·6	0·3	0·6	0·3	0·6	0·3
June	0·6	0·3	0·6	0·3	0·6	0·3	0·6	0·3
July	0·6	0·3	0·6	0·3	0·6	0·3	0·6	0·3
August ...	0·3	0·2	0·3	0·2	5·0	3·4	1·9	1·4
September ...	0·6	0·3	0·3	0·2	3·2	2·2	1·4	1·0

Note
1. On land ploughed after a cereal crop, drilled early August to mid-September.

	1-year ley drilled in autumn (1)		3-year ley drilled in spring		Permanent Pasture	
	Av.	Prem.	Av.	Prem.	Av.	Prem.
March	3·0	2·1	1·4	1·0	0·6	0·3
April	1·8	1·2	0·9	0·7	0·6	0·3
May	0·3	0·3	0·6	0·3	0·6	0·3
June	0·6	0·3	0·6	0·3	0·6	0·3
July	0·6	0·3	0·6	0·3	0·6	0·3
August ...	0·3	0·2	0·2	0·2	0·3	0·2
September ...	—	—	—	0·2	0·2	0·2
October	0·9	0·5	0·6	0·3	—	—
November ...	1·4	1·0	1·0	0·3	—	—
December ...	0·7	0·5	0·6	0·2	—	—

B. Conservation

	Hay				Silage			
	per hectare		per tonne		per hectare		per tonne	
	Av.	Prem.	Av.	Prem.	Av.	Prem.	Av.	Prem.
May	—	—	—	—	6·3	4·7	0·37	0·28
June	7·4	5·6	1·3	1·0	3·2	2·4	0·19	0·14
July	3·7	2·6	0·7	0·5	—	—	—	—

Seasonal Labour Requirements

A. Maincrop

KALE (growing only)

Operations	Labour-Hours per hectare Average	Premium	Time of Year
Plough	1·4	1·0	September onwards
Seedbed Cults.	2·2	1·6	March, April, early May
Fertilizer	0·4	0·3	April, early May
Drill	1·3	1·0	May
Roll	0·6	0·4	Straight after drilling
Spray (weedkiller)	0·3	0·2	6 weeks after drilling

B. Catch Crop

Kale may be drilled up to the first week of July; the crop will be smaller but either an early bite or silage crop may have been taken from a ley earlier in the year, or the ground may have been fallowed and thoroughly cleaned during the spring and early summer. The smaller crop is also easier to graze using an electric fence.

The above operations will still apply although the times of the year will obviously be different, but there may be an additional three or so rotavations and two or three heavy cultivations if fallowed for the first half of the year or ploughed after an early bite. This means approximately an extra 10 (average) or 8 (premium) man-hours per hectare in April, May, June.

FIELD-SCALE VEGETABLES
(Labour hours per hectare unless otherwise stated)

Cabbage Transplanting.	Hand 150-160. Spring cabbage, Sept.-Oct.; summer, April; autumn, May-June
	Machine (3·5 gang). Spring cabbage 75, summer 85, autumn 100.
	Pulling and dipping plants. 20 per hectare transplanted.
Cabbage Harvesting.	Early spring cabbage, 210, Feb.-April; hearted spring, 250, April-June; summer, 220, June-July; autumn, 220, Oct.-Dec.
Brussels Sprouts Transplanting.	45 (machine) to 55 (hand), May-June.
Brussels Sprouts Picking.	320-400: picked over 3-5 times, maximum approx. 3 hectares per picker per season. Early sprouts, Aug.-Dec.; late, Nov.-Mar.
Peas Hand Pulling.	475-525 (150 per tonne). Early, June; maincrop, July-Aug.
Runner Beans (Picked)	Harvesting. 625 (175 per tonne), July-Sept.
Runner Beans (Stick)	Harvesting. 675, July-Sept.
Runner Beans (Stick)	Erecting Canes and String. 100-150, May-June.
Carrot Harvesting.	Elevator-digger: 260 (1 man + 12 casuals, 20 hours per hectare). Earlies, July-Aug.; maincrop, Sept.-Feb. Harvester: 30 (3 men, 10 hours per hectare). Riddle and Grade: (1½ per tonne), Dec.-Feb.
Beetroot Harvest and Clamp.	25, Oct.-Dec. 12-15 man-hours per tonne to wash and pack.

Source: The Farm as a Business, Aids to Management, Section 6: Labour and Machinery (M.A.F.F.). (N.B. This data is now very dated, but it is still the latest known to the author.)

4. LABOUR FOR FIELD WORK: Gang Sizes and Rates of Work

Basic information on *Rates of Work is* given on pages 143 to 145, where both "average" and "premium" rates for many operations are listed.

The following data relate to rates of work with gangs of different sizes. The rates of work are *averages* for good and bad conditions throughout the season, including preparation time and travelling to the field, and *assume an 8-hour day, unless otherwise stated.* Obviously these rates can be exceeded by overtime work in the evenings.

Combine Harvesting

Gang size can vary from 1 to 4 men per combine (excluding straw baling) according to the number of men available, size and type of combine, distance from grain store, crop yield, type of grain drier, and degree of automation in the grain store. The main possibilities are:

1 man: all jobs (trailer in field)

2 men: 1 combining, 1 carting and attending to grain store

3 men: 1 combining, 2 carting and attending to grain store

3 men: 1 combining, 1 carting, 1 attending to grain store

4 men: 1 combining, 2 carting, 1 attending to grain store

Three men is most typical, although two is quite feasible with a fully automated grain store with in-bin or floor drying, unless transport times are excessive owing to distance or lack of good connecting roads. Four men is most usual with two combines, but an extra man may be needed with a continuous drier.

Except in the case of the small area cereal producer operating on his own, the rate of work will normally depend on the speed of the combine, sufficient tractors and trailers being provided to ensure that combining does not have to stop because of their absence.

Assuming a 9-hour combining day, typical rates of work are:

Size of combine (metres cut)	No. of Men	Ha/day
3 to 4·2...	1	4·5 to 7·75
	2 or 3	6 to 10
4·25 to 5·4	2 or 3	8 to 12
5·5 and over	3 or 4	10 to 15

Straw Carting

2 men, 1 or 2 tractors and trailers	"traditional system"	2·5 to 3·25 ha a day
3 men, 1 to 3 tractors and trailers		3·25 ha a day
1 man, 1 tractor with front and rear carriers		2·5 ha a day
2 men, flat 8/10 accumulator mechanised system		10 to 15 ha a day
2 or 3 men, big bale system		8 to 15 ha a day

Potato Planting

Hand planting (chitted seed) 3 men, 16 women	2 ha a day
Hand planting (unchitted seed) 2 men, 12 women	2 ha a day
(women working a 6-hour day only)	
2-row planter (chitted seed) 3 workers	1 ha a day
3-row planter (chitted seed) 4 or 5 workers	1·75 ha a day
2-row planter (unchitted seed) 3 workers	1·5 ha a day
3-row planter (unchitted seed) 4 workers	2·25 ha a day
2-row automatic planter (unchitted seed) 1 worker	2·5 ha a day
(part-time help loading and carting seed additional; this may be full time if fertilizer is applied with an attachment to the planter)	

Potato Harvesting

Hand harvesting (piecework) 3 to 5 men, 10 to 15 women	0·65 to 0·85 ha a day
(women working a 6-hour day only)	
Machine harvesting (1-row) 4 men, 3 women	0·65 to 0·9 ha a day
Machine harvesting (2-row) 5 men, 3 women	1 to 1·5 ha a day
(lower end of range for heavy land, upper end for light land and good work organization)	

Potato Riddling

3 to 5 workers	10 to 15 tonnes a day

Sugar Beet Harvesting (1-row)

Gang can vary from 1 to 5 (1 or 2 on harvester, 2 or 3 carting, 1 at clamp) but is usually 3 or 4.

3 or 4 men	0·9 ha a day
2 men	0·8 ha a day
1 man	0·7 ha a day
(add 20 per cent for light loams and silts)	

Vining Peas

Drilling (2 men)	7 to 10 ha a day
2·5-3 m. cutter (1 man)	2 ha a day
Pea pod picker, and carting, 5 or 6 men	0·4 ha a day
(large-scale growers: two 12 hour shifts worked per day)	

Carting Hay Bales

2 men, 1 or 2 tractors and trailers	7 to 9 tonnes a day
3 men, 1 to 3 tractors and trailers	9 to 14 tonnes a day

Silage-Making with Forage Harvester (excl. mowing, but inc. clamping; 15 tonne/ha crop)

1 man gang (1)	1·25 ha a day
2 man gang (1,3)	2·25 ha a day
3 man gang (1,3)	3·5 ha a day
4 man gang (2,3)	4·5 ha a day
(1) trailers towed behind, in line	
(2) trailers towed alongside	
(3) man with buckrake at clamp full-time	

Farmyard Manure Spreading

1 man: front loader and mechanical spreader	28 tonnes a day
4 men: front loader and 3 mechanical spreaders	90 tonnes a day

5. LABOUR FOR LIVESTOCK

DAIRY COWS

Herd size (no. of cows)	60	80	100 or more
	hours per cow per month		
January	3·3	2·9	2·5
February	3·3	2·9	2·5
March	3·3	2·9	2·5
April	3·0	2·7	2·4
May	2·7	2·4	2·2
June	2·7	2·4	2·1
July	2·7	2·4	2·1
August	2·7	2·4	2·1
September	2·7	2·4	2·2
October	3·0	2·8	2·4
November	3·3	2·9	2·5
December	3·3	2·9	2·5
Total per cow per year...	36	32	28
Total hours per year	2160	2560	2800
Total hours per week	42	49	54
Total cost per annum	£15,425	£18,700	£21,275
Total cost per week	£296·50	£360·50	£409
Total cost per cow per annum ...	£257	£234	£213
Cost per litre: 4750 litres/cow ...	5·41p	4·92p	4·48p
Cost per litre: 5500 litres/cow ...	4·67p	4·25p	3·87p
Cost per litre: 6250 litres/cow ...	4·11p	3·74p	3·40p
Cost per litre: 7000 litres/cow ...	3·67p	3·34p	3·04p
Cost per litre: 7750 litres/cow ...	3·32p	3·02p	2·75p

Note

These *costs* (note, not *earnings)* are *estimates for 2000* and are based on the average number of *direct* hours of work per cow for different herd sizes obtained from University costings; they do not include fieldwork, such as hay and silage making. The costs include craftsman addition and any other premiums paid, overtime, national insurance payments, and holidays with pay. They also include the cost of relief milking, including during annual holidays.

Earnings. The average earnings of all "dairy herdsmen" in 1997, according to MAFF Statistics, were £315·02/week (£16,380/year), for a 52·5 hour week. Wage inflation is likely to raise this to approximately £343/week (£17,825/year) in 2000.

DAIRY FOLLOWERS AND BEEF

Note.

No recent survey work has been published on labour requirements for beef animals and dairy followers. The following data can therefore only be taken as "best estimates". They are for average performance under average conditions. Substantial variations can occur from farm to farm, *e.g.* through economies of scale with widely differing herd sizes.

A. Calves (per head, early weaning)

Age Group	Labour hours per month Average	Premium
0-3 months	2·3	1·6
3-6 months	0·9	0·6
(av. 0-6 months	1·6	1·1)
6-12 months, yarded	1·1	0·8
6-12 months, summer grazed	0·3	0·2
(av. 0-12 months, during winter (1)	1·3	0·9)
(av. 0-12 months, during summer (1)	0·9	0·6)

Note
1. Assuming 6- to 12-month olds yarded in winter and grazed in summer, and calvings or calf purchases fairly evenly spaced throughout the year.

B. Stores (per head)

Yearling, yarded	1·0	0·7
2 year olds and over, yarded	1·4	0·8
Outwintered store	0·7	0·5
12 months and over, summer grazed	0·2	0·1

C. Dairy Followers

(Per "replacement unit", *i.e.* calf + yearling + in-calf heifer.) (1)

During winter	2·9	2·0
During summer	1·2	0·8

Note
1. Assuming calvings fairly evenly spaced throughout the year and heifers calving at 2 to 2·5 years old.

D. Beef Finishing (per head)

Yarded	1·9	1·3
Summer Grazed	0·2	0·1
Intensive Beef (0-12 months)	1·35	1·0

E. Suckler Herds (per cow)

Single suckling (av. whole year)	0·9	0·6
Multiple suckling (av. whole year)	2·9	2·1

SHEEP
(per ewe)

	Labour hours per month	
	Average	Premium
January	0·3	0·25
February	0·3	0·25
March	1·0 (1)	0·75
April	0·4	0·3
May	0·3	0·25
June	0·4 (2)	0·3
July	0·2	0·15
August	0·2	0·15
September	0·25	0·15
October	0·25	0·15
November	0·2	0·15
December	0·2	0·15
Total	4·0 (3)	3·0

Notes
1. Assuming mainly March lambing.
2. 0·3 if shearing is by contract.
3. A full-time shepherd can look after 400 ewes, with lambs (average), to 600 (premium), with help of extra man at lambing time (4 to 6 weeks) and extra men during dipping (one day) and at shearing time. The above labour-hour figures would thus be higher if only full-time shepherds were considered, since 400 ewes per man equals more than 5·5 hours per ewe per year. (With a full-time assistant a shepherd can look after 1,000 ewes or more.)

PIGS

	Labour hours per month	
	Average	Premium
Breeding and Rearing, per sow	1·8	1·5
(Average 125 sows per worker, Premium 150)		
Feeding only, per 10 pigs	1·9	1·4
No. at a time, per worker:		
Average 1,200 per man, Premium 1,600		
No. per year, per worker:		
Average: 5,750 porkers, 4,500 cutters, 4,250 baconers		
Premium: 7,250 porkers, 5,750 cutters, 5,250 baconers		
Breeding, Rearing and Feeding, per sow		
Porkers, average 80 sows per worker (with progeny),		
premium 100	2·8	2·3
Cutters, average 75 sows per worker (with progeny),		
premium 95	3·0	2·5
Baconers, average 70 sows per worker (with progeny),		
premium 85	3·2	2·6

POULTRY
(large-scale, automated)

	Labour hours per month
Laying hens: battery cages (18,000 per full-time worker)	1·1 per 100
free range	4 per 100
Broilers: 32,500 at a time per full-time worker*	
(225,000 a year)	1·0 per 100

*N.B. additional help needed for catching and cleaning out (included in labour hours per month).

V. MACHINERY

1. AGRICULTURAL MACHINERY PRICES

(Estimated Spring 2000 prices for new machinery, net of discounts and excluding V.A.T.)

1. Tractors

(a) Two-Wheel Drive £

27-34 kW (36-45 hp)	10,000-12,000
35-41 kW (47-55 hp)	12,000-14,000
43-49 kW (57-66 hp)	14,000-18,000
50-56 kW (67-75 hp)	16,000-20,000
57-66 kW (76-89 hp)	18,000-22,000
67-75 kW (90-100 hp)	20,000-24,000

(b) Four- Wheel Drive

43-50 kW (57-67 hp)	16,000-20,000
56-65 kW (75-87 hp)	20,000-24,000
66-75 kW (88-100 hp)	24,000-30,000
76-90 kW (101-120 hp)	30,000-38,000
95-100 kW (127-134 hp)	33,000-42,000
115-134 kW (154-180 hp)	44,000-51,000
140-165 kW (187-220 hp)	48,000-58,000
170-200 kW (228-268 hp)	58,000-67,000

(c) High Road Speed

86-105 kW (115-140 hp)...	48,000-53,000
112-139 kW (150-185 hp)	59,000-69,000

(d) Crawlers

60-64 kW (80-85 hp), steel track	20,000-22,000
90-120 kW (120-160 hp), rubber track...	60,000-65,000
150-206 kW (200-275 hp), rubber track	90,000-110,000

2. Cultivating Equipment

(a) Ploughs

Mounted	2-furrow	2,200-2,600
	3-furrow	3,000-3,500
	4-furrow	4,000-5,000
	5-furrow (semi-mounted)	8,000-8,500
Reversible	2-furrow	4,000-5,000
	3-furrow	5,000-6,000
	4-furrow	6,000-8,000
	5-furrow	8,000-10,000
	6-furrow (semi-mounted)	13,000-16,000
	7-furrow (semi-mounted)	17,000-21,000

(b) Furrow Presses

1·3-1·5 m double row	2,300-2,500
1·7-1·9 m double row	2,500-2,800
2·1-2·5 m double row	3,200-3,500
2·7-3·1 m double row	4,000-4,500
3·3-3·5 m double row	4,400-5,500

(c) Front Presses (excluding linkage)

1·5 m single row	1,400-1,600
3·0 m single row	2,100-2,500
4·0 m single row— hydraulic folding	3,400-4,000

(d) Front Press Linkage

Single row	1,500-1,750
Double row	3,200-3,800

(d) *Other Cultivating Equipment*

Sub Soiler 2-3 leg		2,000-2,500
Soil Looseners (3 m)		4,000-4,400
(4 m)		5,500-6,500
Vibrating Compaction Breaker (2·5-3 m)		4,000-4,500
(3·7-4·5 m)		5,500-6,500
Straw Incorporating Cultivator (3-4 m)		3,500-4,500
Stubble Cultivator (2·5-3 m):		2,100-3,000
(4-5 m): hydraulic folding ...		3,000-4,000
(6-7 m): hydraulic folding ...		4.500-5,000
Spring-tine Cultivator (3-4 m):		1,600-2,300
(5-6 m): hydraulic folding		3,500-4,000
Combination Harrows(2·5-4 m)		2,800-4,500
(5-6 m): hydraulic folding		7,000-8,000
Levelling Harrows (2·5-4·2 m)		1,500-2,200
(3·7-6·1 m): hydraulic folding ...		3,000-4,500
Disc Harrows (3-4 m): trailed		9,000-10,000
(4·5-5·5 m): trailed, heavy duty, folding		14,000-16,000
Harrows (5-6 m): light-medium, hydraulic folding		2,000-2,200
Rotovator (up to 80 kW tractor)		5,000-6,000
(80-100 kW tractor)		6,000-7,000
Power Harrow (2·5-3 m)		5,000-6,000
(with crumbler roller)(3·5-4 m)		7,000-8,000
(4·5-5 m)		10,000-13,000
(6 m)		18,000-20,000
Roller Packer for power harrow (2·5-4 m)		1,200-1,700
(4·5-6 m)		2,000-2,600
Rolls: triple gang, hydraulic folding (6 m)		6,000-7,000
five gang, „ „ (12m)		13,000-14,000

3. *Fertilizer Distributors, Seed Drills, Sprayers*

(a) *Fertilizer Distributors*

Mounted Spinner (500-750 litre)	1,500-1,700
(800-1200 litre): twin disc, hydraulic control	2,500-3,000
(800-1200 litre): twin disc, electric control	3,000-3,500
Pneumatic Spreader trailed (12m boom), 4,000 litre hopper	17,000-18,000
trailed (18m boom), 6,000 litre hopper	23,000-25,000

(b) *Seed Drills*

Grain: mounted	2·5-3 m, gravity fed, 21-25 row ...	4,000-5,000
	3-4 m, pneumatic, 24-32 row	9,000-11,000
	6-8 m, pneumatic, 48-64 row	18,000-26,000
Mounted grass seed broadcaster (2·4-4·6 m)		1,000-1,200

(c) *Combine Grain and Fertilizer Drills*

Mounted, 3 m, gravity fed, 23 row	6,500-7,500
Trailed, 4 m, pneumatic, 32 row	22,000-26,000

(d) *Combined Cultivator and Pneumatic Drill*

4 m, 32 row	15,000-17,000

(e) *Combined Power Harrow and Pneumatic Drill*

3-4 m, 24-32 row	14,000-18,000

(f) *Sprayers*

Mounted, 200-300 litre tank, 6-8 m boom	1,200-1,400
Mounted, 600-800 litre tank, 12 m boom	2,500-3,000
Mounted, 800-1,000 litre tank, 24 m hydraulic boom ...	12,000-15,000
Mounted, Air Assisted, 800-1,000 litre tank, 12 m boom ...	12,000-15,000
Trailed, Air Assisted, 2,000-2,500 litre tank, 12 m boom ...	16,000-20,000
Trailed, 1,500-2,000 litre tank 12 m boom	9,000-12,000
Trailed, 2,500-3,000 litre tank 24 m boom	15,000-20,000
Self-propelled, 12-20 m boom, lightweight	27,000-35,000
Self-propelled, 24 m boom, 4-wheel drive	40,000-50,000

4. Grass Conservation and Handling Equipment

(a) Silage Equipment

Forage Harvester: mounted	9,000-11,000
Forage Harvester: trailed	15,000-20,000
Self-propelled (3-4·5 m pick-up 210-285 kW)	100,000-110,000
Maize attachment, 4-6 row	15,000-21,000
Silage Trailer, 6 tonne	3,000-3,500
Silage Trailer, 10 tonne, tandem axle	4,500-5,000
Buckrake (push off)	1,200-1,400

(b) Haymaking Equipment

Mower (1·6-2·0 m, drum)	2,000-3,000
Mower (2·0-2·5 m, disc)	3,500-5,000
Mower (drum) Conditioner, mounted (1·8-2·5 m)	5,000-6,000
Mower (disc) Conditioner (2·4-2·8 m)	6,000-7,000
Tedder (5-7 m, 4-6 rotors)	4,000-6,000
Windrower, (3-4 m)	2,500-3,000
Balers and Bale Handling: see 5(c) and (d) below	

(c) Silage Handling Equipment

Silage shear bucket (1-1·2 m³)	1,600-2,000
Silage grab	1,000-1,200
Big Bale Silage Feeder, mounted	4,000-5,000
Forage Feeder Wagon (6-7 m³)	7,000-8,000
Mixer-feeder Wagon (8-12 m³)	16,000-18,000
Feed Trailer	800-1,000

5. Grain and Straw Harvesting and Handling Equipment

(a) Combines

Engine size kW (hp)	Cutterbar width metres (feet)	
75-89 (100-119)	3·0-3·6 (10-12)	65,000-75,000
90-111 (120-149)	3·6-6·0 (12-19)	70,000-80,000
112-148 (150-199)	3·6-6·0 (12-19)	80,000-100,000
149-185 (200-249)	4·2-6·1 (14-20)	100,000-120,000
186-224 (250-299)	6·1-7·6 (20-25)	120,000-140,000
Over 225 (Over 300)	6·9-9·0 (23-29)	140,000-160,000
(For self-levelling models add 6,000-8,000)		

(b) Straw Disposal Equipment

Straw Chopper (trailed), (2-3 m)	4,500-5,500
Straw Chopper attachment for combines	4,000-5,000
Chaff Spreader attachment for combines	2,000-2,500

(c) Pick-up Balers (twine tying)

Small rectangular bales	8,000-9,000
Small rectangular bales, heavy duty models	10,000-12,000
Big round bales, twine tying	14,000-15,000
net wrap	15,000-16,000
High density rectangular bales	48,000-55,000

(d) Bale Handling Equipment

Big Bale Wrapper: mounted, with loading arm	5,000-6,000
trailed	7,000-8,000
Big Square Bale Wrapper	16,000-19,000
Bale Trailers, 5-8 tonne	2,200-3,000
Accumulator, flat 8, mechanical	1,500-1,700
Loader, flat 8	700-800
Big Bale Spike	150-200
Big Bale Handler	600-800
Big Bale Shredder...	3,200-3,700

(e) *Drying, Handling, Food Processing Equipment*
Grain driers and Grain storage: see pages 156 and 173

Cleaner/grader, 10-20 tonnes/hour	6,000-9,000
Grain augers 100 mm, 3·3-7·3 m	450-550
Grain augers 150 mm, 6-8·5 m, with trolley	1,400-1,600
Grain conveyors, (25t/hour) (excl. motor) ...	1,000-1,200 + 90-100 per m
Bucket elevator, (25-30t/hour)	1,800-2,000 + 125-150 per m
Hammer Mill, 7·5-15 kW	1,400-1,700
Crushing Mill, 2-5·5 kW	1,500-2,000
Mixer, 750-1000 kg	2,500-3,000
Mill and Mixer, 1000kg, 3·7-5·5 kW	4,000-5,000
Seed Dresser, 3 tonne	3,000-3,500

6. Potato, Sugar Beet and Vegetable Machinery

(a) *Potato Machinery*

Stone separator, 1·8-2·0 m	23,000-26,000
Bedformer, 1·5-2 m	2,500-2,800
Bed cultivator, 1·8 m	4,500-5,500
Ridger, 3 5 row	800-1,200
Planter: 2 row automatic, mechanical drive	5,000-6,000
2 row automatic, hydraulic drive	7,500-8,500
3 row automatic, hydraulic drive	10,000-12,000
Fertilizer attachment, 2 row	1,400-1,600
Haulm pulveriser: 2 row	4,500-5,000
2 row cross conveyor	6,500-7,500
Elevator-Digger, 2 row	5,000-5,500
Harvesters: semi-mounted, 1 row, manned/unmanned ...	14,000-16,000
trailed, 1 row, manned	25,000-27,000
trailed, 2 row, manned/unmanned ...	45,000-55,000
Elevator (rubber belt)	6,000-7,000
Flat belt conveyor, 3-8 m	1,750-2,500
Swinging head elevator	9,000-10,000
Soil elevator (rubber belt)	3,000-3,500
Self-unloading hopper, 3-5 tonnes	5,000-6,000
Hopper cleaner, 2-4 tonnes	2,750-4,000
Clod separator	5,000-6,500
Sizer, 5-10 tonnes/hour	6,000-8,000
Sponge drier, 0·9-1·2m	5,500-6,500
Barrel washer, 6-8 tonnes/hour	6,500-8,000
Roller inspection table, 1·2 × 2·4 m	2,500-3,000
Weigher, automatic, 8-10 tonnes/hour	4,000-5,000
Box tipper	3,250-4,000
Box filer, automatic	9,000-10,000
Bag stitcher (hand held)	750-900

(b) *Sugar Beet Machinery*

Precision Drill:	6 row-12 row (mechanical)	8,000-15,000
	12 row-18 row (pneumatic)	18,000-25,000
Hoe:	6 row-12 row (heavy duty)	4,000-7,500
Harvesters:	Trailed, 4-6 row	45,000-50,000
	Trailed, 2 row, tanker	35,000-40,000
	Trailed, 3 row, tanker	42,000-47,000
Self-propelled, 6 row (including power unit) elevator	...	120,000-130,000
Cleaner-loader, with engine, 60 tonnes per hour	... ...	18,000-20,000
Fodder beet harvester		5,000-5,500

(c) *Vegetable Machinery*

Onion windrower		7,000-8,000
Root crop digger: 1 webb		5,000-5,500
2 webbs		6,000-7,000
Top lifting vegetable harvester: single row, bunker ...	...	35,000-40,000
	twin row, bunker/elevator ...	65,000-70,000
	four row, elevator	90,000-100,000
Leek harvester		11,000-12,000

7. General

Trailer, 4 tonne tipping	1,600-1,900
Trailer, 6 tonne tipping; grain/silage	2,500-3,000/3,000-3,500
Trailer, 10 tonne tipping, tandem axle; grain/silage	4,000-4,500/4,500-5,000
F.Y.M. Spreaders, (4-6 m³)	3,000-3,500
F.Y.M. Spreaders, (6-8 m³)	4,000-5,000
Loaders, front mounted...	2,500-3,500
Pallet loader, self levelling (1,000-1,600 kg)	3,000-4,000
Materials Handler, telescopic boom (2·5-3·0 tonne)...	30,000-35,000
Skid steer loader (500-600 kg)	12,000-14,000
Slurry Stores (metal), including base but before grant (assumes large store for 200 cows with a 15-week storage period; stores for 70-80 cows are £150-170 per cow)	£125 per cow
Vacuum Tankers (5,000-6,000 litre)	5,000-6,000
Low Ground Pressure Tankers (9,000-11,000 litre)...	8,000-10,000
Slurry pump	2,500-3,000
Cattle crush	500-700
Cattle crush with weigher	1,000-1,200
Cattle trailer (twin-axle)	1,700-2,000
Yard scrapers	500-600
Rotary brush (2-2·5 m)	1,800-2,200
Grassland roll, ballastable (2·5-3 m)	800-900
Pasture topper (2·0-3·0 m)	1,500-2,000
Pasture aerator (2·5-3 m)	1,700-2,200
Hedger: hydraulic angling; flail head	8,000-9,000
Ditcher: fully slewing	5,000-6,000
Carrier box	300-400
Post hole digger/driver	800-1,000/1,400-1,700
Saw bench	800
Log splitter	450-550

2. TYPICAL CONTRACTORS' CHARGES, AVERAGE FARMERS' COSTS AND RATES OF WORK FOR VARIOUS FARM OPERATIONS

Contractors' charges vary widely according to many factors: those given below are estimates for 2000. Farmer-contractors often charge less, since their overheads and machinery fixed costs are largely covered by their own farming operations, but the service may not always be so complete, including specialist advice.

Farmers' own costs (which include the value of the farmers' own manual labour) vary even more widely; those given below (estimated for Spring 2000) are averages in every respect — covering different types of soil, size of farm, and so on; they are based on accounting cost procedures in that labour, tractor and machinery fuel, repairs and depreciation are included — but no allowance has been added for general farm overheads, interest on capital, supervision/ management or under-occupied labour during slack times. They assume four-wheel drive 75-90 kW (100-120 hp) tractors for ploughing, heavy cultivation and other work with a high power requirement. Four-wheel drive 55-65 kW (75-87 hp) tractors are assumed to be used for most other operations. The figures should not be used for partial budgeting.

For a typical set of farm operations, excluding harvesting, the breakdown of the farmers' costs averages very approximately one third each for labour, tractors and implements/machines. The larger the farm the lower the labour element and the higher the machine element, and vice versa.

The contract charges and average farmers' costs are put side-by-side for tabular convenience, not to facilitate comparisons. Apart from the fact that contractors' charges must cover expenses omitted from the farmers' cost, the advisability or otherwise of hiring a contractor for a particular job depends on many factors, varying widely according to farm circumstances; furthermore, there are advantages and disadvantages not reflected in a cost comparison alone.

Machinery rings. Prices charged by farmers offering services through machinery rings are extremely variable but are generally between average farmers' costs and contractors' charges. There are exceptions, which mainly relate to relatively expensive items of machinery (*e.g.* precision drills, destoners and combine harvesters), where the charges for services offered through machinery rings are close to and often less than average farmers' costs.

Four-wheel drive 120-150 kW (150-200 hp) tractors are assumed where appropriate to achieve the "Premium" rates of work (which will be achieved on most farms with more than 200 hectares (500 acres) of arable land); obviously, still larger wheeled tractors and crawlers could achieve still faster rates of work, particularly on light land. See further page 119, first paragraph.

All charges and costs below are *per hectare* unless otherwise stated.

Operation	Contract Charge	Average Farmers' Cost	Rate of Work (hectares per 8 hr. day)	
			Average	Premium
	£	£		
Ploughing (light/heavy soils) ...	37·00-46·00	31·25-40·50	5-6½	7½-9
Ploughing with furrow press ...	42·00-52·00	36·25-48·25	4½-6½	7-8½
Deep Ploughing (over 300 mm)	51·00-63·00	50·00-62·00	3-3¾	5-6½
Rotavating...	49·00-57·00	54·00 (ploughed land)	4½	6
		80·50 (grass)	3	4

143

Operation	Contract Charge	Average Farmers' Cost	Rate of Work (hectares per 8 hr. day) Average	Premium
	£	£		
Subsoiling	50·00	29·50	6	10
Stubble Cultivating	26·00	16·00	12	16
Heavy Disc Cultivating	31·00	23·00	10	15
Disc Harrowing ...	20·00	11·50	12	16
Power Harrowing	32·00	23·25	9	12
Spring tine Harrowing	23·00	11·50	12	18
Seedbed Harrowing	14·00	9·50	12	20
Rolling (flat 3-4 tonne)	21·00	16·75	6	10
(ring, set of 3, 6 m) ...	13·50	10·25	14	22
Fertilizer Distributing (including loading and carting):				
Broadcast (125-375 kg/ha) ...	7·00-10·00 (fert. in field)	7·00	20	30
Broadcast (500-1,250 kg/ha) ...	—	11·50	15	20
Pneumatic (125-375 kg/ha)...	—	9·75	30	45
Drilling:				
Cereals (direct into stubble) ...	33·00 (seed & fert. in field)	31·00	8	10
Cereals (plain, 1 man)	21·50	16·00	12	16
Grass (broadcast)	16·00	12·00	11	15
Roots (4-row)	—	50·00	3½ (4 row)	5 (6 row)
Sugar Beet—precision drill ...	36·00	30·25	6 (6 row)	10 (12 row)
Power Harrowing and Drilling Cereals	43·00	33·50	8	11
Destoning potato land	160·00	125·00	3·25	4
Potato Planting automatic	—	100·00	2½ (2 row)	3¼
Potato Ridging	35·00	22·00	5½	7
Spraying (excl. materials):				
Low Volume (up to 175 l/ha) ...	10·00	6·00	35	55
Medium Volume (200-300 l/ha) ...	12·00	7·00	30	45
High Volume (over 800 l/ha) ...	—	12·50	25	35
Tractor Hoeing Sugar Beet	—	27·50	5	8
Combine Harvesting Cereals:			(hectares per hour)	
100 ha/year	70-85	90·00	¾-1	1-1½
200 ha/year	70-85	71·00		
300 ha/year	70-85	64·00		
Carting to barn add	16·50	13·00		
Combine Harvesting:				
Oilseed rape (direct)	80-85	as cereals + 10%	²/₃-1	¾-1¼
Beans	70-85	as cereals + 10%	²/₃-1	¾-1¼
Peas	80-90	as cereals	¾-1	1-1½
Windrowing Oilseed Rape	35·00	—	1·2	1·4
Pick-up Baling (incl. string) ...	20-24p per bale	17p per bale	0·8 per hour	1·25 per hour
Big Baling (round)	1·75-2·00 per bale	1·55 per bale	—	—
Crop Drying (inc. pre-cleaning) (per tonne)				
Cereals:				
by 6 per cent	12·00	7·00	—	—
by 10 per cent	15·50	8·50	—	—
Oilseed Rape:				
by 5 per cent	16·50	9·00	—	—
by 10 per cent	21·50	11·50	—	—
Cleaning without drying (per tonne)	7·50	—	—	—
Mobile Seed Cleaning (cereals) (per tonne) (including chemicals)	70-90	—	—	—
Grain Storage (per tonne per week)	27p	(see page 156)	—	—
Handling into store (per tonne)	£1·50	£1		
Handling out of store (per tonne)	£1·50	£1		

Operation	Contract Charge	Average Farmers' Cost	Rate of Work (hectares per 8 hr. day) Average	Premium
	£	£		
Potato Harvesting (2-row unmanned) ...	£42/hour	—	0·75	1
Sugar Beet Complete Harvesting ...	155	145(excl. carting)	3·5	4·5
...	200	182(incl. carting)		
Grass Mowing/Topping (inc. Set-aside)	22·00	18·50	8	12
Swath Turning/Tedding	14·00	12·50	11	15
Forage Harvesting (inc. mowing): Full chop harvester, 17·5 tonnes/ha (driver only)	45·00	—	—	—
Forage harvesting, carting and ensiling grass 17·5 tonnes/ha	110	—	—	—
Forage harvesting, carting and ensiling maize 25-30 tonnes/ha...	125	—	—	—
F.Y.M.: Tractor and Spreader ...	20·00 per hour	—	—	—
F.Y.M.: Tractor and Loader	16·00 per hour	—	—	—
Lime Spreading	3·00 per tonne	—	—	—
Hedge Cutting	15·00 per hour	—	—	—
Tractor Hire (inc. driver and fuel):				
2 wheel drive, 56 kW (75 h.p.) ...	110	—	—	—
2 wheel drive, 75 kW (100 h.p.)	115	per —	—	—
4 wheel drive, 75 kW (100 h.p.)...	128	8 hour —	—	—
4 wheel drive, 112 kW (150 h.p.)	144	day —	—	—
Trailer (with driver and tractor) ...	132	12·75 per hour	—	—

Contract Charge for All Operations (Cereals and Combinable Break Crops, "stubble to stubble" i.e. up to and including Combine Harvesting and Carting the Grain to Store): £220 to £270/ha (£90-110/acre). (Variation according to such factors as distance away, area contracted, size of fields, type of terrain, quality of soil and level of inputs (as affecting weight of crop to be harvested and carted). The charge is typically £222 to £235/ha (£90-£95/acre) but can be even as low as £200/ha (£80/acre) where a proportion of the profit is also taken by the contractor or a neighbouring farmer after payment of a prior charge to the landowner of £250 to £270/ha (£100-£110/acre); the percentage share of total gross margin less these two deductions has been typically 70% to the contractor and 30% to the landowner.

One sometimes sees farmers' total power and machinery costs compared with stubble to stubble contractors' charges. It has of course to be remembered that the former include many cost items not included in the latter, e.g. the cost of farm vehicles, fixed plant such as grain stores and general farm maintenance.

Total Cultivations cost typically £60/ha (£24/acre) on light land, £90/ha (£36/acre) on heavy land.

Grain Haulage Costs

UK average in 1998: £5·40 per tonne, 9·3p per tonne per mile. Average for 20 miles £4·05 per tonne, 50 miles £5·13, 100 miles £6·92. (Home-Grown Cereals Authority).

3. TRACTOR HOURS
(per annum)

Crops

	per hectare	
	Average	Premium
Cereals	9	7
Straw Harvesting	3·5	2·5
Potatoes	25	15
Sugar Beet	20	12
Vining Peas	20	12
Dried Peas	10	8
Field Beans	9	7
Oilseed Rape	9	7
Herbage Seeds:		
1 year undersown or 3 year direct drilled	7	5
1 year direct drilled	11	8
Hops (machine picked)	125	—
Kale (grazed)	8	6
Turnips/Swedes: folded/lifted	12/35	10/25
Mangolds	50	35
Fallow	12	7
Ley Establishment:		
Undersown	2	1
Direct Seed	7	4
Making Hay	12	8
Making Silage:		
1st Cut	12	8
2nd Cut	9	6
Grazing:		
Temporary Grass	3	2·5
Permanent Grass	2	1·5

Livestock

	per head Average
Dairy Cows...	6
Other Cattle over 2 years	5
Other Cattle 1-2 years	4
Other Cattle ½-1 year	2·25
Calves 0-½ year	2·25
Yarded bullocks	3
Sheep, per ewe	1·25
Store sheep	0·8
Sows...	1·75
Other pigs over 2 months	1
Laying Birds	0·04

1. For Livestock, annual requirements are the per head requirements above multiplied by average numbers during the year (*i.e.* average numbers at end of each month).

2. As with labour, the number of tractors required by a farm depends more on the seasonal requirements and number required at any one time than on total annual tractor hours. These can be calculated from the seasonal labour data provided earlier in this book. The soil type and size/power of tractors purchased are obviously other relevant factors.

Tractor Power Requirements		hp/acre		hp/ha		kW/ha	
		av.	prem.	av.	prem.	av.	prem.
Combinable crops:	heavy land	·75	·6	1·85	1·5	1·4	1·1
	light land	·5	·4	1·25	1	·9	·75
Mixed cropping:	heavy land	1	·8	2·5	2	1·85	1·5
	light land	·75	·6	1·85	1·5	1·4	1·1

The average power of tractors registered during the first quarter of 1998 was 77·3 kw (103·7 hp); (AEA).

4. TRACTOR COSTS
(Estimates for Spring 2000)

	Two-Wheel Drive 43-49 kW (56-66 h.p.)		Four-Wheel Drive 56-65kW (75-85 h.p.)	
Initial Cost	£16,000		£22,000	
	per year £	per hour £	per year £	per hour £
Depreciation	960	1·92	1,375	2·75
Tax and Insurance	195	0·39	247	0·49
Repairs and Maintenance	800	1·60	1,100	2·20
Fuel and Oil	527	1·05	841	1·68
Total	2,482	4·96	3,563	7·13

	Four-Wheel Drive			
	76-90 kW (101-120 h.p.)		115-134 kW (154-180 h.p.)	
Initial Cost	£34,000		£48,000	
	per year £	per hour £	per year £	per hour £
Depreciation	2,210	4·42	3,360	6·72
Tax and Insurance	333	0·67	424	0·85
Repairs and Maintenance	1,700	3·40	2,400	4·80
Fuel and Oil	1,164	2·33	1,617	3·23
Total	5,407	10·81	7,801	15·60

	Crawlers			
	60-64 kW (80-86 h.p.)		90 kW (120 h.p.)	
Initial Cost	£21,000		£60,000	
	per year £	per hour £	per year £	per hour £
Depreciation	1,470	2·94	4,200	8·40
Tax and Insurance	191	0·38	510	1·02
Repairs and Maintenance	1,050	2·10	3,000	6·00
Fuel and Oil	828	1·66	1,242	2·48
Total	3,539	7·08	8,952	17·90

Depreciation is based on the assumption that small two-wheel drive tractors are sold for 40% of their original value after ten years and that small, medium and large four-wheel drive tractors (including crawlers) are sold for 37·5, 35 and 30% respectively of their original value after ten years. Annual Repair Costs have been calculated at 5 per cent of initial cost for all tractors. No interest on capital has been included.

The hourly figures are based on a use of 500 hours a year. A greater annual use than this will mean higher annual costs but possibly lower hourly costs. On large arable farms in particular, many tractors do over 750 hours a year, or even 1,000 in some cases. Early replacement at a given annual use will increase depreciation costs per hour but should reduce repair costs. The hourly figures are averages for all types of work: heavy operations such as ploughing obviously have a higher cost than light work.

The average size of wheeled tractor currently purchased is around 82 kw (110 hp), which compares with 60 kw (80 hp) five or six years ago.

5. ESTIMATING ANNUAL MACHINERY COSTS

Annual machinery costs consist of depreciation, repairs, fuel and oil, contract charges, and vehicle tax and insurance. These can be budgeted in three ways, assuming there is no available information on past machinery costs on the farm:

(a) *Per hectare,* by looking up an average figure for the district, according to the size and type of farm. Approximate levels are shown in the tables of fixed costs (pages 157-161). This is obviously a very rough and ready measure.

(b) *Per standard tractor hour.* The crop area and livestock numbers can be multiplied by the appropriate standard (average) tractor hours per hectare and per head as given on page 146. The total can then be multiplied by the machinery cost per standard tractor hour as calculated from farm surveys. The following average figures (estimated for mid-2000) are based on 1995-98 levels in South-East England.

Farm Type	Cost per Standard Tractor Hour
Mainly Sheep/Cattle, over 100 ha	£8·50
Mainly Sheep/Cattle, under 100 ha ... ... Sheep/Cattle and Arable, over 100 ha	£11·00
Sheep/Cattle and Arable, under 100 ha ... ... Mainly Dairying, under 60 ha ... ... Dairying and Arable	£15·00
Mainly Dairying, 60-120 ha ... ... Mainly Arable, over 200 ha	£17·50
Mainly Dairying, over 120 ha	£19·00
Mainly Arable, 100-200 ha	£22·50
Mainly Arable, under 100 ha	£37·50

Premium levels are about 10 per cent lower.

Depreciation is based on the historic cost of the machinery and equipment. The capital element of leasing (but not the interest) is included in depreciation. With depreciation calculated on the current (*i.e.* replacement) cost the above figures are raised by approximately 10%.

The percentage composition of the total cost varies with size and type of farm but averages approximately:

	Depreciation	Repairs	Fuel/Elec.	Contract	VTI*
A.	35	24	14	22	5
B.	40	22	13	20	5

A = Depreciation based on historic cost.
B = Depreciation based on current cost.
*Vehicle tax and insurance.

This method may be used as a check on the per hectare calculation.

(N.B. The standard tractor hour is used only as a convenient measure of machinery input. *The costs incorporate not only tractor costs but all other power and machinery expenses, including field machinery and implements, fixed equipment, landrovers, vans, use of farm car, etc.)*

(c) *Fully detailed calculation,* costing and depreciating each machine in turn, including tractors, estimating repairs and fuel costs for each, and adding the charges for any contract work.

The following tables, giving, for different types of machine, estimated life, annual depreciation, and estimated repairs according to annual use, are mostly taken from "Profitable Farm Mechanisation", by C. Culpin.

ESTIMATED USEFUL LIFE (YEARS) OF POWER OPERATED MACHINERY IN RELATION TO ANNUAL USE

Equipment	Annual Use (hours)				
	25	50	100	200	300
Group 1: Ploughs, Cultivators, Toothed harrows, Hoes, Rolls, Ridgers, Potato planting attachments, Grain cleaners	12+	12+	12+	12	10
Group 2: Disc harrows, Corn drills, Grain drying machines, Food grinders and mixers	12+	12+	12	10	8
Group 3: Combine harvesters, Pick-up balers, Rotary cultivators, Hydraulic loaders	12+	12+	12	9	7
Group 4: Mowers, Forage harvesters, Swath turners, Side-delivery rakes, Tedders, Hedge cutting machines, Semi-automatic potato planters and transplanters, Unit root drills, Mechanical root thinners	12+	12	11	8	6
Group 5: Fertilizer distributors, Combine drills, Farmyard manure spreaders, Elevator potato diggers, Spraying machines, Pea cutter-windrowers	10	10	9	8	7
Miscellaneous: Beet harvesters	11	10	9	6	5
Potato harvesters	—	8	7	5	—
Milking machinery	—	—	—	12	10

	Annual Use (hours)					
	500	750	1,000	1,500	2,000	2,500
Tractors	12+	12	10	7	6	5
Electric motors	12+	12+	12+	12+	12	12

149

DEPRECIATION: AVERAGE ANNUAL FALL IN VALUE
(per cent of new price)
(Source: V. Baker, Bristol University; slightly amended)

Frequency of renewal. Years	Complex. High Depreciation Rate e.g. potato harvesters, mobile pea viners, etc.	Established machines with many moving parts, e.g. tractors, combines, balers, forage harvesters	Simple equipment with few moving parts, e.g. ploughs, trailers
	%	%	%
1	40	30	20
2	27½	20	15
3	20*	16*	12½
4	17½†	14½	11½
5	15‡	13†	10½*
6	13½	12	9½
7	12	11	9
8	11	10‡	8½†
9	(10)	9½	8
10	(9½)	8½	7½‡

* Typical frequency of renewal with heavy use.
† Typical frequency of renewal with average use.
‡Typical frequency of renewal with light use.

Tractors. For the results of a recent study giving variations in tractor depreciation according to size and annual use as well as age when sold see P. Wilson and S. Davis, "Estimating Depreciation in Tractors in the UK (etc)", "Farm Management", Vol. 10, No. 4, Winter 1998/99, pp. 183-193.

VALUATION AND DEPRECIATION OF MACHINERY BY TYPE

(% of total machinery valuation per farm, 1997/98;
% depreciation in brackets; both based on replacement costs)

Type of Farm	Mainly Cereals	Mixed Cropping	Dairy & Arable	ALL FARMS
Tractors	34 (35)	30 (31)	34 (36)	24 (25)
Vehicles	10 (10)	11 (11)	13 (13)	17 (18)
Harvesters	17 (20)	12 (16)	7 (9)	9 (11)
Other Equipment and Plant	39 (35)	47 (42)	46 (42)	50 (46)

Source: M. C. Murphy, Report on Farming in the Eastern Counties of England, 1997/98. University of Cambridge, Rural Business Unit, 1999.

DEPRECIATION: PERCENTAGE RATES

A. Straight-Line

Years Retained	Trade-in, Second-hand or Scrap Value as % of New Price							
	5	10	20	25	33	40	50	60
3	—	—	—	—	—	20	16½	13½
4	—	—	—	—	17	15	12½	—
5	—	—	—	15	13½	12	—	—
6	—	—	13½	12½	11	10	—	—
8	—	11	10	9½	—	—	—	—
10	9½	9	8	—	—	—	—	—
12	8	7½	—	—	—	—	—	—
15	6½	—	—	—	—	—	—	—

Example: If a machine costing £10,000 is retained for 8 years, at the end of which the trade-in value is 20% of the new price (*i.e.* £2,000), the average depreciation per annum has been £8,000 ÷ 8 years = £1,000 (*i.e.* 10% of the new price).

B. Diminishing Balances

Years Retained	Trade-in, Second-hand or Scrap Value as % of New Price							
	5	10	20	25	33	40	50	60
3	—	—	—	—	—	26	21	16
4	—	—	—	—	24	20	16	—
5	—	—	—	24	20	17	—	—
6	—	—	23	20	17	14	—	—
8	—	25	18	16	—	—	—	—
10	25	20	15	—	—	—	—	—
12	22	17	—	—	—	—	—	—
15	18	—	—	—	—	—	—	—

Example: If a machine costing £10,000 is retained for 4 years, at the end of which the trade-in value is 40% of the new replacement price, the annual depreciation on the diminishing balances method is: Year 1, £2,000 (*i.e.* 20% of £10,000); Year 2, £1,600 (*i.e.* 20% of £8,000 [the written-down value]); Year 3, £1,280 (*i.e.* 20% of £6,400); Year 4, £1,024 (20% of £5,120). The total written-down value at the end of Year 4 is therefore £4,096 (*i.e.* £10,000 less the total depreciation of £5,904). This is approximately 41% of the new price. (Taking the percentages in the above table to decimal places would give the trade-in prices stated more precisely).

Note. The trade-in value taken for purposes of the calculation must exclude any "disguised" discount on the price of the new machine.

Calculations of data collected as part of the Farm Management Survey in 1982/83 found the following to be the best estimates of the real diminishing balance rates of depreciation for machines sold during that year: (source: S. Cunningham, University of Exeter, Agricultural Economics Unit, 1987):

Tractors	15%	Potato harvesters	21%
Combine harvesters	15%	Forage harvesters	21%
Balers	18%	Beet harvesters	23%

For other machinery and equipment an average rate of 15% is suggested (author).

Tax Allowances on Machinery. See page 196.

151

ESTIMATED ANNUAL COST OF SPARES AND REPAIRS AS A PERCENTAGE OF PURCHASE PRICE* AT VARIOUS LEVELS OF USE

	Approximate Annual Use (hours)				Additional use per 100 hours
	500	750	1,000	1,500	ADD
	%	%	%	%	%
Tractors	5·0	6·7	8·0	10·5	0·5

	Approximate Annual Use (hours)				Additional use per 100 hours
	50	100	150	200	ADD
	%	%	%	%	%
Harvesting Machinery:					
Combine Harvesters, self-propelled and engine-driven	1·5	2·5	3·5	4·5	2·0
Combine Harvesters, p.t.o. driven, metered-chop forage harvesters, pick-up balers, potato harvesters, sugar beet harvesters	3·0	5·0	6·0	7·0	2·0
Other Implements and Machines:					
Group 1: Ploughs, Cultivators, Toothed harrows, Hoes, Elevator potato diggers (Normal Soils)	4·5	8·0	11·0	14·0	6·0
Group 2: Rotary cultivators, Mowers, Pea cutter-windrowers	4·0	7·0	9·5	12·0	5·0
Group 3: Disc harrows, Fertilizer distributors, Farmyard manure spreaders, Combine drills, Potato planters with fertilizer attachment, Sprayers, Hedge-cutting machines	3·0	5·5	7·5	9·5	4·0
Group 4: Swath turners, Tedders, Side-delivery rakes, Unit drills, Flail forage harvesters, Semi-automatic potato planters and transplanters, Down-the-row thinners	2·5	4·5	6·5	8·5	4·0
Group 5: Corn drills, Milking machines, Hydraulic loaders, Potato planting attachments	2·0	4·0	5·5	7·0	3·0
Group 6: Grain driers, Grain cleaners, Rolls, Hammer mills, Feed mixers Threshers	1·5	2·0	2·5	3·0	0·5

* When it is known that a high purchase price is due to high quality and durability or a low price corresponds to a high rate of wear and tear, adjustments to the figures should be made.

6. IRRIGATION COSTS

(Estimated for 2000)

A. Capital Costs

(before deducting grant)

1. *Pumps* (delivering from 20 to 200 cubic metres per hour from a surface water source, all with portable suction and delivery fittings)

Tractor pto shaft driven	£1,000-4,500
Diesel engine driven	£4,000-25,000
Electric motor driven	£2,000-15,000

2. *Pipelines (averages per m)*

   Portable. (excl. valve take offs) 75 mm, £5·00; 100 mm, £6·50; 125 mm, £7·50; 150 mm, £10·00; (incl. valve take offs) 75 mm, £7·00; 100 mm, £8·50; 125 mm, £10·00; 150 mm, £13·00.

   Permanent (P.V.C. pipe 12·5 bar rating supply and laying): 100 mm, £10·00; 150 mm, £14·00. Hydrants: 100 mm × 100 mm, £200; 150 mm × 100 mm, £300.

3. *Application Systems*

   Self travellers: hose reel equipment capable of irrigating 10 hectares in a 10-day cycle (two moves each day and operating for 22 hours per day) cost approximately £4,000. Larger machines capable of irrigating 20, 32, 50 and 60 hectares in a 10-day cycle cost approximately £6,000, £10,000, £16,000 and £24,000 respectively.

   Sprinkler lines: a 1 hectare setting of a hand-moved sprinkler line costs £5,000 to £7,500 depending on application requirements. For each hectare cover of sprinklers 30 to 40 hectares can normally be irrigated in a 10-day cycle. A one hectare setting of solid set pipework and fittings costs £950.

4. *Total*

   If no source works are needed, as with water from a river, or pond, total capital costs can be as low as £1,000 for each hectare requiring irrigation at regular intervals, but are more typically £1,400 to £2,000.

5. *Source Works*

   Boreholes typically cost £160 to £200 per m depth and require expensive submersible pumps. An overall cost, including electricity supply, pump and well head, to irrigate 4 hectares with 25 mm of water per day would be in the region of £20,000 to £30,000. £500 to £800 per hectare can easily be added to capital costs.

The least expensive large reservoirs typically cost £1 per cubic metre of storage capacity, with smaller reservoirs costing as much as £4.00 per cubic metre where lining is required. £1 per cubic metre equals £1,000 per hectare irrigated if enough water is stored to apply 100 mm per hectare.

B. Operating Costs

A typical depreciation and interest cost for a self traveller capable of covering 30 ha in a 10-day cycle where only limited source works are provided would be £50 per application of 25 mm per hectare. Running costs, including labour (2 man-hours per hectare), repairs, fuel, etc. would cost £31.

Abstraction charges vary widely, depending on the region, season and whether or not the source is supported by National Rivers Authority operations. Winter abstraction charges typically range from £1 to £3 per 1,000 m^3 and summer rates from £15 to £27 per 1,000 m^3 for sources which are not supported by National Rivers Authority operations. Abstraction charges during the summer can be up to £80 per 1,000 m^3 in areas where supplies are supported by National River Authority operations. A charge of £2 per 1,000 m^3 equals 50p per 25mm hectare, whilst a charge of £25 per 1,000 m^3 would cost £6·25 per hectare per 25 mm application. Mains water at 60p per m^3 would cost £150 per application of 25 mm per hectare.

Total costs per application of 25 mm per hectare, based on limited source works and summer abstraction rates, would be in the region of £85 to £90 for a self traveller system. Costs for sprinkler lines are likely to be between 10 and 20 per cent higher, largely because of greater labour requirements (5 man-hours per hectare).

Source works at £1,500 per hectare, together with mainly permanent pipelines, would increase the above figure for depreciation and interest to £90 per 25 mm per hectare, but abstraction and variable costs would be lower, giving a total cost of £105 to £110 per application of 25 mm per hectare.

Where irrigation capacity is under-utilised the effective cost per 25 mm of water applied per hectare can be very much higher.

Note:

The (approximate) imperial equivalents for metric values commonly used in irrigation are as follows:

1 cubic metre = 1,000 litres = 220 gallons.

A pump capacity of 100 cubic metres per hour is equivalent to 22,000 gallons per hour (366 gallons per minute).

In terms of water storage 1,000 cubic metres (1 million litres) is equivalent to 220,000 gallons (1 million gallons = 4,546 cubic metres).

1,000 cubic metres is sufficient to apply 25 millimetres of water over 4 hectares, which is approximately equivalent to applying 1 inch over 10 acres.

7. FIELD DRAINAGE

(Estimated for 2000)

1. Installation (costs per metre of excavating a trench, supplying and laying the pipe and backfilling with soil).

		£ per metre
Plastic pipes:	60mm diameter	1·00—1·25
	80mm diameter	1·15—1·40
	100mm diameter	1·75—2·10
	125mm diameter	2·40 2·80
	150mm diameter	3·30—3·40
	300mm diameter	5·75—7·75

The above rates apply to schemes of 5 hectares or more; smaller areas and patching up work can cost up to 50% more.

Supplying and laying permeable backfill to within 375mm of ground level will add between £1·50 and £2·00 per metre to costs.

Digging new open ditches (1·8m top width, 0·9m depth) costs £1·50-£2·00 per metre compared with improving existing ditches at £1·00 to £1·50 per metre.

Subsoiling or mole draining will cost in the region of £45-£60 per hectare.

2. *Total*

Costs per hectare for complete schemes will vary depending on the distance between laterals, soil type, size of area to be drained, region of the country and the time of year when the work is to be undertaken. The cost of a scheme with 20m spacing between laterals and using permeable backfill will typically be in the range £1,400 to £1,600 per hectare (£565-£650 per acre). Backfilling with soil, rather than with permeable material such as washed gravel, may reduce the cost by almost half but is only possible on certain types of soil. Equally, certain soil types which are particularly suitable for mole drainage may permit spacing between laterals to be increased to 40m or even 80m in some instances. Where this is possible costs will be reduced proportionally.

Grant aid is no longer available for field drainage.

8. GRAIN DRYING AND STORAGE COSTS
(Estimated for 2000)

A. Drying

Capital Costs: vary widely according to type and capacity of drier; assuming 125 to 150 hours of use per season and driers with a rated capacity of 8 to 25 tonnes per hour at 5% extraction, a typical range is £23 to £37 per tonne dried annually.

Annual fixed costs: depreciation and interest £2·40 to £4·30 per tonne.

Running costs: fuel and repairs, £2.20 to £3·20 per tonne (6 per cent moisture extraction) for oil-fired driers or where little heat is used in ventilated plants; £6.00 to £8·00 for electrically-heated driers. Little labour is required for modern automatic driers unless grain has to be passed over the drier several times.

Total operating costs: average £5·90 to £8·80 per tonne (6 per cent) for cereals; costs for oilseed rape are likely to be £2 to £3 per tonne higher when drying in ventilated bins, because of higher labour requirements.

B. Storage

Capital Costs: from approximately £70 per tonne (on-floor storage in a purpose-built building) to over £200 per tonne for an elaborate plant, including pit, elevator, conveyors, ventilated storage bins etc. in a new building.

Typical costs are given on page 173.

Depreciation and Interest: £160 per tonne depreciated over 10 years, with 8 per cent interest, equals £23·85 per annum; over 15 years, at 6 per cent interest, £16·50. (In highly mechanized bulk plants, part of this may be charged against harvesting rather than entirely against storage).

Fuel and Repairs: £1·75 per tonne.

Extra Drying: Additional drying costs will be borne if storage necessitates further moisture reduction. Average £1·60 per tonne where own drier, £3·50 if dried on contract, for an additional 4 per cent moisture extraction.

Loss of Weight: the value of the weight of grain lost should be considered as an additional cost of storage if storage requires extra drying. 2 per cent = £1·40 to £2·00 per tonne.

Interest on Grain Stored: from 35p (£70 per tonne grain, at 6 per cent) to 60p (£90 per tonne grain, at 8 per cent) per month.

Contract Storage: typically £1·10 per tonne per month with a handling charge of around £1·50 per tonne for loading into store and out of store.

(The Intervention Board paid 1·9p/day for wheat storage and 2·17p/day for barley storage at harvest time 1998).

VI. OTHER FIXED COSTS DATA

1. WHOLE FARM FIXED COSTS

The following are a *broad indication* of the levels of fixed costs (£) per hectare (acre) for various types and sizes of farm, estimated for 2000, *including the value of unpaid family manual labour,* including that of the farmer and his wife.

All of these costs can of course vary widely according to many factors, especially the intensity of farming, e.g. the number of cows per 100 farm hectares on the mainly dairying and dairying and arable farms, or the hectares of intensive crops such as potatoes, sugar beet and vegetables per 100 farm hectares on the mixed cropping farms.

Furthermore, *the figures provided are only averages. "Premium" farms of the same level of intensity can have labour, machinery and general overhead costs at least 20% lower.* However, the most profitable farms are often more intensive and therefore have higher fixed costs associated with the great intensity — but with substantially higher total farm gross margins; it is the net amount (TGM-TFC) that matters.

Regional survey results can be obtained from reports published annually by the agricultural economics departments of certain Universities and Colleges. These are listed on page 5.

The term "fixed costs" is used here as it is in gross margin analysis and planning: a full explanation of the differences between fixed and variable costs in this context is given on pages 1 and 2. *Note that all casual labour and contract work have been included under fixed costs.* In calculating enterprise gross margins on the individual farm these costs are normally allocated as variable costs if they are specific to a particular enterprise and vary approximately in proportion to its size, *i.e.* are approximately constant per hectare of a particular crop or per head of livestock. Otherwise they are included as fixed costs. In both cases, however, they could be regarded as substitutes for regular labour and/or the farmer's own machinery — which are both items of fixed cost. It is therefore simpler if both are included, fully, as fixed costs. If one is comparing results from accounts set out on a gross margin basis, and some or all of the casual labour and contract work have been included as variable costs (especially on cropping farms, *e.g.* for potato harvesting by casual labour or contractor's machine), the necessary adjustments need to be made in making the comparisons.

Notes

Unpaid Labour. Refers to the value of family manual labour, including that of the farmer and his wife.

Depreciation. This is based on the "historic" (*i.e.* original) cost of machinery, not on the current (*i.e.* replacement) cost. Although the latter is a truer refection of the *real* loss of value of machinery (as is apparent when replacement becomes necessary), virtually all farm accounts use the historic cost method. Hence the use of the latter facilitates efficiency comparisons. It should, however, be noted that depreciation is based on current costs in the University/College reports listed on the previous page; on average this increases the figure by about a fifth. Both this item and *Repairs* include vehicles.

157

Leasing Charges: The capital element, but not the interest, is included in depreciation; the proportion paid as interest varies according to the rate of interest paid and the length of the leasing period, but is typically 15 to 20 per cent.

Rental Value. Estimated rent for owner-occupied land, based on actual rents of farms of similar type and size (established tenancies; *i.e.* not new / farm business tenancies). "Landlord-type" expenses average about 40 per cent of the estimated rent.

General Overheads include general farm maintenance and repairs, office expenses, water, insurance, fees, subscriptions, etc. 'Farm maintenance', *i.e.* repairs to property (buildings, roads, etc.), average approximately one-quarter of total general farm overhead expenses.

In making comparisons with fixed costs taken from farm accounts it is important to note that in the figures below unpaid manual labour and a rental value for owner-occupied land are included; (but not paid management or interest charges). Very low "target" figures given in press articles often omit these items and can therefore be misleading; usually, too, they relate only to large, very well appointed farms.

Labour, machinery and buildings are the main items of "fixed" costs subject to change with major alterations in farm policy. Each is the subject of a separate section in this book.

	Mainly Dairying		
	Under 50 ha (Under 125 acres)	50-100 ha (125-250 acres)	Over 100 ha (Over 250 acres)
Regular Labour (paid)	150 (61)	260 (105)	320 (129)
Regular Labour (unpaid) ...	520 (210)	260 (105)	115 (47)
Casual Labour	30 (12)	20 (8)	15 (6)
Total Labour	700 (283)	540 (218)	450 (182)
Machinery Depreciation	110 (45)	100 (41)	100 (41)
Machinery Repairs	100 (40)	90 (36)	90 (36)
Fuel, Elec., Oil	75 (30)	65 (26)	65 (26)
Contract	100 (41)	87·5 (36)	100 (41)
Vehicle Tax and Insurance ...	15 (6)	12·5 (5)	10 (4)
Total Power and Machinery ...	400 (162)	355 (144)	365 (148)
Rent/Rental Value	190 (77)	180 (73)	175 (71)
General Overhead Expenses ...	210 (85)	175 (71)	160 (65)
Total Fixed Costs	1500 (607)	1250 (506)	1150 (466)

	Dairying and Arable		
	Under 100 ha (Under 250 acres)	100-200 ha (250-500 acres)	Over 200 ha (Over 500 acres)
Regular Labour (paid)	210 (85)	245 (99)	200 (81)
Regular Labour (unpaid) ...	210 (85)	80 (32)	50 (20)
Casual Labour	15 (6)	10 (4)	15 (6)
Total Labour	435 (176)	335 (135)	265 (107)
Machinery Depreciation	110 (45)	90 (37)	90 (37)
Machinery Repairs	70 (28)	60 (24)	60 (24)
Fuel, Elec., Oil	50 (21)	45 (18)	42·5(17)
Contract	72·5(29)	70 (28)	35 (14)
Vehicle Tax and Insurance ...	12·5 (5)	10 (4)	7·5 (3)
Total Power and Machinery ...	315 (127)	275 (111)	235 (95)
Rent/Rental Value	180 (73)	170 (69)	165 (67)
General Overhead Expenses ...	150 (61)	125 (51)	115 (47)
Total Fixed Costs	1080 (437)	905 (366)	780 (316)

	Mainly Cereals*		
	Under 100 ha (Under 250 acres)	100-200 ha (250-500 acres)	Over 200 ha (Over 500 acres)
Regular Labour (paid)	65 (26)	85 (34·5)	95 (39)
Regular Labour (unpaid) ...	150 (61)	85 (34·5)	35 (14)
Casual Labour	15 (6)	15 (6)	15 (6)
Total Labour	230 (93)	185 (75)	145 (59)
Machinery Depreciation ...	85 (35)	85 (35)	85 (35)
Machinery Repairs	65 (26)	55 (22)	50 (20)
Fuel, Elec., Oil	40 (16)	32·5(13)	32·5(13)
Contract	52·5(21)	52·5(21)	25 (10)
Vehicle Tax and Insurance ...	12·5 (5)	10 (4)	7·5 (3)
Total Power and Machinery ...	255 (103)	235 (95)	200 (81)
Rent/Rental Value	160 (65)	155 (63)	150 (61)
General Overhead Expenses ...	100 (41)	90 (36)	70 (28)
Total Fixed Costs	**745 (302)**	**665 (269)**	**565(229)**

* With combinable break crops.

	Mixed Cropping*		
	Under 100 ha (Under 250 acres)	100-200 ha (250-500 acres)	Over 200 ha (Over 500 acres)
Regular Labour (paid)	55 (22)	130 (53)	145 (59)
Regular Labour (unpaid) ...	190 (77)	70 (28)	40 (16)
Casual Labour	10 (4)	10 (4)	10 (4)
Total Labour	255 (103)	210 (85)	195 (79)
Machinery Depreciation... ...	85 (35)	110 (41)	95 (39)
Machinery Repairs	65 (26)	60 (24)	60 (24)
Fuel, Elec., Oil	40 (16)	37·5 (15)	35 (14)
Contract	50 (20)	50 (20)	25 (10)
Vehicle Tax and Insurance ...	15 (6)	12·5 (5)	10 (4)
Total Power and Machinery ...	255 (103)	260 (105)	225 (91)
Rent /Rental Value	180 (73)	175 (71)	170 (69)
General Overhead Expenses ...	105 (43)	90 (36)	85 (34)
Total Fixed Costs	**795 (322)**	**735 (297)**	**675 (273)**

* With potatoes and/or sugar beet and/or field vegetables; grade 1 or 2 land.

	Mainly Sheep/Cattle (lowland)		
	Under 100 ha (Under 250 acres)	100-200 ha (250-500 acres)	Over 200 ha (Over 500 acres)
Regular Labour (paid)	80 (32)	80 (32)	110 (45)
Regular Labour (unpaid) ...	250 (101)	135 (55)	75 (30)
Casual Labour	20 (8)	10 (4)	5 (2)
Total Labour	350 (141)	225 (91)	190 (77)
Machinery Depreciation... ...	45 (18)	55 (22)	55 (22)
Machinery Repairs	50 (20)	40 (16)	40 (16)
Fuel, Elec., Oil	30 (12)	30 (12)	27·5(11)
Contract	45 (18)	35 (14)	25 (10)
Vehicle Tax and Insurance ...	10 (4)	10 (4)	7·5 (3)
Total Power and Machinery ...	180 (73)	170 (68)	155 (62)
Rent/Rental Value	140 (57)	135 (55)	125 (51)
General Overhead Expenses ...	90 (37)	75 (31)	65 (26)
Total Fixed Costs	**760 (308)**	**605 (245)**	**535 (216)**

Sheep/Cattle and Arable

	Under 100 ha (Under 250 acres)	100-200 ha (250-500 acres)	Over 200 ha (Over 500 acres)
Regular Labour (paid)...	50 (20)	55 (22)	100 (41)
Regular Labour (unpaid)	180 (73)	120 (49)	50 (20)
Casual Labour ...	10 (4)	15 (6)	10 (4)
Total Labour ...	240 (97)	190 (77)	160 (65)
Machinery Depreciation	55 (23)	65 (26)	60 (24)
Machinery Repairs	40 (16)	50 (20)	45 (18)
Fuel, Elec., Oil...	25 (10)	25 (10)	22·5 (9)
Contract...	47·5(19)	25 (10)	20 (8)
Vehicle Tax and Insurance ...	12·5 (5)	10 (4)	7·5 (3)
Total Power and Machinery...	180 (73)	175 (70)	150 (62)
Rent/Rental Value	150 (61)	145 (59)	140 (57)
General Overhead Expenses...	95 (38)	90 (37)	80 (32)
Total Fixed Costs	665(269)	600(243)	535(216)

Arable and Pigs/Poultry*

	Under 100 ha (Under 250 acres)	100-200 ha (250-500 acres)	Over 200 ha (Over 500 acres)
Regular Labour (paid)	375(152)	350(141)	260(105)
Regular Labour (unpaid)	235 (95)	80 (33)	25 (10)
Casual Labour ...	40 (16)	20 (8)	15 (6)
Total Labour ...	650(263)	450(182)	300(121)
Machinery Depreciation	125 (51)	110 (45)	100 (41)
Machinery Repairs	95 (38)	80 (32)	70 (28)
Fuel, Elec., Oil	90 (36)	70 (28)	50 (20)
Contract...	70 (29)	62·5(25)	50 (20)
Vehicle Tax and Insurance ...	15 (6)	12·5 (5)	10 (4)
Total Power and Machinery...	395(160)	335(135)	280(113)
Rent/Rental Value	180 (73)	175 (71)	170 (69)
General Overhead Expenses ...	220 (89)	180 (73)	120 (49)
Total Fixed Costs	1445 (585)	1140 (461)	870 (352)

* The number of pigs in relation to the total farm area varies widely, and so, therefore, can these per hectare (per acre) figures.

Livestock Rearing

	Upland	Hill
	(per *adjusted* hectare (acre))*	
Regular Labour (paid)	90 (37)	40 (16·5)
Regular Labour (unpaid)	70 (28)	60 (24·5)
Casual Labour	7·5 (3)	12·5 (5)
Total Labour	167·5 (68)	112·5(46)
Machinery Depreciation ...	50 (20)	27·5(11)
Machinery Repairs...	25 (10)	15 (6)
Fuel, Elec., Oil	17·5 (7)	12·5 (5)
Contract	22·5 (9)	7·5 (3)
Vehicle Tax and Insurance	5 (2)	2·5 (1)
Total Power and Machinery	120 (48)	65 (26)
Rent/Rental Value ...	75 (30)	45 (18)
General Overhead Expenses	62·5 (25)	32·5(13)
Total Fixed Costs ...	425 (171)	255 (103)

*Divisors to give the *actual* area figure = upland 1·5, hill 1·85.

Large (Lowland) Farms

The following data are based on the Cambridge University Farm Business Survey results for non-fenland farms in 1997/8 approximated for 2000 (with historic cost depreciation and including all contract work):

	All Farms		Farms excluding livestock	
	400-500 ha (1000-1250 acres)	Over 500ha (Over 1250 acres)	400-500 ha (1000-1250 acres)	Over 500 ha (Over 1250 acres)
Regular Labour (paid)	201 (81)	175 (71)	180 (73)	158 (64)
Regular Labour (unpaid)	17 (7)	2 (1)	10 (4)	2 (1)
Casual Labour	2 (1)	3 (1)	5 (2)	5 (2)
Total Labour	220 (89)	180 (73)	195 (79)	165 (67)
Power and Machinery	280 (113)	215 (87)	350 (142)*	190 (77)
Rent/Rental Value	150 (61)	150 (61)	135 (55)	150 (61)
General Overhead Expenses	85 (34)	80 (32)	85 (34)	65 (26)
Total Fixed Costs	735 (297)	625 (253)	765 (310)	570 (231)

*An exceptionally high figure (and note only 5 farms in the group).

N.B. **Horticultural holdings**—see page 44.

2. RENTS

The following figures relate to farms let with a combination of crops, grass and rough grazing in England; they include housing and buildings, as available. They are per hectare (with per acre in brackets) to the nearest 50p per ha and 25p per acre.

On land with full agricultural tenancies (under the Agricultural Holdings Act 1986) the average increase in rents (including farms with no change) in 1998 compared with 1997 was 2%. The average increase for those rents reviewed in 1998 was estimated to be 6%. Rents for farm tenancies for 1 year and over fell by 5% and seasonal lets of less than one year by 7%.

It has to be borne in mind that rough grazing, including upland, is included in the figures in this section. **The average rent for lowland, excluding woodland and rough grazing, for land under full agricultural tenancies is likely to be approximately £145 per ha, a little under £60 per acre, in 2000.** The levels on large mixed arable farms (*i.e.* including potatoes, sugar beet and/or vegetables) on very good soil, or well-equipped dairy farms, will tend to average £160 to £210 per ha, £65 to £85 per acre. Rents on moderate, below average, quality farms, particularly with full repairing and insuring leases, are likely to average £115 to £125 per ha, £45 to £50 per acre, or even less.

Farm Business Tenancy rents will be higher still, although future levels are likely to be lower than those initially offered when such tenancies first became available, in 1996, at a relatively prosperous time, unless 1994-96 levels of agricultural prosperity (unexpectedly) reoccur. Farmers who already own land, with little or no mortgage, can afford to offer a higher figure than bidders with no other farm.

The following data all relate to 1998.

Average Rent by Type of Agreement

	£ per ha (acre)	Agreements in sample
Full Agricultural Tenancies	119·50 (48·25)*	2492
Farm Business Tenancies for 1 year and over	177·00 (71·75)	1802
Seasonal Lets of less than one year	131·50 (53·25)	664

*126·75 (51·25) where there was a provision for a rent review.

Average Rent by Farm Type
(£ per ha [acre])

A. Full Agricultural Tenancies.

	Land only	Other	All
Cereal	125·50 (50·75)	133·50 (54·00)	131·75 (53·25)
General Cropping	136·75 (55·25)	148·25 (60·00)	146·00 (59·00)
Dairy	116·25 (47·00)	144·25 (58·50)	141·50 (57·25)
Cattle and Sheep (Lowland)	89·75 (36·25)	92·50 (37·50)	92·00 (37·25)
Cattle and Sheep (LFA)	29·50 (12·00)	42·75 (17·25)	41·25 (16·75)
All	115·00 (46·50)	120·50 (48·75)	119·50 (48·25)

B. Farm Business Tenancies for 1 year and over (All).

Cereal	185·00 (75·00)
General Cropping	232·00 (94·00)
Dairy	177·25 (71·75)
Cattle and Sheep (Lowland)	142·50 (57·75)
Cattle and Sheep (LFA)	55·75 (22·50)
All	177·00 (71·75)

Average Rent by Rented Area
(Full Agricultural Tenancies only, 1997)

Less than 10 ha	157·50 (63·75)
10 to 49·9 ha	136·00 (55·00)
50 to 99·9 ha	126·50 (51·25)
100 to 249·9 ha	113·50 (46·00)
250 ha and above	101·00 (41·00)

Source of Data

MAFF (Government Statistical Service): Annual Survey of Tenanted Land, England, 1998. There were 5,787 agreements included in the survey, covering 220,000 ha (543,125 acres). This survey replaced the Annual Rent Enquiry in 1996.

3. LAND PRICES

Sale Value of Farmland, England and Wales (£ per hectare (acre))

(1) Auction Sales (with Vacant Possession only)

(a) Oxford Institute/Savills series*

Year	Current Prices		Real Values**		Index***	Year	Current Prices		Real Values**		Index***
1937-9	60	(24)	2030	(822)	33	1981	4272	(1729)	8525	(3450)	139
1945	111	(45)	2246	(909)	37	1982	4557	(1844)	8373	(3389)	136
1950	198	(80)	3274	(1325)	53	1983	5145	(2082)	9041	(3659)	147
1955	198	(80)	2643	(1070)	43	1984	4888	(1978)	8180	(3310)	133
1960	304	(123)	3608	(1460)	59	1985	4781	(1935)	7542	(3052)	123
1965	581	(235)	5857	(2370)	95	1986	4193	(1697)	6398	(2589)	104
1970	605	(245)	4872	(1972)	79	1987	4944	(2001)	7242	(2931)	118
1971	647	(262)	4761	(1927)	77	1988	6716	(2718)	9376	(3794)	153
1972	1473	(596)	9603	(3886)	156	1989	6558	(2654)	8493	(3437)	138
1973	1871	(757)	11793	(4773)	192	1990	6346	(2568)	7505	(3037)	122
1974	1572	(636)	8529	(3452)	139	1991	6007	(2431)	6708	(2715)	109
1975	1332	(539)	5817	(2354)	95	1992	5441	(2202)	5859	(2371)	95
1976	1814	(734)	6798	(2751)	111	1993	5456	(2208)	5783	(2340)	94
1977	2449	(991)	7922	(3206)	129	1994	5028	(2035)	5204	(2106)	85
1978	3279	(1327)	9794	(3964)	160	1995	6140	(2484)	6140	(2485)	100
1979	4371	(1769)	11513	(4659)	188	1996	8797	(3560)	8591	(3477)	140
1980	4265	(1726)	9521	(3853)	155	1997	8065	(3263)	7636	(3090)	124
						1998	7250	(2934)	6637	(2686)	108

*Savills since 1988. ** At 1995 general price levels. ***Real Values, 1995 = 100.
Since 1970, figures based on sales reports in the *Estates Gazette* and the *Farmers Weekly*, plus some unpublished sales, with a minimum size of 10 hectares.

(b) Farmland Market series

Size Group (hectares)	10-20	20-40	40-60	60-80	80-100	100-140	Over 140	All Farms	
1973	2530	2080	1815	1805	1885	1735	2100	1975	(799)
1974	2245	1745	1490	1565	1415	1335	1280	1685	(682)
1975	2115	1545	1340	1165	1200	1190	1090	1485	(601)
1976	2560	2015	1855	1830	1670	1610	1730	1965	(795)
1977	2825	2660	2365	2425	2230	2530	2325	2525	(1020)
1978	3970	3425	3125	3265	3180	3480	3595	3380	(1368)
1979	6280	4385	4220	3975	4330	4890	4315	4515	(1828)
1980	5585	4905	4270	4305	4405	4435	4130	4705	(1904)
1981	6135	4680	3880	4315	3760	4710	4355	4500	(1821)
1982	6455	4950	4465	4065	4705	4510	4325	4815	(1949)
1983	6825	5630	5160	5110	5095	5495	5130	5450	(2206)
1984	6565	5815	5300	5520	5435	5360	4625	5480	(2218)
1985	8410	5190	4455	4555	4210	4405	4645	5245	(2123)
1986	7825	5180	3930	3745	N/A	3155	N/A	4185	(1949)
1987	7280	7115	5130	4285	4325	N/A	N/A	5980	(2421)
1988	13255	9035	6225	5825	5320	6220	4275	7205	(2916)
1989	14140	9260	6660	6610	5770	5980	5260	7520	(3044)
1990	8225	6680	7440	6420	5820	N/A	N/A	6505	(2635)
1991	7335	7790	6575	4455	4985	N/A	N/A	6460	(2615)
1992	8920	6255	4280	4890	N/A	4400	N/A	5650	(2285)
1993	8910	7185	5410	5305	4725	N/A	5585	5890	(2385)
1994	10265	6095	5565	5335	5535	5220	N/A	5765	(2335)
1995	13115	9755	7705	6765	7075	N/A	5855	7785	(3150)
1996	19005	10140	10145	7015	N/A	8605	N/A	9745	(3945)
1997	14650	10650	8060	8510	7040	7615	N/A	8780	(3555)
1998	10710	12280	9400	5485	5855	7020	N/A	8920	(3610)

Bare land prices (over 2 ha): 1987, £3955 (1600); 1988, £5040 (2040); 1989, £5620 (2275); 1990, £7885 (3190); 1991, £4800 (1945); 1992, £3970 (1605); 1993, £4320 (1750); 1994, 4940 (2000); 1995, 5960 (2410); 1996, 6780 (2745); 1997, 7250 (2935); 1998, 5905 (2390).

(2) **Current Agricultural Prices (CALP and CALP/RICS) series (vacant possession only)**

Cover sales of 5 ha and above but excludes land sold for development or forestry, gifts, inheritances and compulsory purchases. Includes sales of bare land as well as land with dwellings, buildings, etc. (see [iii] [d] below).

CALP series (England only) data collected jointly by ADAS (Agricultural Development and Advisory Service) AMC (Agricultural Mortgage Corporation) and CLA (Country Landowners Association) and were published by the AMC until 1993. A CALP/RICS Farmland Price Index (England and Wales) began in 1995.

(i) *CALP Annual Figures*

	Average price (A)	Average price (B): in 1995 £	Index (of B) (1995 = 100)
1978	3160 (1280)	9438 (3820)	176
1979	4140 (1675)	10497 (4248)	196
1980	3975 (1610)	8874 (3591)	166
1981	3940 (1595)	7863 (3182)	147
1982	4125 (1670)	7579 (3067)	142
1983	4630 (1875)	8288 (3354)	155
1984	4555 (1845)	7622 (3085)	142
1985	4340 (1755)	6846 (2771)	128
1986	3675 (1485)	5608 (2270)	105
1987	3780 (1530)	5537 (2241)	103
1988	5350 (2165)	7469 (3023)	139
1989	5595 (2265)	7245 (2932)	135
1990	4440 (1795)	5251 (2125)	98
1991	4145 (1675)	4629 (1873)	86
1992	3658 (1480)	3939 (1594)	74
1993	3608 (1460)	3824 (1548)	71
1994*	5085 (2060)	5263 (2130)	98
1995	5355 (2170)	5355 (2170)	100
1996	6940 (2810)	6778 (2743)	127
1997	7295 (2955)	6907 (2795)	129
1998	7055 (2855)	6459 (2613)	121

Total value of sales divided by total area sold.

*Based on a very small sample.

(ii) *Royal Institution of Chartered Surveyors Farmland Price Survey*

	1996	1997	1998	1999
Jan. — March	6023 (2437)	6906 (2795)	7494 (3033)	6375 (2580)
April — June	6731 (2724)	7263 (2939)	7530 (3047)	7010 (2837)
July — Sept.	7019 (2841)	7870 (3185)	6573 (2660)	
Oct. — Dec.	7046 (2851)	7166 (2900)	6888 (2788)	

Sales of vacant possession land in England and Wales, excluding residential sales. Averages weighted to dilute the influence of exceptional sales.

(3) **Inland Revenue Returns** (England only; Oct. 1-Sept. 30 years)*

Year[1]	Vacant Possession Farms[2]	Bare Land	Tenanted Farms[2]	Bare Land
1980/1	3568 (1444)	3325 (1346)	2334 (945)	2354 (953)
1981/2	3503 (1418)	3281 (1328)	2644 (1070)	1340 (542)
1982/3	3766 (1524)	3525 (1427)	2549 (1032)	2210 (894)
1983/4	3761 (1522)	3835 (1552)	2389 (967)	2511 (1016)
1984/5	4258 (1723)	3466 (1403)	2879 (1165)	2310 (935)
1985/6	4055 (1641)	3477 (1407)	2192 (887)	2217 (897)
1986/7	3703 (1499)	3023 (1223)	2141 (866)	1777 (719)
1987/8	3750 (1518)	3140 (1271)	2252 (911)	2476 (1002)
1988/9	4739 (1918)	3521 (1425)	3178 (1286)[3]	1929 (781)
1989/90	5355 (2167)	4080 (1651)	2143 (867)	2093 (847)
1990/91	5515 (2231)	3750 (1517)	2090 (846)	2505 (1014)
1991/92	5015 (2030)	3370 (1363)	2505 (1015)	1465 (592)
1992/93	4405 (1785)	3120 (1265)	1680 (680)	2045 (830)[3]
1993/94	4319 (1748)	3235 (1309)	2102 (851)	1116 (452)
1994/95	4661 (1886)	3608 (1460)	1860 (753)	1720 (696)
1995/96	5058 (2047)	3936 (1593)	2605 (1054)	1490 (603)
1996/97	6224 (2519)	4548 (1841)	4513 (1826)	2623 (1062)

* *This series has recently been substantially amended: see below.*

1. There is a delay between the dates when a price is agreed and when it is notified to the Inland Revenue and thus included in the above figures; this time-lag is thought to average about 9 months; hence, for example, the 1997/98 figures roughly approximate to 1997 calendar year prices.
2. Farms = Land and Buildings, including the farmhouse.
3. High figure caused by a few untypically high-priced transactions.

The above figures relate to all sales of agricultural properties of 5 ha and over except those for development and other non-agricultural purposes. They include any sales at prices below ruling open market value (as between members of a family), sales where the vendor retains certain (e.g. sporting) rights, sales in which the farmhouse represents a substantial part of the total value, and sales of land which may, in the purchaser's view, have an element of development value.

Vacant Possession Premium
On the basis of the Inland Revenue Returns above the average price of tenanted land as a percentage of vacant possession land in the five years 1992/93 to 1996/97 was 50% for whole farms and 49% for bare land. In individual years the figure varied from 38% to 73% for whole farms and from 35% to 65% for bare land. A sudden jump (for whole farms) from a previous high of around 50% to 72·5% in 1996/97 could be attributed to the introduction of farm business tenancies in 1995.

(4) **Valuation Office Agency Transactions** (England only)
This new series, issued by MAFF, uses the same basic data source as the Inland Revenue Returns series above, which it has replaced, but the sales are now analysed on the basis of the time period when the transactions actually take place, not when validated by the Inland Revenue on an average nine months later. Hence there is no longer a time-lag. Some restrictions and technical adjustments mean that the new series is not strictly comparable with the old one. The figures are subject to revision for up to three years, but the later revisions are expected to be minor. The 1997 figures below are denoted as provisional estimates. (Number of sales in 1997: 3,943).

A. By Property Type

	Land and Buildings	Land only
1993	4,252 (1,721)	3,297 (1,334)
1994	4,854 (1,964)	3,565 (1,443)
1995	5,451 (2,206)	4,177 (1,690)
1996	6,803 (2,753)	5,333 (2,158)
1997	7,470 (3,023)	5,532 (2,239)

B. By Tenure

	Vacant Possession	Tenanted
1993	3,829 (1,550)	1,855 (751)
1994	4,323 (1,750)	2,069 (837)
1995	4,946 (2,002)	2,566 (1,038)
1996	6,132 (2,482)	3,227 (1,306)
1997	6,557 (2,654)	3,690 (1,493)

(Vacant Possession Premium: average 48% in 1993/1994, 56% in 1997).

C. By Size Group (area sold in hectares)

	5-49.9	50-99.9	100 and over	All sales
1993	4,487 (1,816)	3,808 (1,541)	2,944 (1,191)	3,791 (1,534)
1994	5,138 (2,079)	4,272 (1,729)	3,145 (1,273)	4,229 (1,711)
1995	5,933 (2,401)	4,902 (1,984)	3,555 (1,439)	4,788 (1,938)
1996	6,962 (2,817)	5,737 (2,322)	5,161 (2,089)	6,058 (2,452)
1997	7,217 (2,921)	6,197 (2,508)	5,601 (2,267)	6,448 (2,609)

D. By Land Class (predominant grade of land)

	1 and 2	3	4 and 5	Ungraded
1995	5,144 (2,082)	5,473 (2,215)	2,677 (1,083)	3,397 (1,375)
1996	6,798 (2,751)	6,396 (2,588)	3,700 (1,497)	4,474 (1,811)
1997	7,304 (2,956)	7,258 (2,937)	3,158 (1,278)	3,691 (1,494)

% total area, England and Wales: grade 1, 2.3%; 2, 16.9%; 3, 54.7% (a 19.3, b 35.4); 4, 15.0%; 5, 11.1%.

E. By Region

	1995	1996	1997
North East	2,606 (1,055)	3,728 (1,509)	3,300 (1,335)
North West	6,440 (2,606)	5,511 (2,230)	5,805 (2,349)
Yorkshire/Humberside	3,287 (1,330)	4,897 (1,982)	5,594 (2,264)
East Midlands	5,005 (2,025)	5,867 (2,374)	6,089 (2,464)
West Midlands	5,736 (2,321)	7,770 (3,144)	6,915 (2,798)
Eastern	5,229 (2,116)	6,453 (2,611)	7,302 (2,955)
South East	5,947 (2,407)	6,845 (2,770)	8,172 (3,307)
South West	4,889 (1,979)	6,067 (2,455)	7,174 (2,903)

Woodland

Average price range of average quality established lowland woodland: £1250-1750/ha (£500-700/acre).

4. BUILDINGS

A. Building Costs

Building costs are notoriously variable. Many factors influence a contractor's price, including distance from his yard, size of contract, site access, site conditions, complexity of work, familiarity with the type of work and his current work load. There will also be differences in efficiency and standard of work between contractors and, as is often the case with farm buildings, the absence of detailed specification by the client may mean that different contractors will not have quoted for identical buildings. The number of extras that are found to be required after a contract has been agreed will also vary.

The costs given below can only be taken as an approximate guide. They refer to new buildings, erected by contractor on a clear level site and exclude VAT and any grants that may be available. Prices are forecasts for mid 1999.

Sources of Further Information

The costs below are based on information gathered by the SAC Buildings Design Unit, Aberdeen, cross-checked with other sources to ensure general applicability. More detailed information is available in the following publications. The books and journals giving general building cost information generally assume knowledge of how to take off quantities for building work.

Specialised Information on Farm Building Costs

Farm Building Cost Guide published annually by the Building Design Unit, SAC, Craibstone, Aberdeen.

Standard Costs Part 1: Specifications; Part 2: Costs. Published by MAFF and the Agricultural Departments in Scotland, Wales and Northern Ireland. Used when claiming government grants on a standard-cost basis.

General Building Cost Information

Books are produced by a number of publishers with annual or more frequent new editions and updates. Examples are *Laxton's Building Price Book, Spon's Architects' and Builders' Price Book,* and *Wessex Comprehensive Building Price Book.* Regularly updated cost information is also given in several professional and trade journals.

I. *Constituent Parts*

Frame, Roof and Foundations   *per m² floor area*

1. Open-sided timber framed pole barn with round pole uprights on concrete bases, sawn timber rafters and purlins, high-tensile galvanised steel cladding to roof and gable ends above eaves, hardcore floor, eaves height 4·8 m, 9 m span, no side cladding, rainwater drainage to soakaways.   £43

2. Open-sided steel portal-framed building with fibre-cement or plastic coated steel cladding to roof and gables above eaves, hardcore floor, eaves height 4·8 m, no side cladding, rainwater drainage to soakaways.

9 m span	£89
13·2 m span	£77
18 m span	£70

3. Cost breakdown of 2 above

Materials:	portal frame and purlins	26%
	foundations	3%
	roofing	16%
	rainwater and drainage	3%
	hardcore and blinding	2%
	Total Materials	50%
Erection:	portal frame and purlins	19%
	foundations	2%
	roofing	19%
	rainwater and drainage	5%
	hardcore and blinding	5%
	Total Erection	50%

Roof cladding   per m²

1. Natural grey fibre-cement, 146 mm corrugations fixed with drive screws
   Materials   £6·30
   Fixing   £11·35

Total	£17·65
2. Extra for coloured sheet	£2·85
3. Deduct for translucent sheets	£0·10
4. Deduct for PVC-coated steel	£5·25
5. Deduct for high-tensile corrugated galvanised steel sheeting	£8·45
6. PVC 150 mm half-round gutter on fascia brackets, including stop-ends and outlets	£19·45
7. PVC 100 mm rainwater pipe with fixings, swanneck and shoe	£24·45

per m run

8. Fibre-cement close-fitting ridge   £20·95
9. Fibre-cement ventilating ridge   £23·35

Walls and Cladding   per m²
1. Concrete blockwork, fair faced and pointed both sides
   150 mm thick   £27·80
   215 mm thick   £40·35
   215 mm thick hollow blocks   £43·25
   215 mm thick hollow blocks, filled and reinforced   £59·30
2. Extra for rendering or roughcast to blockwork on one
   side   £12·70
3. Vertical spaced boarding 21 × 145 mm with 19 mm gaps
   including horizontal rails, all pressure treated   £20·60
4. Fibre-cement vertical cladding, including rails   £30·90
5. Corrugated high-tensile steel side cladding, including rails £25·35
6. Wall element: 215 mm thick blockwork, including strip
   foundation (base 750 mm below ground level), 2.5 m
   height above ground level   £130 per m run

Floors   per m²
1. Concrete floor 100 mm thick, Gen 3 mix, on 150 mm
   hardcore, including excavation: £22·20

   Breakdown:
   (a) excavate, level and compact   £1·82
   (b) hardcore   £2·52
   (c) blinding   £1·59
   (d) damp-proof membrane   £1·22
   (e) premixed concrete spread and
       compacted   £13·18
   (f) float finish   £1·88
2. Extra to above for
   (a) 150 mm instead of 100 mm   £4·89
   (b) laying concrete to falls   £1·41
   (c) broom or textured finish   £1·88
   (d) Carborundum dust non-slip finish   £2·55
   (e) insulating concrete   £6·17
3. Reinforced concrete slatted floors for cattle
   (a) cattle loading   £51
   (b) tractor loading   £54
4. Reinforced concrete slats for pigs   £40
5. Insulating floor, including excavation and base
   (a) 27 mm expanded polystyrene, 38 mm screed   £35
   (b) insulating concrete with lightweight aggregate   £28
   (c) as (b) with 20 mm screed   £36
6. Form channel in concrete   £2.83 per m run
7. Excavate for cast 1 m³ in-situ concrete bases for
   stanchions   £90 each

Services and Fittings
1. Drainage: 100 mm PVC pipe laid in trench,
   including 750 mm deep excavation and
   backfill   £16.95 per m run
   Breakdown:
   (a) excavate and backfill   £8·50
   (b) 100 mm PVC pipe laid   £8·45
   Extras:
   (c) add to (a) for 1 m deep   £2·65
   (d) add to (b) for 150 mm pipe   £8.70
2. Excavate soakaway and fill with stones   £83 each
3. Trap and grid top, 100 mm PVC   £55.50 each
4. Yard gully with heavy duty road grating
   400 × 300 mm   £215 each
5. Inspection chamber 900 mm deep,
   450 × 600 mm opening and medium duty
   cast iron cover   £355 each
6. Above-ground vitreous enamel slurry tank
   on concretebase, 1000 m^3 £22,455 each
7. Reception pit, 20 m^3 £1,340 each
8. Slurry channel beneath (not including) slats,
   1·8 m deep, 3 m wide   £327 per m run
9. Lighting: 1.5 m 60W single fluorescent unit,
   including wiring and switch   £92 each
   Extras:
   (a) PVC conduit   £63
   (b) screwed steel conduit   £83
10. Power: 13A switched outlet   £64 each
11. Diagonal feed fence, fixed, including posts
    (painted)   £48 per m run
12. Tombstone feed fence, fixed, including posts
    (painted)   £69 per m run
13. Feed bunker   £43 per m run
14. Hay rack, wall fixing   £45 per m run
15. Cubicle division, galvanised, fixed in place   £63 each
16. Fencing: three-rail timber with posts, all
    pressure treated   £14 per m run
17. Gate, 3 m wide, galvanised steel, including
    posts set in concrete
    (a) medium duty   £152 each
    (b) heavy duty   £201 each
    Deduct for painted instead of galvanised finish   £38

II Complete Buildings

Fully Covered and Enclosed Barn
Portal frame, 18 m span, 6 m bays, 6 m to eaves, 3
m high blockwork walls with sheet cladding above,
6 m sliding doors at either end, 150mm thick concrete
floor   £136 perm^2 floor area

Cows and Cattle Housing

1. Covered strawed yard, enclosed with ventilated cladding, concrete floor, pens only, with 4·0 m² per head floor area — £517 per head
2. Extra to 1 for 4·0 m wide double-sided feeding passage, barrier and troughs — £218 per head
3. Kennel building — £300 per head
4. Portal framed building with cubicles — £556 per head
5. Extra to 4 for feed stance, feeding passage, barriers and troughs — £327 per head
6. Extra to 4 for slatting of cubicle passages — £330 per head
7. Covered collecting yard, 1·1 m² per cow — £160 per head
8. Milking parlour building, example: 5·5 × 11·5 m for 8/16 parlour — £11,075
9. Parlour equipment, herringbone parlours:
   - (a) low level, 1 stall per point — £2,255 per point
   - (b) pipeline — £2,075 per point
   - (c) extra for meter and auto cluster removal — £1,775 per point
   - (d) auto feed dispenser — £627 per stall
10. Dairy building — £175 per m² floor area
11. Bulk tank and washer — £5·06 per litre
12. Loose box, 16 m² floor area laid to falls, rendered walls — £266 per m² floor area
13. Bull pen and open run — £8,005
14. Cattle crush and 20 m race — £2,730
15. Slatted floor cattle building for 120 growing cattle (1·7 m² pen space per head) with drive-through feed passage/troughs — £565 per head

Silage	per tonne stored
1. Timber panel clamp on concrete base with effluent tank	£48
2. Precast concrete panel clamp with effluent tank	£45
3. Glass-lined forage tower and unloader	£165

Waste Storage	per m³ stored
Lined lagoon with safety fence	£20
Glass-lined steel slurry silo	
small (400 m³)	£33
medium (1,200 m³)	£24
large (3,600 m³)	£19
GRP below-ground effluent tank, encased in concrete	per m³ stored
small (12 m³)	£365
large (36 m³)	£290

Sheep Housing
1. Penning, troughs, feed barriers and drinkers
   installed in suitable existing building £17 per ewe
2. Purpose-built sheep shed with 1·35 m² per ewe
   pen space, concentrate troughs, feed passage
   and barrier for forage feeding £97 per ewe
   Extras:
   (a) softwood slatted floor panels, materials
        only £4·12 per m²
   (b) slatted panels as (a), made up, plus
        supports £16·00 per m²

Pig Housing *per sow and litter*
1. Farrowing and rearing
   (a) Prefabricated farrowing pens with crates,
        side creep areas, part-slatted floors,
        including foundations, electrical and
        plumbing work £1,585
   (b) Steel-framed farrowing house with
        insulated blockwork walls, part-slatted
        pens with side creeps in rooms of eight
        with off main passage £2,410 *per weaner*
   (c) Flat-deck rearing house 3-6 weeks with
        fully perforated floors to pens, 0·25 m²
        per pig pen area £102
   (d) Prefabricated verandah house including
        foundations, electrical and plumbing
        work, 0·3m² per pig internal lying area £75

2. Finishing *per baconer*
   (a) Prefabricated fattening house with
        part-slatted floors, trough feeding £147
   (b) Prefabricated fattening house with
        part-slatted floors, floor fed £131
   (c) Steel framed building with insulated
        blockwork walls, part-slatted floors,
        trough fed £213
   (d) Automatic feeding systems for items (a),
        (b) and (c) above:
        dry-feed system with ad-lib hoppers £5
        dry on-floor feeding £10
        wet feeding £12

3. Dry sows and boars *per sow*
   (a) Yards with floor feeding £211
   (b) Sow cubicle system £420
   (c) Yards with electronic feeders £740
   (d) Yards with individual feeders £825
   (e) Two-yard system with flat-rate feeding £825
   (f) Boar pens as part of sow house £1,850 each

4. Complete pig unit
   Building costs calculated on basis of three-week
   weaning, 23 pigs per sow per year to bacon,
   excluding external slurry or dung storage,
   feed storage and handling/weighing facilities:
(a) Breeding and rearing only	£980 per sow
(b) Breeding with progeny to bacon	£1,745 per sow

Poultry Housing and Equipment   *per bird*
Intensive cages with automatic feeding and egg
collection, 5 layers per cage   £11·00-£12·00
Perchery/barn   £12·80-£16·50
Free Range: maximum stocking rate of 1,000/ha.
(Cost varies with size of unit and degree of automation)   £12·00-£17·00
Broiler Breeders, deep litter, 0·167 m² per bird   £18·00
Pullets (cage and floor reared)   £7·80
Broilers, deep litter, 0·05 m² per bird   £4·70-£5·00
Turkeys, 20,000 pole barn fattening unit   £12·00-£17·50
(Cost varies with size of unit and degree of automation)
(N.B. Source of Poultry Housing costs: as for poultry, see page 113)

Grain Storage and Drying per tonne stored
1. Intake pit, conveyor, elevator, overhead
   conveyor and catwalk, storage bins within
   existing building   £134
   extra for low volume ventilation of bins   £55
2. As 1 in new building   £214
3. Portable grain walling for on-floor storage in
   existing building   £31
4. On floor grain storage in purpose-built
   building   £73
   Extras:
   (a) low volume ventilation   £5-£6
   (b) on-floor drying with above-ground main
       duct and laterals   £89
   (c) add to (b) for below-ground laterals   £9·25
5. Sealed towers for moist grain, including loading
   and unloading equipment   £95-£130

Potato Storage   *per tonne stored*
1. Pallet-box store with recirculation fans   £143
   Pallet boxes, 1 tonne   £50
2. Bulk store, building only   £135
   Ventilation system: fans, main duct, below-floor
   lateral ducts   £26

Roads and Fences	*per m length*
3·2 m wide hardcore road with drainage ditches	
using locally excavated material	£20
using imported hardcore (£6·15/m³)	£32
extra for bitumen macadam surfacing, two coats	£24
Traditional 7-wire stock fence	£2·80
High tensile 7-wire stock fence	£2·60

Construction Equipment Hire	*hourly rate, with driver*
Excavator	£16-£20
Tipping lorry	£19
10-tonne crane	£22
	weekly rate
Concrete mixer, 100 litre (5/3)	£30
Compressor and heavy breaker	£82

B. Standard Costs

Standard costs are published by MAFF and the Scottish Office and Welsh Office Agriculture Departments on the basis of the cost of farm or casual labour and new materials. They do not include an allowance for overheads and profit: in most cases building contractors would add 15-30% to cover them. Standard costs are therefore usually lower, sometimes by a larger percentage than this, particularly where the labour content of the item is high. The following examples are based on standard costs issued in 1992. Farm buildings costs generally will have risen between 15% and 20% between that year and 1999.

	per m² floor area
Open-sided framed building with cladding to roof and gable peaks only, hardcore floor, rainwater drainage to soakaways:	
9 × 18 m	£32
13·2 × 24m	£29

	per m² wall or roof
Corrugated cladding to roof or walls, *including supports* (purlins or rails):	
fibre cement sheeting	£13·10
extra for coloured sheeting	£0·72
extra for PVC coated steel instead of fibre cement	£0·72
deduct for metallic coated (*e.g.* galvanised) steel	£3·75
Spaced boarding	£15·00
Wall element, concrete blockwork 190-324 mm thick with strip foundation (base 750 mm below ground level) and 2·5 mm height above ground level	£72 per m run
Extra for rendering blockwork on one side	£4·85 per m²
Concrete floor, 100 mm thick, including excavation, hardcore and waterproof membrane	£11·05 per m²
Concrete floor, 150 mm thick as above	£13·90 per m²

Reinforced concrete slats for cattle (supports not included)	£38 per m²
Yard gully with heavy grating	£195 each
Drainage pipes, 100 mm, jointed in UPVC, clayware or spun concrete including 900 mm trench and backfill	£8·30 per m run
Drainage pipes 150 mm as above	£14·90 per m run
Tank for water, effluent etc., 20 m³	£2,332 each
Gate, 3 m wide, steel, including posts concreted in: light duty	£84 each
cattle yard type	£112 each
Fully covered enclosed building with concrete floor, and rainwater drainage to soakaways	

	per m² floor area
10 × 18 m	£64
15 × 24 m	£57

C. Storage Requirements

Bulk (cubic metres (feet) per tonne):

Beans		1·2	(43)
Wheat, peas		1·3	(46)
Barley, rye, oilseed rape, linseed, fodder beet		1·4	(50)
Oats		1·9	(68)
Potatoes		1·6	(57)
Dry bulb onions		2·0	(71)
Concentrates:	meal	2·0	(71)
	cubes	1·6	(57)
Grass silage:	18% DM	1·3	(46)
	30% DM	1·6	(57)
Maize silage		1·3	(46)
Silage; large round bales		2·5	(88)
Wheat straw ⎫		13·0	(464)
Barley straw ⎬ small bales		11·5	(411)
Hay ⎭		6·0	(214)
Wheat straw ⎫		20·0	(714)
Barley straw ⎬ large round bales		18·0	(643)
Hay ⎭		8·0	(286)
Brewers' grains		0·9	(32)

(With straw and hay the storage requirement clearly depends on the packing density; the above are simply typical averages).

Boxes (floor area in square metres (feet) per tonne):

Potatoes:	0·5 tonne boxes, 5 boxes high	0·52	(5·6)
	1·0 tonne boxes, 4 boxes high	0·52	(5·6)
	1·0 tonne boxes, 5 boxes high	0·45	(4·8)

Bags (floor area in square metres (feet) per tonne):

Feedingstuffs:	2 bags high	1·6	(17)
Fertilizer:	6 bags high	1·1	(12)
	10 bags high	0·7	(8)

VII. CAPITAL, TAXATION AND GRANTS

1. CAPITAL

(i) Tenant's Capital consists of:

(a) *Machinery.* Costs of new machinery are given on pages 138-142. Written-down values in 2000 are likely to be averaging about £550 per hectare (£225 per acre) taking all farm types together — based on current (*i.e.* replacement) costs (approximately £450/ha (£180/acre) based on historic costs).

(b) *Breeding Livestock.* Over all types of farm the 2000 average is estimated to be about £650 per hectare (£265 per acre), but the figure can vary from zero to over £2,000 (£800) for grazing livestock alone. Approximate average market values (£) of various categories of breeding livestock (of mixed ages in the case of adult stock) are as follows (actual value will vary according to average age and weight, quality and breed):

Holstein Friesian Dairy Cows (inc. dry cows): 600.
Channel Island Dairy Cows (inc. dry cows): 350.
Other Dairy Cows (inc. dry cows): 500.
Beef Cows: 525.

Other Cattle:	Dairy Followers		Beef Cattle
	Holstein Friesians	Ayrshires and C.I. Breeds	
In-calf heifers	575	340	450
Stores over 2 years	425	255	390
Stores 1-2 years	350	210	325
Stores 6-12 months	275	175	275
Calves under 6 months	160	95	175

Ewes: 50. Rams 250.
Sows and In-pig Gilts: 150. Boars 525.

(c) *Working Capital.* This is the capital needed to finance the production cycle, the length of which varies considerably between different crop and livestock enterprises and different combinations of these enterprises. Because of this, no generalizations are possible, but it can include the cost of purchased fattening stock, feed, seed, fertilizers, regular labour, machinery running costs, general overhead costs, rent and living expenses. This capital may be only a few pounds per hectare on an all-dairying farm but £500 or more per hectare on an all-cereals farm where the crop is stored until the spring. The average is likely to be about £300 per hectare (£120 per acre) in 2000.

(ii) *Return on Capital*

(a) *Tenant's capital.* For all lowland farms (excluding intensive pig and poultry units, fruit and glasshouse production), total tenant's capital will average about £1,500 per hectare (approximately £610 per acre) in 2000, with the (written-down) machinery valuations based on current ('replacement') costs £1,400 (565) based on historic costs); (for range, see table on page 178). If the average U.K. management and investment in year 2000 were, say, £100 per hectare (£40 per acre), the average return on tenant's capital would be approximately 6·75 per cent. 'Premium' levels (the average of the top 50 per cent of farms) would be likely to be some 50 per cent higher (*i.e.* close to 10 per cent), with the levels achieved for mixed cropping on the very best soils and top dairy farms possibly double the average. Note that no charge has been included for management (but that a rental value for owner-occupied land and the value of the unpaid labour of the farmer and wife have been deducted).

(b) *Landlord's Capital (i.e.* land, buildings, roads, etc.). With farms towards the end of the 1990s averaging, say, £6,000 per hectare (£2,425 per acre), with vacant possession (assuming no special amenity or house value), an average lowland rent of, say, £150 per hectare (£60 per acre) (see p. 162), and assuming ownership expenses at £60 per hectare (£24 per acre), the (net) return (which is £90 per hectare (£36 per acre)) averages 1·5 per cent. If land is taken at its tenanted value, with a vacant possession premium of say 50 per cent, the return obviously doubles, to 3·0 per cent. If business tenancy rents were paid, at say 50% above the average level for established tenants (*i.e.* £225/ha [£91/acre]), and many have been much higher, the return would average 2·75 per cent with land at the vacant possession price assumed and 5·5 per cent with land at the tenanted value assumed. Full repairing and insurance leases clearly raise the returns above these levels. Above average quality farms acquire higher rents but also obviously command higher prices than the average levels quoted above.

(c) *Total Owner-Occupier's Capital (i.e.* land plus 'tenant's' capital). The combined (net) return on the above assumptions (£190 per hectare, or £76 per acre) on total capital, (£7,500 per hectare, or £3,035 per acre), with land at its vacant possession value, averages 2·5 per cent. This increases to 4·2 per cent if land is taken at its tenanted value and this is half the vacant possession value. If higher rent levels are assumed (given the same farming return), the overall return remains the same, the distribution simply being reallocated in favour of the land ownership share at the expense of the farming share. 'Premium' farming returns (as defined above), assuming the same capital requirements, raise the returns to 3·2 per cent with land at the vacant possession price and 5·3 per cent with tenanted land values. (To repeat, the above figures all assume that machinery depreciation and valuation are based on its current cost.)

(iii) *Average Tenant's Capital per hectare* (per acre in brackets) for Different Farm Types, as estimated for 2000, are as follows:

177

Farm Type Group	Average No. Hectares	Livestock £	Crops, Cultivns., Stores £	Machinery and Equipment* £	Total Tenant's Capital £ £
Mainly Dairying:					
under 50 ha ...	40	1400	250	850	2500 (1010)
50 to 100 ha ...	75	1225	250	750	2225 (900)
Over 100 ha ...	150	1050	250	650	1950 (790)
Mainly Arable:					
under 100 ha ...	70	125	425	650	1200 (485)
100 to 200 ha ...	150	125	450	650	1225 (495)
over 200 ha ...	350	125	450	550	1125 (455)
Dairy and Arable:					
under 100 ha ...	70	1000	300	700	2000 (810)
100 to 200 ha ...	150	750	350	675	1775 (720)
over 200 ha ...	350	550	375	650	1575 (635)
Mainly Sheep/Cattle:					
under 100 ha ...	65	650	125	300	1075 (435)
over 100 ha ...	170	550	150	300	1000 (405)
Sheep/Cattle and Arable:					
under 100 ha ...	65	650	200	400	1250 (505)
100 to 200 ha ...	150	550	250	375	1175 (475)
over 200 ha ...	240	500	300	350	1150 (465)
Dairy, Sheep/Cattle and Arable: ...	275	500	275	350	1125 (455)
Intensive Arable:					
Fruit	80	0	4000	1000	5000 (2025)
Field Vegetables ...	35	0	1000	2250	3250 (1315)
Mainly Pigs Poultry:					
(per £1000 output)	—	300	25	150	475
Glasshouse salads:					
(per £1000 output)	—	0	100	1000	1100

* Based on current *(i.e.* replacement) costs.

Note: The above (deliberately rounded) data are based on Farm Business Survey results compiled annually by University/Colleges centres (as listed on page 5), where actual figures for previous years can be found. None includes the value of milk quota on farms with dairying, even though a case can be made for this on the grounds of opportunity cost; obviously the cost of additional quota must be included when budgeting for, and calculating the return on capital of, introducing or expanding a dairy herd — whether by increasing yield per cow or the number of cows or both.

(iv) *Return on Capital to Individual Enterprises* on a mixed farm is virtually impossible to ascertain, except perhaps for a full-time pig or poultry enterprise, nor would it be of very much use even if it could be determined. It would require the arbitrary allocation both of costs and capital inputs that are common to several, in some cases all, of the enterprises on the farm.

What is relevant and important is the extra (net) return from an enterprise either to be introduced or expanded, as calculated by a partial budget, related to the extra (net) capital needed. The "net" in brackets relates, as regards return, to the addition to gross margins less any addition to (or plus any reduction in) "fixed" costs, bearing in mind that another enterprise may have to be deleted or reduced in size; and, as regards capital, to the fact that deletion or reduction of another enterprise may release capital.

In most cases of "marginal" substitution, it is differences in the value of breeding livestock and differences in variable costs that are particularly relevant, but the timing of both inputs and sales are also obviously very important.

(v) *"Marginal" Capital Requirements for* small changes in crop areas or livestock numbers can be estimated as follows:

Crops: variable costs till sale.

Dairy Cows and Egg Production: value of the cow* or hens, plus one month's food.

Other Breeding Livestock: average value of stock*, plus variable costs to sale of the progeny (*e.g.* lambs)—or their transfer to another enterprise (*e.g.* weaners to the pig fattening enterprise). Rearing Breeding Livestock (*e.g.* heifers, tegs, gilts, pullets). cost of the calf, lamb, weaner or chick, plus variable costs till they produce their first progeny/eggs.

Fattening Livestock and Production of Stores: cost of stock, plus variable costs till sale.

* Value of breeding stock, including dairy cows: either the average value over their entire breeding or milk producing life (see table on page 000) or their value when they first produce progeny can be taken. The latter will give the lower return on (marginal) capital and is thus the severer test.

Home-reared stock: where stock to be used for milk or egg production, breeding or fattening are home-reared, there are two possibilities:

(i) either they can be valued at variable costs of production when they are transferred from the rearing to the "productive" enterprise; in this case the return on (marginal) capital will be estimated over the combined rearing and "productive" enterprise.

(ii) or they can be valued at market value at point of transfer. This is the procedure if one wishes to work out a return on (marginal) capital for the rearing and the "productive" enterprises separately.

(vi) *Return on "Marginal" Capital.* This is sometimes expressed as the gross margin less fuel and repair costs of the enterprise expanded as a percentage of the "marginal", or extra, capital. However, two points have to be remembered:

(i) If another enterprise has had to be reduced in size to enable the enterprise under consideration to be expanded, the capital released and the gross margin forfeited by reducing the size of the first enterprise must be brought into the calculation in estimating the net result of the change.

(ii) All the above statements on "marginal" capital refer to small changes. If the change is large enough to cause changes in labour, machinery or building requirements the capital changes brought about may be considerably greater.

(vii) *Return on Investments in Medium-Term and Long-Term Capital. Rate of Return and the Discounted Yield.*

Example: If £5,000 investment results in an annual net return of £500 (after deducting depreciation, but ignoring interest payments):

$$Rate\ of\ Return\ on\ Initial\ Capital = \frac{500}{5,000} \times 100 = 10\%$$

$$Rate\ of\ Return\ on\ Average\ Capital = \frac{500}{2,500} \times 100 = 20\%$$

It is more accurate to calculate the *"Discounted Yield"*, which is the discount rate that brings the present value of the net cash flows (which means ignoring depreciation) to the value of the investment.

The tables on pages 182 and 183 may be used.

"Short-Cut" Estimates of the Discounted Yield on depreciating assets.

The Discounted Yield falls between the simple Rates of Return on Initial and Average Capital. In fact, for investments lasting 5 to 15 years, when the Rate of Return on Initial Capital is 10 per cent and on Average Capital 20 per cent, the Discounted Yield will be almost exactly halfway between, *i.e.* about 15 per cent. However, this is only so providing the anticipated annual net cash earnings are fairly constant — or fluctuate unpredictably around a fairly constant level.

There are three circumstances when the Discounted Yield will get closer to the Rate of Return on Initial Capital (*i.e.* the lower per cent return) and further from the Rate of Return on Average Capital:

(a) The longer the life of the investment.
(b) The higher the Rate of Return.
(c) The higher the net cash flow is in the later years of the investment compared with the earlier years.

When the opposite circumstances obtain, the Discounted Yield will be closer to the Rate of Return on Average Capital (*i.e.* the higher per cent return).

Granted that there are inevitably varying degrees of estimation and uncertainty in calculating future net annual earnings of investments, the following short-cuts might reasonably be used where the annual net cash earnings are expected to be fairly constant — or fluctuate unpredictably (*e.g.* through weather effects on yields) around a fairly constant level. (W.O. period = write-off period; R.R.I.C. = rate of return on initial capital).

1. Where   (i) the W.O. period is 5 years or less,
         (ii) the W.O. period is 6 to 10 years and the R.R.I.C. is
              15 per cent or less,
        (iii) the W.O. period is 11 to 20 years and the R.R.I.C. is
              10 per cent or less,
calculate the Return on Capital as being approximately midway between
the Rates of Return on Initial and Average Capital, *i.e.* by calculating
the Rate of Return on $^2/_3$ of the original investment.

For example, following the earlier example (page 180):

$$\frac{500}{3,333} \times 100 = 15\%.$$

2. Where   (i) the W.O. period is 6 to 10 years and the R.R.I.C.
              exceeds 15 per cent,

         (ii) the W.O. period is 11 to 20 years and the R.R.I.C. is
              between 10 per cent and 25 per cent,

        (iii) the W.O. period exceeds 20 years and the R.R.I.C. is
              10 per cent or less,

calculate the Return on Capital on 80 per cent of the original investment.

For example, again following the earlier example:

$$\frac{500}{4,000} \times 100 = 12\frac{1}{2}\%.$$

3. Where (i) the W.O. period is 11 to 20 years and the R.R.I.C.
              exceeds 25 per cent,

         (ii) the W.O. period exceeds 20 years and the R.R.I.C.
              exceeds 10 per cent,

take the Return on Capital to be the R.R.I.C.

In borderline cases, use method 1 rather than 2, or 2 rather than 3 if
there is a tendency for the cash flow to be higher in the earlier years,
e.g. because of tax allowances on machinery. Take 2 rather than 1, and
3 rather than 2, if the likelihood is that the cash flow will be lower in
earlier years and increase in later years.

However, where the annual cash flow is expected to vary (apart from
unpredictable fluctuations) it is safer to make the full D.C.F. calculation.
This is particularly so where the variation is both up and down and
where further periodic investments are to be made during the life of
the project.

Discounting Table A

Discount Factors for Calculating the Present Value of Future (irregular) Cash Flows.

Year									Percentage								
	3%	4%	5%	6%	7%	8%	9%	10%	11%	12%	13%	14%	15%	16%	18%	20%	25%
1	0.971	0.962	0.952	0.943	0.935	0.926	0.917	0.909	0.901	0.893	0.885	0.877	0.870	0.862	0.847	0.833	0.800
2	0.943	0.925	0.907	0.890	0.873	0.857	0.842	0.826	0.812	0.797	0.783	0.769	0.756	0.743	0.718	0.694	0.640
3	0.915	0.889	0.864	0.840	0.816	0.794	0.772	0.751	0.731	0.712	0.693	0.675	0.658	0.641	0.609	0.579	0.512
4	0.888	0.855	0.823	0.792	0.763	0.735	0.708	0.683	0.659	0.636	0.613	0.592	0.572	0.552	0.516	0.482	0.410
5	0.863	0.822	0.784	0.747	0.713	0.681	0.650	0.621	0.593	0.567	0.543	0.519	0.497	0.476	0.437	0.402	0.328
6	0.837	0.790	0.746	0.705	0.666	0.630	0.596	0.564	0.535	0.507	0.480	0.456	0.432	0.410	0.370	0.335	0.262
7	0.813	0.760	0.711	0.665	0.623	0.583	0.547	0.513	0.482	0.452	0.425	0.400	0.376	0.354	0.314	0.279	0.210
8	0.789	0.731	0.677	0.627	0.582	0.540	0.502	0.467	0.434	0.404	0.376	0.351	0.327	0.305	0.266	0.233	0.168
9	0.766	0.703	0.645	0.592	0.544	0.500	0.460	0.424	0.391	0.361	0.333	0.308	0.284	0.263	0.225	0.194	0.134
10	0.744	0.676	0.614	0.558	0.508	0.463	0.422	0.386	0.352	0.322	0.295	0.270	0.247	0.227	0.191	0.162	0.107
11	0.722	0.650	0.585	0.527	0.475	0.429	0.388	0.350	0.317	0.287	0.261	0.237	0.215	0.195	0.162	0.135	0.086
12	0.701	0.625	0.557	0.497	0.444	0.397	0.356	0.319	0.286	0.257	0.231	0.208	0.187	0.168	0.137	0.112	0.069
13	0.681	0.601	0.530	0.469	0.415	0.368	0.326	0.290	0.258	0.229	0.204	0.182	0.163	0.145	0.116	0.093	0.055
14	0.661	0.577	0.505	0.442	0.388	0.340	0.299	0.263	0.232	0.205	0.181	0.160	0.141	0.125	0.098	0.078	0.044
15	0.642	0.555	0.481	0.417	0.362	0.315	0.275	0.239	0.209	0.183	0.160	0.140	0.123	0.108	0.084	0.065	0.035
20	0.554	0.456	0.377	0.312	0.258	0.215	0.178	0.149	0.124	0.104	0.087	0.073	0.061	0.051	0.037	0.026	0.012
25	0.478	0.375	0.295	0.233	0.184	0.146	0.116	0.092	0.074	0.059	0.047	0.038	0.030	0.024	0.016	0.010	0.004
30	0.412	0.308	0.231	0.174	0.131	0.099	0.075	0.057	0.044	0.033	0.026	0.020	0.015	0.012	0.007	0.004	0.001

Example: The Present Value of £500 received 10 years from now, at 12 per cent discount rate of interest = 500 × 0.322 = £161.
Conversely, £161 invested now, at 12 per cent compound interest, will be worth £500 in 10 years' time.

Discounting Table B
Discount Factors for Calculating the Present Value of Future Annuity (i.e. Constant Annual Cash Flow) Receivable in Years 1 to n inclusive.

Percentage

Year	3%	4%	5%	6%	7%	8%	9%	10%	11%	12%	13%	14%	15%	16%	18%	20%	25%
1	0·971	0·962	0·952	0·943	0·935	0·926	0·917	0·909	0·901	0·893	0·885	0·877	0·870	0·862	0·847	0·833	0·800
2	1·913	1·886	1·859	1·833	1·808	1·783	1·759	1·736	1·713	1·690	1·668	1·647	1·626	1·605	1·566	1·528	1·440
3	2·829	2·775	2·723	2·673	2·624	2·577	2·531	2·487	2·444	2·402	2·361	2·322	2·283	2·246	2·174	2·106	1·952
4	3·717	3·630	3·546	3·465	3·387	3·312	3·240	3·170	3·102	3·037	2·974	2·914	2·855	2·798	2·690	2·589	2·362
5	4·580	4·452	4·329	4·212	4·100	3·593	3·890	3·791	3·696	3·605	3·517	3·433	3·352	3·274	3·127	2·991	2·689
6	5·417	5·242	5·076	4·917	4·767	4·623	4·486	4·355	4·231	4·111	3·998	3·889	3·784	3·685	3·498	3·326	2·951
7	6·230	6·002	5·786	5·582	5·389	5·206	5·033	4·868	4·712	4·564	4·423	4·288	4·160	4·039	3·812	3·605	3·161
8	7·020	6·733	6·463	6·210	5·971	5·747	5·535	5·335	5·146	4·968	4·799	4·639	4·487	4·344	4·078	3·837	3·329
9	7·786	7·435	7·108	6·802	6·515	6·247	5·995	5·759	5·537	5·328	5·132	4·946	4·772	4·607	4·303	4·031	3·463
10	8·530	8·111	7·722	7·360	7·024	6·710	6·418	6·145	5·889	5·650	5·426	5·216	5·019	4·833	4·494	4·192	3·570
11	9·253	8·760	8·306	7·887	7·499	7·139	6·805	6·495	6·207	5·938	5·687	5·453	5·234	5·029	4·656	4·327	3·656
12	9·954	9·385	8·863	8·384	7·943	7·536	7·161	6·814	6·492	6·194	5·918	5·660	5·421	5·197	4·793	4·439	3·725
13	10·635	9·986	9·394	8·853	8·358	7·904	7·487	7·103	6·750	6·424	6·122	5·842	5·583	5·342	4·910	4·533	3·780
14	11·296	10·563	9·899	9·295	8·745	8·244	7·786	7·367	6·982	6·628	6·302	6·002	5·724	5·468	5·008	4·611	3·824
15	11·938	11·118	10·380	9·712	9·108	8·559	8·061	7·606	7·191	6·811	6·462	6·142	5·847	5·575	5·092	4·675	3·859
20	14·877	13·590	12·462	11·470	10·594	9·818	9·129	8·514	7·963	7·469	7·025	6·623	6·259	5·929	5·353	4·870	3·954
25	17·413	15·662	14·094	12·783	11·654	10·675	9·823	9·077	8·422	7·843	7·330	6·873	6·464	6·097	5·467	4·948	3·985
30	19·600	17·292	15·372	13·765	12·409	11·258	10·274	9·427	8·694	8·055	7·496	7·033	6·566	6·177	5·517	4·979	3·995

Example: The Present Value of £500 a year for the next 10 years, at 12 per cent discount rate of interest = 500 × 5·650 = £2,825. This is the same answer that would be obtained by multiplying 500 by each discount factor (at 12 per cent) in Table A for each year from 1 to 10, and adding together the ten resulting figures.

To obtain the Discounted Yield of a constant annual net cash flow, divide this into the original investment and look up the resulting figure in the table above, against the number of years. *Example:* an investment of £1,000 is estimated to produce £80 a year additional profit over 10 years (before charging interest). Add £100 depreciation a year = £180 annual net cash flow. 1000 ÷ 180 = 5·56. This equals just over 12 per cent (the 10 years/12 per cent figure being 5·650).

Compounding Table A

The Future Money Value of £1 after n Years.

Rate of Interest

Year	3%	4%	5%	6%	7%	8%	9%	10%	11%	12%	13%	14%	15%	16%	18%	20%	25%
1	1·03	1·04	1·05	1·06	1·07	1·08	1·09	1·10	1·11	1·12	1·13	1·14	1·15	1·16	1·18	1·20	1·25
2	1·06	1·08	1·10	1·12	1·14	1·17	1·19	1·21	1·23	1·25	1·28	1·30	1·32	1·35	1·39	1·44	1·56
3	1·09	1·12	1·16	1·19	1·23	1·26	1·30	1·33	1·37	1·40	1·44	1·48	1·52	1·56	1·64	1·73	1·95
4	1·13	1·17	1·22	1·26	1·31	1·36	1·41	1·46	1·52	1·57	1·63	1·69	1·75	1·81	1·94	2·07	2·44
5	1·16	1·22	1·28	1·34	1·40	1·47	1·54	1·61	1·69	1·76	1·84	1·93	2·01	2·10	2·29	2·49	3·05
6	1·19	1·27	1·34	1·42	1·50	1·59	1·68	1·77	1·87	1·97	2·08	2·19	2·31	2·44	2·70	2·99	3·81
7	1·23	1·32	1·41	1·50	1·61	1·71	1·83	1·95	2·08	2·21	2·35	2·50	2·66	2·83	3·19	3·58	4·77
8	1·27	1·37	1·48	1·59	1·72	1·85	1·99	2·14	2·30	2·48	2·66	2·85	3·06	3·28	3·76	4·30	5·96
9	1·30	1·42	1·55	1·69	1·84	2·00	2·17	2·36	2·56	2·77	3·00	3·25	3·52	3·80	4·44	5·16	7·45
10	1·34	1·48	1·63	1·79	1·97	2·16	2·37	2·59	2·84	3·11	3·39	3·71	4·05	4·41	5·23	6·19	9·31
11	1·38	1·54	1·71	1·90	2·10	2·33	2·58	2·85	3·15	3·48	3·84	4·23	4·65	5·12	6·18	7·43	11·64
12	1·43	1·60	1·80	2·01	2·25	2·52	2·81	3·14	3·50	3·90	4·33	4·82	5·35	5·94	7·29	8·92	14·55
13	1·47	1·67	1·89	2·13	2·41	2·72	3·07	3·45	3·88	4·36	4·90	5·49	6·15	6·89	8·60	10·70	18·19
14	1·51	1·73	1·98	2·26	2·58	2·94	3·34	3·80	4·31	4·89	5·53	6·26	7·08	7·99	10·15	12·84	22·74
15	1·56	1·80	2·08	2·40	2·76	3·17	3·64	4·18	4·78	5·47	6·25	7·14	8·14	9·27	11·97	15·41	28·42
20	1·81	2·19	2·65	3·21	3·87	4·66	5·60	6·73	8·06	9·65	11·52	13·74	16·37	19·46	27·39	38·34	86·74
25	2·09	2·67	3·39	4·29	5·43	6·85	8·62	10·83	13·59	17·00	21·23	26·46	32·92	40·87	62·67	95·40	264·7
30	2·43	3·24	4·32	5·74	7·61	10·06	13·27	17·45	22·89	29·96	39·12	50·95	66·21	85·85	143·4	237·4	807·8

Compounding Table B

The Future Money Value of £1 per annum after n Years *

Rate of Interest

Year	3%	4%	5%	6%	7%	8%	9%	10%	11%	12%	13%	14%	15%	16%	18%	20%	25%
1	1·03	1·04	1·05	1·06	1·07	1·08	1·09	1·10	1·11	1·12	1·13	1·14	1·15	1·16	1·18	1·20	1·25
2	2·09	2·12	2·15	2·18	2·21	2·25	2·28	2·31	2·34	2·37	2·41	2·44	2·47	2·51	2·57	2·64	2·81
3	3·18	3·25	3·31	3·37	3·44	3·51	3·57	3·64	3·71	3·78	3·85	3·92	3·99	4·07	4·22	4·37	4·77
4	4·31	4·42	4·53	4·64	4·75	4·87	4·98	5·11	5·23	5·35	5·48	5·61	5·74	5·88	6·15	6·44	7·21
5	5·47	5·63	5·80	5·98	6·15	6·34	6·52	6·72	6·91	7·12	7·32	7·54	7·75	7·98	8·44	8·93	10·26
6	6·66	6·90	7·14	7·39	7·65	7·92	8·20	8·49	8·78	9·09	9·40	9·73	10·07	10·41	11·14	11·92	14·07
7	7·89	8·21	8·55	8·90	9·26	9·64	10·03	10·44	10·86	11·30	11·76	12·23	12·73	13·24	14·33	15·50	18·84
8	9·16	9·58	10·03	10·49	10·98	11·49	12·02	12·58	13·16	13·78	14·42	15·09	15·79	16·52	18·09	19·80	24·80
9	10·46	11·01	11·58	12·18	12·82	13·49	14·19	14·94	15·72	16·55	17·42	18·34	19·30	20·32	22·52	24·96	32·25
10	11·81	12·49	13·21	13·97	14·78	15·65	16·56	17·53	18·56	19·65	20·81	22·04	23·35	24·73	27·76	31·15	41·57
11	13·19	14·03	14·92	15·87	16·89	17·98	19·14	20·38	21·71	23·13	24·65	26·27	28·00	29·85	33·93	38·58	53·21
12	14·62	15·63	16·71	17·88	19·14	20·50	21·95	23·52	25·21	27·03	28·98	31·09	33·35	35·79	41·22	47·50	67·76
13	16·09	17·29	18·60	20·02	21·55	23·21	25·02	26·97	29·09	31·39	33·88	36·58	39·50	42·67	49·82	58·20	85·95
14	17·60	19·02	20·58	22·28	24·13	26·15	28·36	30·77	33·41	36·28	39·42	42·84	46·58	50·66	59·97	71·04	108·7
15	19·16	20·82	22·66	24·67	26·89	29·32	32·00	34·95	38·19	41·75	45·67	49·58	54·72	59·93	71·94	86·44	137·1
20	27·68	30·97	34·72	38·99	43·87	49·42	55·76	63·00	71·27	80·70	91·47	103·8	117·8	133·8	173·0	224·0	428·7
25	37·55	43·31	50·11	58·16	67·68	78·95	92·32	108·2	127·0	149·3	175·8	207·3	244·7	289·1	404·3	566·4	1318
30	49·00	58·33	69·76	83·80	101·1	122·3	148·6	180·9	220·9	270·3	331·3	406·7	500·0	615·2	933·3	1418	4034

* Payments made at the beginning of each year.

Amortisation Table
Annual Charge to write off £1,000

Write-off Period (Years)	Rate of Interest															
	3	4	5	6	7	8	9	10	11	12	13	14	15	16	18	20
5	218	225	231	237	244	250	257	264	271	277	284	291	298	305	320	334
6	185	191	197	203	210	216	223	230	236	243	250	257	264	271	286	301
7	161	167	173	179	186	192	199	205	212	219	226	233	240	248	262	277
8	142	149	155	161	167	174	181	187	194	201	208	216	223	230	245	261
9	128	134	141	147	153	160	167	174	181	188	195	202	210	217	232	248
10	117	123	130	136	142	149	156	163	170	177	184	192	199	207	223	239
11	108	114	120	127	133	140	147	154	161	168	176	183	191	199	215	231
12	100	107	113	119	125	133	140	147	154	161	169	177	184	192	209	225
13	94	100	106	113	120	127	134	141	148	156	163	171	179	187	204	221
14	89	95	101	108	114	121	128	136	143	151	159	167	175	183	200	217
15	84	90	96	103	110	117	124	131	139	147	155	163	171	179	196	214
16	80	86	92	99	106	113	120	128	136	143	151	160	168	176	194	211
17	76	82	89	95	102	110	117	125	132	140	149	157	165	174	191	209
18	73	79	86	92	99	107	114	122	130	138	146	155	163	172	190	208
19	70	76	83	90	97	104	112	120	128	136	144	153	161	170	188	206
20	67	74	80	87	94	102	110	117	126	134	142	151	160	169	187	205
25	57	64	71	78	86	94	102	110	119	127	136	145	155	164	183	202
30	51	58	65	73	81	89	97	106	115	124	133	143	152	162	181	201
40	43	51	58	66	75	84	93	102	112	122	131	141	151	160	180	200

Example: £3,000 is borrowed to erect a building. The annual charge to service interest and capital repayment on the £3,000, repayable over 10 years at 12%, is 3 × £177 = £531. Where the write-off period of the building (10 years) is equal to the repayment period of the loan, then the average annual depreciation and interest will also equal £531.

The proportion of the total annual charge representing the average amount of capital repaid per annum can be readily determined by dividing the sum borrowed by the number of years of the loan: (in the above example this is £3,000 ÷ 10 = £300/year). The remainder is clearly the average amount of interest paid per annum: (in the above example, £531 — £300 = £231/year). The year to year variations between the two items (i.e. capital repaid and interest) are shown in the tables on pages 178 to 180, which demonstrate the way in which the capital repayment part increases and the interest part decreases over time.

Sinking Fund Table

The annual sum required to be set aside at the end of each year to accumulate to £1,000 at the end of the period

No. of Years	Rate of Interest															
	3	4	5	6	7	8	9	10	11	12	13	14	15	16	18	20
5	188	185	181	177	174	170	167	164	161	157	154	151	148	145	140	134
6	155	151	147	143	140	136	133	130	126	123	120	117	114	111	106	101
7	131	127	123	119	116	112	109	105	102	99	96	93	90	88	82	77
8	112	109	105	101	97	94	91	87	84	81	78	76	73	70	65	61
9	98	94	91	87	83	80	77	74	71	68	65	62	60	57	52	48
10	87	83	80	76	72	69	66	63	60	57	54	52	49	47	43	39
11	78	74	70	67	63	60	57	54	51	48	46	43	41	39	35	31
12	70	67	63	59	56	53	50	47	44	41	39	37	34	32	29	25
13	64	60	56	53	50	47	44	41	38	36	33	31	29	27	24	21
14	59	55	51	48	44	41	38	36	33	31	29	27	25	23	20	17
15	54	50	46	43	40	37	34	31	29	27	25	23	21	19	16	14
16	50	46	42	39	36	33	30	28	26	23	21	20	18	16	14	11
17	46	42	39	35	32	30	27	25	22	20	19	17	15	14	11	9
18	43	39	36	32	29	27	24	22	20	18	16	15	13	12	10	8
19	40	36	33	30	27	24	22	20	18	16	14	13	11	10	8	6
20	37	34	30	27	24	22	20	17	16	14	12	11	10	9	7	5
25	27	24	21	18	16	14	12	10	9	7	6	5	5	4	3	2
30	21	18	15	13	11	9	7	6	5	4	3	3	2	2	1	1
40	13	11	8	6	5	4	3	2	2	1	1	1	1	—	—	—

MORTGAGE REPAYMENT DATA

Items per £1,000 invested where I = Interest, P = Principal repaid, L = Loan outstanding

Loan through 5 years	6% I	6% P	6% L	8% I	8% P	8% L	10% I	10% P	10% L	12% I	12% P	12% L	14% I	14% P	14% L	16% I	16% P	16% L
1	60	177	823	80	170	830	100	164	836	120	157	834	140	151	849	160	145	855
2	49	188	635	66	184	645	84	180	656	101	175	670	119	172	677	137	169	686
3	38	199	435	52	199	447	66	198	458	80	197	469	92	196	481	110	196	490
4	26	211	224	36	215	232	46	218	240	56	221	248	67	224	257	78	227	263
5	13	224	0	19	232	0	24	240	0	30	248	0	32	257	0	42	263	0
10 years																		
1	60	76	924	80	69	931	100	63	939	120	57	934	140	52	948	160	47	953
2	55	80	844	75	75	856	94	69	868	113	64	879	133	59	889	152	54	899
3	51	85	758	69	81	776	87	76	792	106	71	808	124	68	821	144	63	836
4	46	90	668	62	87	689	79	84	709	97	80	728	115	77	744	134	73	762
5	40	96	572	55	94	595	71	92	617	87	90	638	104	88	656	122	85	677
6	34	102	471	48	101	494	62	101	516	77	100	538	92	100	556	108	99	579
7	28	108	363	39	110	384	52	111	405	65	112	425	78	114	442	93	114	465
8	22	114	249	31	118	266	40	122	282	51	126	299	62	130	312	74	133	332
9	15	121	128	21	128	138	28	134	148	36	141	158	44	148	164	53	154	178
10	8	128	0	11	138	0	15	148	0	19	158	0	23	164	0	29	178	0

MORTGAGE REPAYMENT DATA *(continued)*

Loan through 20 years	6% I	6% P	6% L	8% I	8% P	8% L	10% I	10% P	10% L	12% I	12% P	12% L	14% I	14% P	14% L	16% I	16% P	16% L
1	60	27	973	80	22	978	100	17	983	120	14	986	140	11	989	160	9	991
5	53	34	847	72	30	872	92	26	893	112	22	912	132	19	927	153	16	940
10	41	46	642	58	44	683	76	41	722	95	38	756	115	36	788	136	33	815
15	26	61	367	38	64	407	51	66	445	66	68	483	82	69	518	99	69	552
20	5	82	0	8	94	0	11	107	0	14	120	0	19	132	0	23	145	0
30 years																		
1	60	13	987	80	9	991	100	6	994	120	4	996	140	3	997	160	2	998
5	57	16	929	77	12	948	97	9	963	118	7	974	138	5	986	158	3	987
10	51	21	833	71	18	872	92	14	903	113	11	927	134	9	951	155	7	960
15	44	29	706	63	26	760	83	23	807	104	20	846	126	17	890	147	15	903
20	34	38	535	51	38	596	69	37	652	88	36	701	108	35	751	130	32	782
25	21	51	306	33	56	355	46	60	402	61	63	488	83	60	494	95	66	530
30	4	69	0	7	82	0	10	96	0	13	111	0	16	127	0	22	140	0

MORTGAGE REPAYMENT DATA *(continued)*

Loan through 40 years	6%			8%			10%			12%			14%			16%		
	I	P	L	I	P	L	I	P	L	I	P	L	I	P	L	I	P	L
1	60	6	994	80	4	996	100	2	998	120	1	999	140	1	999	160	0	1000
5	58	8	964	79	5	977	99	3	986	119	2	992	139	2	995	160	1	997
10	56	11	915	76	8	944	97	5	964	118	4	977	138	3	989	159	2	991
15	52	15	850	73	11	895	94	9	928	115	6	951	136	5	973	157	3	978
20	47	20	762	67	17	823	88	14	871	110	11	906	130	11	942	153	7	951
25	40	26	645	59	24	718	80	22	778	102	20	826	123	18	874	145	15	894
30	31	35	489	48	36	563	66	36	628	86	35	685	109	32	742	129	31	775
35	20	47	280	31	53	335	45	58	388	60	61	437	85	56	487	95	66	525
40	4	63	0	6	78	0	9	93	0	13	108	0	18	123	0	22	138	0

Note—All figures rounded to nearest £.

190

Rates of Interest: Further Points

(i)   Rate of Interest on Bank Loans. Typically 2·25% to 2·5% above
Base Rate. Main range is 1·5% above to 3·5% above. Extremes
are likely to be 1% above (minimum) and 5% above (maximum).

(ii)   Annual Percentage Rate (APR). This is the effective rate of interest
calculated on an annual basis and should be used when seeking
to make a true comparison between interest charges on money
borrowed from different sources. The *APR* allows for the fact that
when interest is applied to accounts at half yearly, quarterly or
monthly intervals an element of compounding will arise. For
example, £100 borrowed for one year at a quoted annual *nominal*
interest rate of 12% *(e.g.* 2% over base rate of 10%) with interest
charged quarterly, will lead to an accumulated interest charge of
£12·55 *(i.e.,* giving an APR of just under 12·6%). The higher the
annual nominal interest rate and the more frequently the interest
charges are applied to the account, the more pronounced the
compounding element becomes. For example, an annual nominal
interest rate of 20% produces an APR of 21% with half yearly
charging, 21·6% with quarterly charging and 21·9% with monthly
charging.

In the case of some loans and hire purchase agreements, interest
charges may be quoted as a *flat rate* on the original amount
borrowed. The APR will be considerably greater than the flat rate
if the loan is repaid by equal periodic instalments, comprising part
capital and part interest, so that the borrowing is completely repaid
by the end of the agreed term. For example, the APR for a loan
at a flat rate of interest of 8% repaid by monthly instalments over
5 years will be 15%. The shorter the repayment period, and the
more frequent the payments, the higher is the APR compared with
the flat rate.

(iii) The Real Rate of Interest. When preparing simple profit and
loss budgets to estimate the worthwhileness of an investment in
a fixed asset (machinery, buildings, land), it is usual to price inputs
and outputs at present-day values even when most costs and
returns are expected to rise due to inflation over the life of the
investment. Where this *real terms* approach is adopted a more
realistic estimate of the effect on profitability can be gained by
basing charges for capital on the *real rate of interest* rather than
the APR. The real rate of interest is the APR adjusted for the
annual rate at which prices relevant to the investment are expected
to increase. A crude estimate of the real rate of interest can be
obtained by simply subtracting the expected rate of price increase
from the APR; for example, if the APR were 11% and the
expected rate of inflation 6%, the real rate of interest would be
11 — 6 = 5%.

Financial Ratios

1. *Common Ratios*

The following ratios are often quoted as rough guidelines:

		% of Gross Output
Variable Costs		30-35%
Labour	15-17½%	
Machinery	15-17½%	35-40%
Sundry Fixed Costs	5%	
Rent & Interest		15%
Margin*		15%

* to cover drawings, tax, capital repayments, reinvestments

It has to be borne in mind, however, that these are indeed only rough guidelines and need to be considered with great care. Values vary, for example, with type of farming and size of farm. Furthermore, it is often unclear how certain items are being measured, especially whether unpaid manual labour of the farmer and family has been included or whether a rental value has been allowed for owner-occupied land.

2. *Farm Survey Ratios*

The following are rounded averages over recent years on a large sample of *all types of farm*. It is to be noted that Total Output includes the market value of any production retained for use/consumption on the farm (*e.g.* cereals for feed or seed), Rent includes the rental value of owner-occupied land and Interest charges are not included in the costs. Casual labour and all Contract work are included in fixed costs. The costs were a lower proportion and the margin a higher proportion in the more profitable years 1993-6 (see the previous edition) but vice-versa in the low profit years of the early 1990s and in 1997 and 1998. Obviously, too, within years the more profitable farms have lower percentage costs, leaving higher percentage margins and vice-versa.

	% Total Output	% Total Gross Margin	% Total Fixed Costs
Variable Costs (excl. casual labour and contract work)	35		
Fixed Costs:			
Labour: Paid (inc. casuals)	10 } 20	15 } 30	18 } 36
Labour: Unpaid	10	15	18
Power & Machinery (inc. contract work)	17·5	27·5	31·5
Labour & Machinery	37·5	57·5	67·5
Rent/Rental Value	10	16	17·5
Occupier's Repairs	2·5	4	5
Sundry Fixed Costs	5	7·5	10
Total Fixed Costs	55	85	100
Margin	10	15	—

Total Gross Margin = 65% of Total Output

3. Lending Criteria

Another set of standards widely used by lending and leasing institutions is as follows:

Finance Charges

(rent, interest, leasing charges, etc.)

% of Gross Output	% of Gross Margin	Lending Criteria
0-10%	0-15%	Normally very safe
11-15%	16-22·5%	Common range, should be safe
16-20%	23-29%	Care required
20% plus	30% plus	Potentially dangerous

As lenders will be well aware, however, these ratios too must be regarded with caution and in conjunction with the farm's level of net worth (% equity) and its trend in recent years, recent trends in its profitability and the potential borrower's record of expenditure both on and off the farm, together with his or her character and potential. Also, of course, some enterprises / types of farming are more risky than others.

2. TAXATION

1. *Income Tax*

Husbands and wives have been taxed independently since April 1990.

(a) *Rates of Tax (1999-2000)*

Slice of taxable income £	Rate per cent	Cumulative Tax (at top of slice) £
0-1,500	10	150
1,501-28,000	23	6,245
Over 28,000	40	—

Savings income, other than dividends, below the basic rate limit of £28,000 will be taxed at 20% and at 40% above that. Dividends will be taxed at 10% for income below the basic rate limit and 32·5% above that.

(b) *Allowances and Reliefs (1999-2000)*

   (i) Personal Allowance: £4,335 (£5,720 if aged 65 to 74 and £5,980 if aged over 75).

  (ii) Married Couple's Allowance: £1,970 (£5,125 where at least one spouse is aged 65 to 74 and £5,195 where one spouse is 75 or older, but reduces if income exceeds £16,800).

Couples are able to choose to allocate this allowance either all to the husband or all to the wife or to share it equally between them. Action is required before the start of the tax year from which election is to have effect. For the 1999-2000 tax year this allowance will be at the reduced rate of 10%. The Married Couple's Allowance is to be abolished from 5 April 2000 except for couples where at least one spouse is 65 or more on that date.

 (iii) Personal Pension Plans. Subject to a maximum income rule of £90,600 a year, full relief is obtainable for premiums which fall within the following limits:

Age at start of tax year	Max. % of earnings
35 or less	17·5
36-45	20·0
46-50	25·0
51-55	30·0
56-60	35·0
61-	40·0

Different percentages apply for continuing Retirement Annuity Premiums.

2. *Private Company Taxation*
   (i) Profits are chargeable to Corporation Tax at 30 per cent (1999-
       2000) except where profits are less than £300,000 and where
       there are no associated companies, when the rate is reduced to
       20 per cent. There is also marginal relief between £300,000 and
       £1·5 million: within this band the marginal rate is 32·5%, the
       rate on the first £300,000 being 20%. A new small companies
       starting rate of tax of 10% will apply to profits of up to £10,000
       from April 2000. Profits between £10,000 and £50,000 will also
       get marginal relief.
   (ii) Capital Gains of companies are charged at the appropriate rate
        of Corporation Tax.
   (iii) Distributions, *e.g.* dividends are not deductible in arriving at
         the amount of Corporation Tax profit. However, the recipient
         of distributions will be credited with a tax payment of 10%
         of distributions received, which will be deemed to discharge
         the liability of lower (10%) and basic rate (23%) taxpayers;
         however, higher rate taxpayers will have to pay additional tax
         of 10% of the net dividend; dividends are treated as the top slice
         of income.
   (iv) Losses. Restricted carry back to one year (previously 3 years)
        with effect from 2 July 1997.

3. *Agricultural Businesses: Other Items.*
   (a) *Assessing Self-Employed Profits*
       From 1997-98 self-employed people will be assessed for tax
       in any tax year on the basis of the profits recorded in the annual
       accounts which end in that tax year, *i.e.* on a 'current year basis'.
   (b) *Livestock*
       Dairy cows or breeding livestock may be treated on the herd
       basis or on a trading stock basis.
       Herd basis: valuation changes are not included in the trading
       account, nor are additions to the herd, but sales from the herd
       and replacements are. On the sale of all or a substantial
       proportion (normally taken as 20% or more) of the herd, no tax
       is paid on any profit over the original cost price, nor is there
       any relief for loss.
       Trading stock basis: purchases, sales and valuation changes
       are all included in the trading account. Under this method stock
       should be valued at the lower of cost (or cost of production) and
       net realisable value. Where animals are home-produced and it
       is not possible to ascertain actual costs from farm records the
       "deemed" cost may be used. This is 60% of market value for
       cattle and 75% for sheep and pigs.
   (c) *Stock Valuations: Crops*
       The deemed cost method allows 75% of market value to be
       used, but market value must include a proportion of the relevant
       area aid payment (including set-aside).

(d) *Allowances for Capital Expenditure*

Machinery and Plant (whether new or second hand). For machinery purchased after 30 October 1993 a 25 per cent annual writing down allowance is available on a reducing balance basis. As a temporary measure small and medium-sized businesses will be eligible to claim a 50 per cent allowance for the first year for machinery and plant purchased in the year ending 1 July 1998 and a 40 per cent first year allowance for machinery and plant purchased in the years ending 1 July 1999 and 1 July 2000. The writing down allowances will normally be calculated on a "pool" basis. However, where it is expected that a machine will be sold within five years of acquisition and realise less than its written-down value for tax it will be possible for the taxpayer to elect to have allowances calculated separately for each machine. Although the annual writing down allowance will still be 25 per cent this system will enable balancing allowances to be claimed when a machine is sold for less than its written-down value. If at the end of five years the machine has not been sold its tax written-down value will be transferred to the main machinery pool. Motor cars are included in a separate "pool" in the year of purchase, on which a 25 per cent writing down allowance is available. The allowance is restricted to a maximum of £3,000 for motor cars with a written-down value of more than £12,000. Special rules apply where a motor car is only partly used for business purposes.

Machinery Leasing. Tax allowances for rental payments on financial leases are spread to reflect the commercial depreciation of the asset. This may mean that full tax relief for rental payments may not be gained in the years in which the payments are made.

Buildings. Farm buildings, fencing, drainage and other improvements (including up to one-third of farmhouses) qualify for a writing-down allowance of 4 per cent annually, given equally over 25 years. These annual allowances are normally available to succeeding owners during the 25 year period. Balancing allowances can now be claimed where buildings are demolished and also on the transfer of the land, but only with the new owner's consent.

(e) *Losses*

Losses can normally be set off against other income in the year in which they are incurred and in the prior year. If other income is insufficient in the year when the loss occurs and in the prior year, any unrelieved losses can be carried forward and set off against future profits from farming. Special rules apply to prevent abuse of loss relief provisions by "hobby" farmers who are not running their farms on a commercial basis with a view to producing a profit: normally losses are disallowed against other income after 5 consecutive years of loss.

With effect from 5 April 1991 trading losses may be set against capital gains.

(f) *Profit Averaging*

This relief is to enable farmers, other than companies, to average their taxable profits over two consecutive years. Where the difference between the profits of two consecutive years is 30 per cent or more of the higher profits, the total profits for the two years are equally divided between the two years. Marginal relief is available where the difference is less than 30 per cent but more than 25 per cent of the higher profits. Profit for the purposes of tax averaging calculations used to be before the deduction of capital allowances. Under the new current year basis profit will be after the deduction of capital allowances. There is a two year limit in which to make the claim.

4. Capital Gains Tax

Applies to capital gains by an individual. Capital gains accruing to companies are chargeable to Corporation Tax. A capital gain is the difference between the acquisition value and the sale price. In the case of agricultural property, allowance would be made for any capital expenditure undertaken to improve the property, even though the expenditure may have obtained a buildings allowance referred to at 3 (d) above. Capital Gains Tax is chargeable only on the disposal (including gifts) of assets.

For assets owned on 31st March, 1982 and disposed of subsequently, providing an appropriate election is made (within two years), only the gain attributable to the period after that date is taxable, *i.e.* the chargeable gain is the gain from a valuation at 31st March, 1982 to the date of disposal.

An indexation allowance for inflation applies to periods of ownership between 31 March 1982 and 1 April 1998. The acquisition value of the asset (or its value at 31 March 1982, if it was owned prior to that date) is indexed-up for changes in the Retail Price Index. Tapering relief was introduced in 1998 to replace the indexation allowance and applies to periods of ownership after 5 April 1998. The taper reduces the amount of the gain that is liable to tax according to the length of the period of ownership and it is more generous for business assets than for non-business assets. The operation of the taper is illustrated below.

Number of complete years of ownership after 5 April 1998	Percentage of gain chargeable to tax	
	Business assets	Non-business assets
0	100	100
1	92·5	100
2	85·0	100
3	77·5	95
4	70·0	90
5	62·5	85
6	55·0	80
7	47·5	75
8	40·0	70
9	32·5	65
10	25·0	60

The first £7,100 of capital gains realised by an individual in a tax year are free of tax. Capital gains in excess of £7,100 are treated as the top slice of income and are charged to tax as savings income, *i.e.* below the basic limit of £28,000 they will be taxed at 20% and 40% above that.

Retirement Relief. Relief is also available to farmers who retire over the age of 50. The first £250,000 of gain and half the gains between £250,000 and £1 million are exempt (subject to claimants meeting conditions) where they accrue from the disposal by sale or gift of a family business or shares or securities in a family trading company. This exemption also applies to individuals who have to retire before reaching 50 because of ill-health. The relief only applies in full where the business has been owned for at least 10 years and the person has been either the proprietor, a partner or a full-time working director in a family company. Relief is also available in part for those over the age of 50 who have held the assets for more than one year, increasing to full relief after 10 years. However, as a result of tapering relief in 1998, retirement relief is to be phased out over a five year period as follows:—

Year	100 per cent relief on gains up to £	50 per cent relief on gains between £
1998-1999	250,000	250,001-1 million
1999-2000	200,000	200,001-800,000
2000-2001	150,000	150,001-600,000
2001-2002	100,000	100,001-400,000
2002-2003	50,000	50,001-200,000

Payment of tax may be deferred on gains accruing from the sale of business assets (including land and buildings occupied and used for trade purposes, fixed plant and machinery, milk, ewe and suckler cow quotas, and from the sale of shares in a family business) if part or all of the proceeds are spent on acquiring new assets liable to the tax. The tax is deferred by deducting the gain from the acquisition price of the new asset. Normally it can only be done if the new asset is acquired within 12 months before and 3 years after the disposal of the old assets. Disposal and acquisition dates for Capital Gains purposes are almost always contract, not completion, dates.

Payments of tax may be deferred where disposal is by gift. This relief only applies to gifts of business assets, land which qualifies for agricultural property relief at either the 100 per cent or 50 per cent rate under Inheritance Tax (see next section) and gifts which lead to an immediate charge to Inheritance Tax (*e.g.* gifts into a discretionary trust). The amount of the chargeable gain which would normally have accrued to the donor will be held over; the value at which the donee is deemed to acquire the asset will be its market value reduced by the amount of the donor's chargeable gain held over. The held over gain is netted down by any time apportionment, indexation allowance, or any retirement relief available to the donor, but not tapering relief. Where deferral is not available payment of tax by interest bearing annual instalments over 10 years will be allowed for gifts of land, controlling share holdings and minority share holdings in unquoted companies.

Should a transaction produce a loss, this may be set against any long term chargeable gains arising in the same year or, if these are insufficient, those accruing in subsequent years. Losses brought forward will be used only to the extent necessary to reduce gains for the year to £7,100. For disposals after 30th November 1993 indexation allowances (for inflation) may not be utilised to create or increase a capital loss. Losses brought forward are set against any gains before applying tapering relief, so that claims need to be made very carefully.

After 5th April 1991, where a trading loss can be set off against other income in the same or following year, for income tax purposes, any unused loss can be set against capital gains for those years.

Payment of Capital Gains Tax is due on 31st January following the tax year of disposal on the self-assessment return.

5. *Inheritance Tax*

This tax, which replaced Capital Transfer Tax, is charged on lifetime gifts and transfers on death.

Slice of Chargeable Transfer	Rate per cent
£1- 231,000	0
Over 231,000	40

Outright gifts to individuals, accumulation and maintenance trusts and interest in possession trusts will be exempt from tax at the time of the gift. All other gifts will be taxed at half the above rates at the time of the transfer. Tax will be charged on the value of an individual's estate at death plus the value of all gifts made within seven years of death. Allowance is made for any tax paid on lifetime gifts included in the value of the estate on death. Relief is given for outright gifts made more than three years before death according to the following scale:

Years between gift and death	Percentage of the full charge to tax
0-3	100
3-4	80
4-5	60
5-6	40
6-7	20

Exemptions include: transfers between husband and wife; the first £3,000 of gift made by a donor in the income tax year and separately up to £250 per year to any number of persons; gifts made out of income which form part of normal expenditure; marriage gifts within limits of £5,000 for a parent, £2,500 for a lineal ancestor and £1,000 for other donors.

Relief may be available for agricultural land. Subject to a general rule that the agricultural land must have been occupied by the transferor (or by his controlled company) for two years, or owned by the transferor for 7 years and occupied for agricultural purposes by someone else before any relief is granted, the relief is at two different rates. If the basis of valuation is vacant possession, the taxable value of the land is reduced by 100%. If the basis of valuation is tenanted value, the taxable value of the land is reduced by 50% of that tenanted value. Ownership and occupation periods normally include prior periods of ownership or occupation by husbands and wives. From 1st September 1995 100% relief will apply to new lettings of agricultural land as farm business tenancies.

Relief is also available in respect to "business property" transferred during lifetime or on death. The relief extends to the business assets of a proprietor and the interest of a partner or controlling shareholder of a company in the business capital. The value of such property, providing certain tests are satisfied (*e.g.* it has been owned by the transferor for two years preceding transfer), is reduced by 100 per cent. Where a partner or controlling shareholder owns assets (*e.g.* land) that the business uses the value will be reduced by 50 per cent. Shareholdings in unquoted companies are eligible for a 100 per cent reduction in market value.

Lifetime gifts of property eligible for Agricultural and Business Property Relief have to be retained (or replaced by similar property) until the death of the donor (or earlier death of the donee) if those reliefs are to be available when the tax (or additional tax) becomes payable subsequent to the donor's death.

In the case of the transfer of property eligible for Agricultural Relief and Business Property Relief the tax can be paid by annual instalments over ten years free of interest.

6. *Stamp Duty*

Stamp Duty arises when the title to property changes hands. In the case of land the duty will usually be paid by the purchaser; the rate payable is 1 per cent on the full value where the consider-ation (purchase price) or value is over £60,000 and less than £250,000, 2·5 per cent if the consideration is more than £250,000 and less than £500,000, and 3·5 per cent if the consideration is more than £500,000. However, the 1 per cent ad valorem duty does not apply on lifetime voluntary gifts. Such gifts are only liable to a 50p fixed duty. Stamp duty on share purchases and sales is at the rate of 0·5 per cent.

7. Value Added Tax

Agricultural businesses with a turnover of taxable goods and services in excess of £51,000 per annum (from 1 April 1999) are required to register for VAT. Businesses with a turnover below this limit may apply for voluntary registration. The standard rate of VAT is 17·5 per cent. Most agricultural products are zero rated for VAT purposes. VAT has to be paid on certain inputs. Registered businesses are eligible to reclaim the tax paid where the goods or services purchased have been used in the production of zero-rated supplies.

A flat rate scheme is available to farmers as an alternative to registering for VAT. Farmers under the flat rate scheme do not have to submit tax returns and consequently cannot reclaim tax.

They can, however, charge (and keep) a flat rate addition of 4 per cent when they sell to VAT registered customers goods and services which qualify. This addition is not VAT but acts as compensation for losing input tax on purchases. The local VAT office may refuse to issue a certificate to participate in the flat rate scheme if this would mean the farmer would recover substantially (£3,000) more than through the normal system.

8. National Insurance Contributions (1999/2000)

Class 1.

Employee's weekly earnings Not contracted out	Employee	Employer
Below £66·00	Nil	Nil
£66·01 to £83·00	10%	Nil
£83·01 to £500·00	10%	12·2%
Over £500·00	No additional liability	12·2%

Contracted out.

	Employee	Employer	
	Salary related scheme	Salary related scheme	Money purchase scheme
Below £66·00	Nil	Nil	Nil
£66·01 to £83·00	8·4%	Nil	Nil
£83·01 to £500·00	8·4%	9·2%	11·6%
Over £500·00	No additional liability	12·2%	12·2%

Class 2.

Self-employed flat rate (no liability if earnings below £3,770 a year) £6·55 a week

Class 3.

Non-employed (voluntary) flat rate £6·45 a week

Class 4.

Self-employed. On profits or gains between £7,530 a year and £26,000 a year) 6% (max. £1,108·20 a year)

3. GRANTS

1. *GRANTS FOR PROCESSING AND MARKETING AGRICULTURAL PRODUCTS*

A. MARKETING DEVELOPMENT SCHEME

This scheme was withdrawn in England from 5 November 1996 but continues to operate in Scotland, Wales and Northern Ireland. It is administered by MAFF and provides grant aid to individual farmers and growers or groups of producers, food processors or manufacturers and trade associations or industry bodies, towards the non-capital costs of projects designed to improve the efficiency of the food marketing chain. Assistance is given at the rate of 50 per cent of approved expenditure on:—

— Feasibility studies and market research.
— Costs of establishment, expansion and merger of producer groups including legal and accountancy costs, redundancy costs of key staff and the costs of recruiting new members.
— Salaries of key staff of a project including recruitment costs.
— Production and dissemination of suitable promotional material intended to encourage the take-up of industry-wide projects.
— Promotional events to demonstrate marketing innovation or excellence of marketing practice.
— Training of directors and key staff members.
— Expenses of outside directors.

The maximum grant payable for a project is £150,000.

B. PROCESSING AND MARKETING GRANT

Under EU Regulation 866/90 the UK Government and the European Agricultural Guidance Fund jointly fund grant aid towards the cost of investment aimed at the improvement, rationalisation of the treatment, processing and marketing of agricultural produce. Grants at the rate of 30% will be available for projects costing a minimum of £70,000. The maximum grant will be £1·2 million in most cases. As funds for this scheme are limited it is likely that there will be stiff competition for these grants. The scheme was withdrawn in England from 31st March 1996 but continues to operate in Scotland, Wales and Northern Ireland.

C. FRESH FRUIT AND VEGETABLE PRODUCER ORGANISATIONS

Producer organisations recognised under European Commission Regulations 2200/96 may apply for a contribution towards an operating fund which the organisation has set up to finance a planned programme to improve performance in marketing, produce quality and environmental considerations. The contribution from the European Commission will be a minimum of 2·5 per cent and a maximum of 4·5 per cent of the producer organisation's turnover and may be no more than 50 per cent of eligible expenditure under the planned programme. Further details are obtainable from the Intervention Board.

2. *OBJECTIVE 5B FUNDING*

Six areas in England have been designated under the European Union Objective 5b (rural development) programme. They may thereby benefit from EAGGF (European Agricultural Guidance Fund) assistance towards the cost of projects which provide new opportunities for developing and diversifying the rural economy. Projects should have the potential to generate business opportunities which sustain rural development and employment and, where appropriate, conserve and enhance the environment. They could include farm diversification, the development of speciality products, promoting rural tourism, and environmental initiatives.

Funding is limited and projects are considered on a competitive basis. Projects serving the needs of individual businesses may be submitted but those which benefit groups of farms are more likely to be successful. EAGGF funding should be matched by an equivalent level of UK public money. Application forms can be obtained from MAFF Regional Service Centres.

The programme ceases at the end of 1999 and discussions are taking place concerning the arrangements for its replacement.

3. *GRANTS FOR ENVIRONMENTAL IMPROVEMENT*

A. ENVIRONMENTALLY SENSITIVE AREAS (ESAs)

The first ESAs were designated in 1987. Currently there are 43 designated areas in the UK, of which 22 are in England, covering a total area of 1,150,000 hectares, some 10% of its agricultural land. Within these areas farmers are offered annual payments if they enter into 10 year agreements to manage their land, buildings, walls and other features in ways which will conserve the traditional environment. The levels of annual payments vary between ESAs and between different tiers within ESAs depending upon the severity of the restrictions imposed upon farming activities and any extra costs associated with additional work which farmers are required to undertake. They can be substantial, *e.g.* £430 per ha under tier 3 of the Somerset Levels and Moors ESA, where the requirement is to create wet winter and spring conditions. Farmers may submit a Conservation Plan which is aimed at enhancing the environment, *e.g.* by planting new hedgerows, which, if accepted, will entitle them to grant aid towards the cost of undertaking the work. Farmers in ESAs can enter a voluntary public access option and will be paid £274 per mile (£170 per km) of access route plus grants of up to 80% of relevant capital work.

Arable land which is subject to an ESA agreement will qualify for area payments or set-aside if it is used to grow eligible arable crops. Arable land reverted to grassland or heathland under an ESA agreement is not eligible for area payments.

B. GRANTS FOR LANDSCAPE CONSERVATION

See pages 207-8

C. COUNTRYSIDE STEWARDSHIP SCHEME

This scheme offers capital and annual payments for conserving, managing and re-creating valued landscapes. The following landscape types and features have been targeted: chalk and limestone grassland, lowland heath, waterside landscapes, coastal areas, historic landscapes (such as deer parks), old orchards, meadows and pastures, arable field margins, Community Forests, countryside around towns, and uplands. Participants must enter a 10 year agreement. Annual payments range from £4 per hectare for managing heather moorland up to £275 per hectare for recreating lowland heath and £280 per hectare for recreating grassland on cultivated land. They are reviewed on a fixed three-year cycle. An additional payment of £35 per hectare is available for allowing public access, with further supplements for linear access strips for walking, horse riding, cycling and the disabled. The scheme also offers grant aid towards the cost of restoring hedgerows and field boundaries which are either long-established features of the landscape, important wildlife habitats or of high amenity value. The scheme is administered by MAFF and is available throughout England, except in ESAs, where it only applies for items which are not available under the ESA scheme. Priority is given to proposals offering the best potential for environmental improvement and public benefit.

D. ARABLE STEWARDSHIP SCHEME

This scheme provides aid to encourage farmers to manage arable land in ways which encourage wildlife. It is being piloted in two areas, one in the East Midlands and the other in East Anglia, as part of Countryside Stewardship. Five main land management options are available under five or six year agreements:

1. Overwintered stubbles
1. Undersown spring cereals
3. Crop margins and conservation headlands
4. Field margins
5. Wildlife seed mixtures

Payment rates can be substantial, *e.g.* £540 per hectare for overwintered cereal stubbles followed by a spring/summer fallow. Priority for acceptance will be given to applications which offer the greatest benefit to wildlife.

E. NITRATE SENSITIVE AREAS (NSAs)

In 1990 ten pilot NSAs were set up in England with the aim of reducing nitrate levels in water supplies to below the EC-permitted levels of 50 mg/litre. A further 22 new NSAs were established in 1994 under the EU AgricEnvironmental Regulation (2078/92), adding a further 25,000 ha to the 10,500 ha of the pilot NSAs. The ten pilot schemes are now incorporated within the scheme for the 22 new NSAs. The scheme is now closed to new entrants but existing agreements continue until the end of the five-year term.

Under the scheme, farmers who change their farming practices to reduce nitrate leaching receive payments of between £65 and £625 per hectare. Entry into the scheme is voluntary. Farmers will have to enter whole fields, or, in the case of the arable conversion option, parts of fields of at least 4 hectares in area. Agreements are for five years' duration. Farmers will have three main options available to them:

(i) Arable conversion—which requires the conversion of arable land to extensive grassland. Sub-options include:

a.	Grassland with no fertilizer and no grazing	£450-£550/ha
b.	As A but with native grass species	£525-£625/ha
c.	As A but with limited grazing	£420-£520/ha
d.	Reversion to grassland with limited fertilizer and grazing	£340-£440/ha

Alternatively, arable land which is planted to a MAFF approved mix of native grass species and maintained as unfertilized, ungrazed grassland for 5 years counts towards set-aside obligations. Payment is at the annual set-aside rate (£306 per ha in England in 1998/9) plus an additional environmental payment of £50 per ha.

(ii) Low nitrogen grassland—which requires a change from intensive to extensive grassland management. Payment is £250/ha.

(iii) Low nitrogen arable—where the level of nitrogen applied is restricted. Two sub-options include:

a.	Nitrogen usage restricted to 150 kg/ha for all 5 years of the scheme and no potatoes or vegetable brassicas	£80-£105/ha
b.	Nitrogen usage restricted to 200 kg/ha in 1 out of 5 years and to 150 kg/ha in remaining 4 years. No restrictions on cropping.	£65/ha

F. FARM WASTE GRANT SCHEME

This scheme provides grant aid to farmers in Nitrate Vulnerable Zones who undertake investment in farm waste handling facilities in order to comply with restrictions on the spreading of livestock manures. Grant is available at 25 per cent of eligible expenditure up to an investment ceiling of £85,000. Eligible expenditure includes manure, slurry and silage effluent stores, and ancillary items and costs integral to the storage facility. Landscaping and professional fees associated with the work may also be eligible for grant aid.

G. HABITAT SCHEME

Introduced in 1994, this scheme was designed to encourage farmers to take land out of production for up to 20 years to create important wildlife habitats. A number of options were available. The annual payments were intended to reflect the cost of entering land into the scheme.

	Annual Payment (£ per Ha)	
	Land currently in arable/temporary grass	Land currently in permanent grass
Creation of intertidal habitats, particularly salt marshes for birds	525 (448*)	250
Establish/enhance water fringe habitats in designated pilot areas by:		
— creating buffer strips with no agricultural production	485 (405*)	240
— extensive grazing	435	125

(*where the land is counted as set-aside)

A supplement of £40/ha may be paid where measures are then taken to raise the water level.

In June 1999 MAFF announced that it would be consulting on proposals to bring the scheme to an end, integrating its more successful elements into the Countryside Stewardship Scheme

H. MOORLAND SCHEME

Introduced in 1995, this scheme is designed to encourage the conservation and enhancement of heather and other shrubby moorland vegetation in those parts of the Less Favoured Areas which are not part of Environmentally Sensitive Areas. Sheep farmers who adopt a more extensive system of production will receive an annual payment for each ewe eligible for Hill Livestock Compensatory Allowances by which their flock is reduced. Applicants must enter at least 20 hectares of moorland containing at least 25% heather and the flock must be reduced by at least 10 animals. Compensation is at the rate of £30 per ewe removed.

The scheme is scheduled to close to new entrants in 1999. The menu of items available under the Countryside Stewardship Scheme has been expanded to include options for managing moorland habitat.

4. *GRANTS FOR REDUNDANT FARM BUILDINGS*

Grants may be available for the refurbishment of redundant buildings. The scheme, which was originally administered by the Rural Development Commission, has been transferred to regional Rural Development Agencies, which may target specific areas for assistance — usually those where the need to create employment opportunities is greatest. Grant aid may be available for up to 25% of refurbishment or conversion costs entailed in bringing redundant buildings back into use for various qualifying activities, which include manufacturing, servicing, craft, office accommodation, retail accommodation, tourism and leisure *but not agriculture.*

5. *OTHER GRANTS/SCHEMES*

Woodland Grant Scheme and Farm Woodland Premium Scheme (See pages 55-57), Countryside Access Scheme (See page 63), Organic Farming Scheme (See page 47), Beef and Sheep (including Hill Livestock) (See page 92).

VIII. MISCELLANEOUS DATA

1. CONSERVATION COSTS

Note: Costs can vary quite widely, depending on geographical location and the type and size of the job.

(N.B. *Abbreviations.* CA: Countryside Agency; FC: Forestry Commission; EN: English Nature; BTCV: British Trust for Conservation Volunteers).

Hedge Trimming (flail). Contract labour, £13 to £15/hour. 3 miles a day (maximum; much less if overgrown or difficult). Aug.-Feb. *(not* April-July). Every 2 or 3 years; *(possibly* annually).

Hedge Laying. Contract labour, £3-£5 a metre, or £5 per hour. Contractor, 15 metres/day; BTCV, 5 metres/day per person. Nov./ March. Every 8 to 20 years. Grant aid: CA, MAFF, EN. LANTRA quotes £1·50 a metre plus 60p a metre for stakers and pleachers, 40 metres a day.

Hedge Planting. Transplants av. £25/100; netlon guards av. 25p; canes av. 10p; fencing (labour and materials): stock proof £2/metre, stock and rabbit proof up to £3/metre. Overall, £1·80/metre unguarded and unfenced, £6·50/metre guarded and fenced. Contract labour: planting up to £2/metre, fencing up to £2·50/metre. Contractor 100-150 metres/day; BTCV 20 metres/day. Pref Oct./March. Above includes repair. Grant aid: CA, MAFF, EN.

Hedge Coppicing. By hand: 2 men and a chain saw, 100 metres/day, £2/metre. Contractor: tractor mounted saw, driver and 2 men, 13 metres/ hour, £27/hour. Grant aid: CA, MAFF.

Dry Stone Walling £12.50/square metre with skilled contract labour. Cornish Hedging: £25-£40/metre length depending upon type of stone. Grant aid: CA, MAFF.

Amenity Tree Planting; (half acre block or less). Transplants av. 75p; shelter plus stake and tie av. £1; stake av. 50p; whip av. 70p. (50p-£1); rabbit spiral guard 30p; netlon guard av. 50p (but 15p in a 50 m roll); cane av. 10p. Trees per man day: farmer 200, contractor 400; (large-scale, 33 man days/ha). Nov.-April. Grant aid: CA, MAFF.

Shelter Belts. Per 100 metre length: 100 large species (oak, lime, etc.) £35; 66 medium species (cherry, birch, etc.) £25; 100 shrubs, £30; 166 tree stakes, shelters and ties, £250; total £340; (site preparation, weed control, labour and fencing extra). MAFF standard costs £637·50/ha; windbreaks £33·85/ha. Grant aid: CA, MAFF.

Woodland Establishment. Conifers £150/1000. To supply and plant oak or beech transplants in tubes £2 each. Rabbit fencing £2·80/ metre. Contract labour: conifers at 2m (inc. trees) £580/ha; broadleaves at 3m (inc. trees) £800/ha; forest transplants (not inc. trees) £70/1000. 12·5 days/ha (contractor). Nov.-April. (Above not inc. maintenance). Grant aid: FC, CA, MAFF.

Forestry: General. Contract labour: chain sawing £8/hr., brush cutting £7·15/hr., extracting timber/pulp £4-£10/tonne, chemical spot weeding 5p-7p/tree, rhodedendron control £600-£800/acre.

Pond Construction. Butyl lining (0·75mm) £5/m²; other lining £2·5/ m². Contract labour: Hymac £12·50/hr., 150 Komatsu £16/hr.; bulldozer D6C £16·50/hr. Autumn (dry ground conditions). Grant aid: MAFF, CA (discretionary), EN (possibly).

Pond Maintenance. Hymac £15/hr.; Backhoe £12·50/hr. 5m²/day (BTCV); 100 m²/day (contractor). Timing: probably winter; time depends on ground condition and species whose life cycles may be disturbed. Every 5 to 50 years. Grant aid: CA, EN.

Ditch Maintenance. Backhoe excavator £12·50/hr. Preferably in winter. Every 3 to 7 years on rotation. Grant aid: MAFF (improvement plan), EN (conservation interest).

Pollarding and Tree Surgery. Pollard: £40-£60/stool; surgery: £150/ tree. Pollarding: 2 or 3 trees/day. Surgery: 2 days/tree. Winter. Pollard every 20-40 years. Grant aid: CA (discretionary).

Grassland Establishment. Grass seed/wild flower mixes: £400-£1800/ ha. Grasses only mix, low seed rate, £200-£350/ha. 11 ha/day. Pref. Aug.-Oct. Grant aid: possibly CA for small areas as part of whole farm plan.

Reducing Pesticide Drift. Use of appropriate spray nozzles: tilt jets £22-£25 for 6; lo-drift nozzles £15 for 6.

Permanent Grass Margins at Field Edges. To provide wildlife benefits and help control pernicious weeds, reducing herbicides at the field edge. A sterile strip provides virtually no wildlife benefit and the initial establishment costs may be offset by savings in maintenance costs in future years. Establishment costs (2m wide) per 100m run, approximately £3, with maintenance (mowing) 50p. Subsequent years, mowing only.

Fertilizer Losses at Field Boundaries. For a 12m spread pattern, at 150 kg/ ha, loss is approx. 30p per 100m per application, or £3 for a 6 ha field (450 × 150m). Loss avoided by driving further away from the field boundary/using a tilting hopper mechanism/using an appropriate border disc or deflector, costing £90.

GRANT AID. A summary of "Grants for Landscape Conservation" is available from the CA, FC, MAFF and EN. Countryside Agency grants are usually available through local authorities.

Acknowledgement. Above information supplied by Farming and Wildlife Advisory Group (FWAG). Sources: County FWAG personnel, BTCV, local authorities.

2. FERTILIZER PRICES

A. *Compounds*

Analysis			Price per tonne
N	P₂O₅	K₂O	£
0	24	24	117.50
0	18	36	117.50
0	20	30	117.50
0	30	15	117.50
0	30	20	120
5	24	24	127·50
8	24	24	130
10	24	24	132.50
10	10	30	127·50
12	15	20	125
13	13	20	110
15	15	20	120
15	15	19	117.50
17	17	17	122.50
20	4	14	102·50
20	10	10	105
20	8	12	102.50
22	11	11	112.50
24	4	4	90
25	5	5	100
25	0	16	90

B. *Straights*

Type	Price per tonne
	£
Ammonium Nitrate: UK (34·5% N.)	87.50
Ammonium Nitrate: Imported (34·5% N.)	77.50
Sulphate of Ammonia (21% N.)	108
Urea (46% N.): granular/ prills	102·50/87·50
Liquid Nitrogen	70
Triple Superphosphate (47% P_2O_5)	132·50
Muriate of Potash (Granular) (60% K_2O)	112·50

Average price (p) per kg: N   :   25.5   (UK AN)
                        P_2O_5 :   28   (triple supers).
                        K_2O :   18·75   (muriate).

The prices above are for fertilizer *delivered* in *bags*; delivery in bulk averages £7/tonne less. They are approximate average prices in mid-1999; they vary according to area and bargaining power. Discounts for cash payment approximately £2·50/tonne. Where separate prices are quoted for granular and blended the former are generally a few pounds more. They assume delivery in 20 tonne lots; add approximately £2 for 10 tonne lots, £4 for 6-9 tonne lots, £6 for 4-5 tonne lots.

3. MANURIAL VALUE OF SLURRY AND FARMYARD MANURE

1. *Composition (% by weight)*

	N	P_2O_5	K_2O
Undiluted Slurry			
(faeces plus urine, or droppings):			
Cow	0·5	0·2	0·5
Pig	0·6	0·2	0·2
Poultry	1·7	1·4	0·7
Farmyard Manure:			
Cattle	0·5	0·4	0·6
Pig	0·6	0·6	0·4
Poultry...	1·8	1·8	1·2

2. *Available Nutrients* (kg)

	N	P_2O_5	K_2O
Undiluted Slurry (per 10m³*):			
Cow	35	11	58
Pig	42	11	23
Poultry...	118	82	82

(* = 10 tonnes; 10,000 litres)

Farmyard Manure (per 10 tonnes):	N	P_2O_5	K_2O
Cattle	17	20	46
Pig	20	31	31
Poultry	110	92	92

3. *Amount per head*

(faeces plus urine, or droppings)	litres per day	N	kg per year (1) P_2O_5	K_2O
1 dairy cow	40	51	16	84
1 pig (dry meal fed)	4·5	6·8	1·8	3·7
100 laying hens	13	55	39	39

(1) `housed all year and no losses.

4. AGROCHEMICAL COSTS (1999)

Only the names of the active ingredients are given below, with their principal use. These materials should only be applied in accordance with the manufacturers' recommendations. Application rates can vary and there are differences between the prices of various proprietary brands. The list is not intended to be exhaustive and there is no implied criticism of materials omitted

Crop	Function	Material	Approx. Cost £ per ha per application
Cereals	Herbicides: General	MCPA	3·10- 7·70
		Mecoprop	8·75-10·50
		Dicamba+Mecoprop+MCPA	20·00
		Ioxynil+Bromoxynil	10·00-20·00
		Ioxynil+Bromoxynil+ Mecoprop	24·00-34·00
		Metsulfuron-methyl	13·00-15·00
	Undersown	MCPA+MCPB	28·00-29·00
	Crops	Benazolin+2, 4-DB+MCPA	38·50
		Linuron+2, 4-DB+MCPA	36·25
	Blackgrass	Chlorotoluron	14·00-17·50
		Isoproturon	8·00-14·00
		Isoproturon+Diflufenican	21·00-24·00
		Isoproturon+Trifluralin	15·00-22·00
		Clodinafop-propargyl+ trifluralin	22.00-25.00
	Cleavers	Fluroxypyr	15·00-20.00
	Wild Oats	Difenzoquat	38·00-50·00
		Tri-allate	25·00
		Diclofop-methyl	19·00-38·00
	Wild Oats	Clodinafop-propargyl	30.00
	and Blackgrass	Fenoxaprop-P-ethyl	25.00
	Growth Regulator	Chlormequat	3·50
		Chlormequat + Choline Chloride	2·80- 4·00
		Chlormequat + Mepiquat Chloride + 2 - chloroethylphosphonic acid	15·00-20·00
		2-chloroethylphosphonic acid + Mepiquat Chloride	10·50-21·00
		Trinescapac-ethyl	12.00-16.00
	Fungicides	Azoxystrobin	40·00
		Benomyl	13·00
		Fenpropimorph	15·00-20·00
		Prochloraz	14·00-18·00
		Propiconazole	12·50
		Triadimefon	23·50
		Expoxiconazole	25.00
		Tebuconazole	14.00-20.00
		Cyproconazole	21.75
	Seed Dressing	Ethirimol + Flutriafol + Thiabendazole	12·00-18·50
		Fuberidazole + Triadimenol	11·00-16·00
		Fludioxonil	5.50-8.25
	Aphicide	Cypermethrin	3.00
		Deltamethrin	3·50- 4·25
		Pirimicarb	10·00-12·00
	Slug Killer	Metaldehyde	12·00-13·00
		Methiocarb	37·00-40·00

Crop	Function	Material	Approx. Cost £ per ha per application
Oilseed Rape	Herbicides	Propyzamide	27·00-38·00
		Trifluralin	5·50- 6·00
		Metazachlon	31·50
		Cyonazine	9·00-12·00
	Insecticide	Deltamethrin	4·25- 5·50
		Pirimicarb	11·00-18·00
		Alphacypermethrin	3·50- 7·00
	Fungicide	Iprodione	30·00-45·00
		Prochloraz + Carbendazim	19·00-27·00
		Tebuconazole	10·00-20·00
Potatoes	Herbicides: Pre-emergence	Monolinuron	31·00-47·00
	Pre-and post-	Metribuzin	25·00-50·00
	emergence	Terbutryne + Terbuthylazine	21·00-31·00
	Blight Control	Fentin Acetate + Maneb	14·50
		Oxadixyl+Cymoxanil+Mancozeb	25·00
		Mancozeb	5·00-6·00
		Mancozeb+Metalaxyl	19·00-24·00
	Haulm Dessicant	Diquat	43·50
	Sprouting Suppressant	Tecnazene	£4·60/tonne
Sugar Beet	Herbicides: Pre-emergence	Chloridazon:	
		overall	15·00-45·00
		band spray	5·00-15·00
		Metamitron:	
		low dose	28·00-30·00
		band spray	25·00-34·00
	Post-emergence	Phenmedipham:	
		low dose	9·00
		band spray	6·00- 8·00
	Insecticide	Aldicarb	50·00-52·00
		Pirimicarb	10.00-12.00
Beans	Herbicide	Simazine	3·75- 5·00
	Fungicide	Chlorothalonil	15.00-18·00
		Tebuconazole	20·00
		Cyproconazole+Chlorothalonil	31·25
Peas	Herbicide	Terbutryne + Terbuthylazine	21·00-31·00
Beans and Peas	Insecticide	Pirimicarb	10·00-12·00
		Deltamethrin	5·50- 7·00
Maize	Herbicide	Atrazine	5·75- 7·50
Brassicas	Herbicides	Desmetryne	53·00-81·00
		Propachlor	59·00-85·00
		Trifluralin	5·50- 6·50

Crop	Function	Material	Approx. Cost £ per ha per application
Broadleaved Crops	Grass weeds and volunteer cereals	Fluazifop-P-butyl	33·00-65·00
		Propaquizafop	21·00-45·00
		Cycloxydim	35·00
Grassland	Herbicides	Limuron+2, 4-DB+MCPA	36·00
		MCPA	6·50-11·00
		MCPA + MCPB	28·50
		Mecoprop+ Dicamba	62·00
General	Weed and Grass Killer		
	General	Paraquat	9·00-24·00
	Prior to Direct Drilling	Paraquat	18·00-42·00
	Couch Grass Control	Glyphosate	9·00-12·00
	WoodyWeed Control	Triclopyr	110·00

Note. The above prices are based largely on retail prices paid by farmers (spring 1999) and reflect the discounts available where there are competing products from several manufacturers.

5. FEEDINGSTUFF PRICES

		£ per tonne
Cattle	Dairy: High Energy	110 - 140
	Medium Energy	100 - 120
	Low Energy	95 - 110
	Concentrate	185 - 245
	Beef: Pellets	87 - 115
	Concentrate	175 - 205
	Calf: Milk Substitute	1,175 -1,225
	High Fat (bags)	880 - 900
	Calf Weaner Pellets	120 - 135
	Calf Rearer Nuts	115 - 128
Sheep	Lamb Pellets	105 - 120
	Sheep/lamb cake	90 - 105
	Ewe cake	100 - 115
Horses	Horse and Pony Pencils	165 - 185
Goats	Goat Nuts	155 - 175
Pigs	Piglet Weaner	160 - 180
	Sow Nuts	100 - 120
	Early Grower Pellets	140 - 170
	Grower/Finisher Pellets	110 - 140
	Sow Concentrate	220 - 230
	Grower Concentrate	225 - 235
Poultry	Chick and Rearer Feeds	175 - 200
	Layers Feeds	155 - 170
	Broiler Feeds	165 - 190
	Turkey Feeds	165 - 190
Straight Feeds	Fishmeal (English; 66/72%)	275 - 475
	Soya Bean Meal (45/48%)	105 - 150
	Rapeseed Meal (34/36%)	60 - 95
	Palm Kernel Meal/Cake (17%CP)	55 - 80
	Linseed Cake	105 - 120
	Sunflower Seed Pellets (30/33%)	55 - 80
	Cottonseed Exp. pellets (40/42%)	75 - 110
	Grass Cubes (16%)	60 - 90
	Wheatfeed	60 - 90
	Maize Germ Meal	80 - 105
	Maize Gluten (20-23%)	65 - 100
	Molasses	70 - 90
	Sugar Beet Pulp Nuts/Pellets	75 - 90
	Molassed Sugar Beet Feed	70 - 80
	Pressed Sugar Beet Pulp	20 - 30
	Brewers' Grains	13 - 28
	Supergrains	22 - 28
	Fodder Beet	20 - 30

The straight feed prices are approximate ranges between late 1998 and mid-1999 (including delivery). The other prices are approximate ranges of purchased compounds in mid-1999.

They are (mainly) delivered prices on the farm *in bulk* in 15-20 tonne loads, and exclude any credit charges. The additional cost for *bags* ranges from £8 to £20 a tonne.

Delivery in bags is assumed for horse and pony pencils, goat nuts, chick and rearer feeds.

ME requirements for Friesian cows (590kg LW) (see page 215)

Liveweight Change		Milk yield (kg/day)			
(kg/day)	Maintenance	20	25	30	35
−0·5		147	172	196	221
0	62	161	186	210	235
+0·5		178	203	227	252

Source: Broster, W.H. and Alderman, G., Livestock Production Science, 4 (1977).

6. FEEDINGSTUFFS: NUTRITIVE VALUES

Type of Feed	Dry Matter Content g/kg	Metabolizable Energy MJ/k DM	Digestible Crude Protein g/kg DM
Pasture, rotational close grazed (monthly)	200	11·2	130
Ryegrass, perennial post flowering	250	8·4	72
Hay—moderate digestibility grass	850	8·8	39
Silage—moderate digestibility grass	200	8·8	102
Pea Haulm and Pods (Canning) Silage...	210	8·7	95
Barley (spring) Straw	860	7·3	9
Oat (spring) Straw...	860	6·7	11
Threshed Ryegrass Hay (approximate)...	850	7·0	38
Kale (marrow stem)	140	11·0	114
Mangels	100	12·4	80
Swede	105	13·9	64
Turnips	100	12·7	70
Fodder Beet	180	12·5	50
Sugar Beet Tops	160	9·9	88
Rape...	140	9·5	144
Potatoes	205	13·3	80
Brewers' Grains (barley)—fresh...	280	10·4	154
Barley	860	12·9	82
Oats	860	12·0	84
Maize	860	13·8	69
Wheat	860	13·5	105
Flaked Maize	900	15·0	106
Maize Gluten Feed	900	12·5	195
Maize Gluten Meal	900	17·2	736
Pressed Sugar Beet Pulp	180	12·3	60
Dried Molassed Sugar Beet Pulp	860	12·5	80
Beans, field spring	860	12·8	248
Cassava	880	12·8	18
Dec. Groundnut Cake	900	12·3	449
Dec. Cotton Cake	900	12·3	393

Source: M.A.F.F. (1984) Reference Book 433, Energy Allowances and Feeding Systems for Ruminants.

For relative value of different feeds see page 104.

7. STANDARD OUTPUTS, STANDARD GROSS MARGINS AND STANDARD MAN-DAYS (1)

Crops (per hectare)

	S.O.	S.G.M.	S.M.D.
Winter Wheat	785	540	
Spring Wheat	610	420	
Winter Barley	670	465	1·25/2 (2)
Spring Barley	615	455	
Winter Oats	715	550	
Spring Oats	595	440	
Winter Oilseed Rape ...	710	475	1·25
Spring Oilseed Rape ...	565	420	1·25
Linseed	505	335	1·25
Field Beans	555	420	1·25
Dried Peas	585	395	1·5
Vining Peas	1015	765	3·0
Potatoes	3000	1050	10/20 (3)
Sugar Beet	1660	1040	3
Herbage Seeds... ...	925	590	1·5
Hops	6000	4750	7·5
Mangolds (carted) ...	—	—	25
Turnips/Swedes:			
folded	—	—	4
lifted	—	—	10
Kale: cut and carted ...	—	—	10
Kale: grazed	—	—	1·5
Hay/Silage: 1 cut ...	—	—	2·5
Hay/Silage: 2 cuts ...	—	—	4
Grazing only	—	—	0·5
Hay for sale	450	350	2·25
Keep let	175	150	0·75
Bare Fallow	—	—	1·25
Set-aside	—	—	0·25
Rough grazing	—	—	0·2

Livestock (per head) (4, 5)

	S.O.	S.G.M.	S.M.D.
Dairy Cows	1100	700	4·25
Bulls	—	—	3·5
Beef Cows (S.S. inc. Calf):			
Lowland	310	170	1·4
Upland	395	250	1·7
Hill	425	280	2·0

Livestock (per head) (4, 5)

	S.O.	S.G.M.	S.M.D.
Cereal Beef			
(0-12 months) (6) ...	455	155	1·5
18 month Beef (6) ...	505	275	1·5
Grass Silage Beef (6)...	415	210	
Other Cattle over 2 years	250	150	1·4
Other Cattle 1-2 years	250	150	1·0
Other Cattle ½-1 year	135	85	1·0
Calves, M.S.-to 6 months (add to S.S.) ...	105	70	0·75
Calves, Others, to 6 months (6):			
steers	185	65	1·25
heifers	150	50	1·25
Ewes: lowland ...	57·5	32·5	0·5
upland... ...	60	40	0·45
hill ...	57·5	45	0·4
Rams	—	—	0·5
Other Sheep over 6 months ...	27·5	15	0·3
Sows	640	270	3
Boars	—	—	2
Other Pigs over 1 month ...	110	22·5	0·3
Laying Birds:			
battery cages ...	6·5	0·65	0·017
free range ...	13·5	6·75	0·06
Pullets reared (6) ...	1·75	0·4	0·005
Broilers (6) ...	0·95	0·16	0·002
Turkeys (6) ...	15	5·5	
Capons (6) ...	10	7	
Ducks (6) ...	7·5	5	
Geese (6) ...	26	21	

1. *Author's estimates for 2000 for average performance under average conditions. Wide variations can occur from farm to farm. Some of the S.M.D. estimates are based on only limited data — though all that is available; these are subject to substantial variations with scale and production methods.*
2. 1·25 if straw ploughed in; 2 if straw harvested. Highly mechanised larger farms will require no more than 0.75 S.M.D./ha of direct labour for cereals and other combinable crops (assuming straw ploughed in).
3. Automatic planter and mechanical harvester/hand-fed planter and hand harvesting. Including casual labour.
4. In calculating the Standard Outputs and Standard Gross Margins for livestock, herd depreciation or livestock (*e.g.* calf) purchases or the value of transfers in have been deducted.
5. Note that for grazing livestock, the S.M.D. per head exclude field work, *e.g.* grass production and silage making, *i.e.* the labour for these has to be added to give the *total* labour for these enterprises.
6. For these livestock, S.O., S.G.M. and S.M.D. per annum should be based on numbers produced (sold) during the year. *For all other livestock, average numbers on the farm at any one time during the year should be used* (i.e. average of numbers at end of each month).

For number of Standard Man-Days per worker per year, see page 117.

8. FARM RECORDS

The following records should be kept for management purposes:

1. *Basic Whole Farm Financial Position*
   1. Cash Analysis Book, fully detailed.
   2. Petty Cash Book.
   3. Annual Valuation, including physical quantities, with crops in store and livestock at (near) market value, less any variable costs yet to be borne. Fertilizers, seeds, sprays, casual labour or contract work applied to growing crops should be recorded, but "cultivations" and manurial residues can be ignored for management purposes.
   4. Debtors and creditors at the end of the financial year.

2. *Other Financial and Physical Records*
   1. Output (quantities and value) of each Crop and Livestock Enterprise for the "Harvest Year" (or Production Cycle). It may be possible to get information of Sales from a fully detailed cash analysis book (although, for crops, the financial year figures will then have to be allocated between crops from the current harvest and those from the harvest in the previous financial year, in order to check on the accuracy of the opening valuation of crops in store; this is particularly a problem with Michaelmas ending accounts). The following records of Internal Transfers and Consumption will also be required:
      (a) Numbers and Market Value of livestock transferred from one livestock category to another, *e.g.* dairy calves to Dairy Followers or Beef Enterprise, or dairy heifers to Dairy Enterprise.
      (b) Quantity and Market Value of Cereals fed on farm and used for seed.
      (c) Quantity and Market Value of Milk and other produce consumed by the farmer or his employees, used on the farm (*e.g.* milk fed to calves), or sold direct.
   2. A Monthly record of Livestock Numbers; preferably reconciled with the previous month according to births, purchases, deaths, sales and transfers.
   3. Costs and Quantities of Concentrate Feed to each category of livestock, including Home-Grown Cereals fed on the farm.
   4. Allocation of costs of seed, fertilizer, sprays, casual labour and contract work specific to an enterprise. This is in order to calculate gross margins, where required. It is less essential than the other records listed.

5. Breeding record for cows, including bulling dates, date(s) served, type of bull used, pregnancy testing, estimated calving date, actual calving date, and date when dried off.

6. For each crop, total output and yield per hectare, in both quantity and value. Include each field where the crop has been grown and its approximate yield, where this can be satisfactorily obtained.

7. For each field, keep one page to cover a period of say, ten years. Record on this, each year, crop grown, variety sown, fertilizer used, sprays used, date sown, date(s) harvested, approximate yield (if obtainable), and any other special notes that you feel may have significance for the future.

8. A rotation record. On a single page, if possible, list each field down the side and say, ten years along the top. Colour each field-year space according to the crop grown, *e.g.* barley yellow, potatoes red, etc.

9. DEFINITIONS OF FARM MANAGEMENT TERMS

Mainly abstracted from "Terms and Definitions used in Farm and Horticulture Management", M.A.F.F., 1970.

1. Valuations and Capital

Valuations. Valuation is essentially a process of estimation. Thus alternative bases are sometimes possible, according to the purpose intended. The basis should be consistent throughout the period of any series of figures.

    (i) *Saleable crops in store.* At estimated market value less costs still to be incurred, e.g. for storage and marketing. Both may be estimated either at the expected date of sale or at the date of valuation.

    (ii) *Growing crops.* Preferably at variable costs to the date of valuation, although estimated total cost can alternatively be used.

    (iii) *Saleable crops ready for harvesting* but still in the ground. Preferably valued as (i), less estimated harvesting costs, although they can alternatively be treated as (ii).

    (iv) *Fodder stocks (home-grown).* Preferably at variable costs when calculating gross margins. Alternatively at estimated market value (based on hay-equivalent value according to quality). Fodder crops still in the ground, e.g. kale, treated as (ii).

    (v) *Stocks of purchased materials (including fodder).* At cost net of discounts (where known) and subsidies

    (vi) *Machinery and equipment.* Original cost net of investment grants, less accumulated depreciation to date of valuation.

    (vii) *Livestock.* At current market value, less cost of marketing. Fluctuations in market value expected to be temporary should be ignored.

Tenant's Capital. The estimated total value of capital on the farm, other than land and fixed equipment. There is no easy way of determining this sum precisely and estimates are made in several ways depending on the information available and the purpose for which the estimate is required. One method is to take the average of the opening and closing valuations (at either market value or cost) of livestock, crops, machinery and stores (feed, seed, fertilizers). See also pages 176-7.

Landlord's Capital. Value of the land and fixed equipment (including buildings).

2. Output Terms

Revenue (or Income). Receipts adjusted for debtors at the beginning and end of the accounting period. Items such as subsidies, grants, contract receipts and wayleaves are included.

Returns. Revenue adjusted for valuation changes (add closing, deduct opening, valuation).

Gross Output. Returns plus the value of produce consumed in the farmhouse or supplied to workers for which no payment is made, less purchases of livestock, livestock products and other produce bought for resale.

Enterprise Output. The total value of an enterprise, whether sold or retained on the farm. It therefore equals Gross Output of the enterprise plus the market value of any of the products kept on the farm (transfers out). Products transferred from another enterprise to be used in the production of the enterprise whose output is being calculated are deducted at market value (transfers in). Instead of the accounting year the "harvest year" can be used for crops; valuations are then not relevant.

(Enterprise) Output from Forage. Primarily the sum of the enterprise outputs of grazing livestock, but includes keep let and occasional sales, *e.g.* of surplus hay, together with an adjustment for changes in the valuation of stocks of home-grown fodder. However, fortuitous changes in stocks caused by yield variations due to the weather, the severity or length of the winter, or minor changes in livestock numbers or forage area can be either ignored (if small in relation to total annual usage) or included in miscellaneous output.

Adjusted Forage (Enterprise) Output is Output from Forage less rented keep and purchases of bulk fodder.

Net Output. Gross Output less the cost of purchased feed, livestock keep, seed, bulbs and plants.

Standard Output. The average enterprise output per hectare of a crop or per head of livestock calculated from either national or local average price and average yield data.

3. Input Terms

Expenditure. Payments adjusted for creditors at the beginning and end of the accounting period. Capital expenditure is not included.

Costs. Expenditure adjusted for valuation changes (add opening, deduct closing, valuation), with the following adjustments. Add: depreciation on capital expenditure including machinery, any loss made on machinery sales (add to depreciation) and the value of payments in kind to workers if not already included in their earnings. Deduct: purchases of livestock, livestock products and other produce bought for resale, any profit made on machinery (deduct from depreciation), allowance for private use of farm vehicles (deduct from machinery costs), the value of purchased stores used in the farmhouse (*e.g.* electricity) or sold off the farm (deduct from the relevant item).

Inputs. Costs with the following adjustments, made in order to put all farms on a similar basis for comparative purposes. Add: the value of unpaid family labour, including the manual labour of the farmer and his wife, and, in the case of owner-occupiers, an estimated rental value (based on average rents of similar farms in the area), less any cottage rents received. Deduct: any mortgage payments and other expenses of owner-occupation, interest payments and the cost of paid management. A proportion of the rental value of the farmhouse may also be deducted.

Fixed Costs. See pages 1-2, 157.

Variable Costs. See page 1.

4. Margin Terms

Management and Investment Income. Gross Output less Inputs. It represents the reward to management and the return on tenant's capital invested in the farm, whether borrowed or not. It is mainly used for comparative purposes, all farms having been put on a similar financial basis by the adjustments made to costs in calculating Inputs.

Net Farm Income. Management and Investment Income, less paid management, plus the value of the manual labour of the farmer and his wife.

Profit (or Loss). Gross Output less Costs. This represents the surplus or deficit before imputing any notional charges such as rental value or unpaid labour. In the accounts of owner-occupiers it includes any profit accruing from the ownership of land.

Gross Margin. See page 1.

Net Margin. A term sometimes used to denote Gross Margin less direct labour and machinery costs charged to an individual enterprise. This is not, however, nationally accepted terminology.

5. Area Terms

Total Hectares. All hectares comprising the farm.

Hectares. Total hectares less the area of woods, waste land, roads, buildings, etc.

Adjusted Hectares. Hectares reduced by the conversion of rough grazings into the equivalent hectares of average quality grassland. This is the figure often used for lowland farms when calculating "per hectare" results.

Forage Hectares. Total hectares of forage crops grown, less any hectares exclusively used by pigs or poultry and the area equivalent of any home-grown fodder fed to barley beef. Usually, too, the area of rough grazings is converted to its grassland equivalent (see Adjusted Hectares). Forage crops are all crops, grass and rough grazings grown specifically for grazing livestock, other than catch crops and crops harvested as grain and pulses.

Adjusted Forage Hectares. Forage hectares adjusted as follows. Add area equivalent of keep rented, deduct area equivalent of keep let; deduct the area equivalent of occasional sales of fodder, *e.g.* surplus hay, and seed cuts (note: hay and seed grown regularly for sale should be regarded as cash crops, not forage crops); add or deduct the area equivalent of planned changes in the valuation of stocks of home-grown fodder (fortuitous changes in stocks resulting from weather conditions may be ignored); convert rough grazings into their grassland equivalent if not already done. The following adjustments also may be made: add the area equivalent of catch crops and of grazing from cash crops of hay or seed: add the area equivalent of purchased fodder.

In calculations such as *Gross Margins per Forage Hectare,* Adjusted Forage Hectares are usually used. If the area equivalent of purchased fodder has been added the cost of purchased fodder must not be charged as a variable cost: this is probably the best calculation for comparative purposes. Alternatively, when considering all the grazing enterprises taken together, purchased fodder can be deducted as a variable cost and no addition made for its area equivalent.

10. AGRISTATS

Some basic agricultural statistics relating to U.K. agriculture.
(All figures are for the U.K. in 1998 unless otherwise stated.)

A. Structure

1. *Agriculture's contribution to Gross Domestic*   £7,298 million
    Product (provisional):   1·0%

2. (a) *Agriculture's proportion of total workforce in*
    employment: 2·3%

2. (b) *Numbers of Persons Engaged in Agriculture* (June, provisional):

    A. Employed:

        (i) Regular Whole-time:

	male	88,000
	female	13,000
	Total	101,000

        (ii) Regular Part-time*:

	male	30,000
	female	25,000
	Total	55,000

        (iii) Seasonal or Casual:

	male	55,000
	female	25,000
	Total	80,000

        (iv) Salaried managers   12,000

                 Total Workers   248,000

B.   Farmers, Partners, Directors and Spouses:

	Whole-time	190,000
	Part-time*	177,000
	Total	367,000
	Total Labour Force**	615,000

*   Part-time is 39 hours or less per week.

**   Total labour force excludes schoolchildren and most trainees.

223

3. *Crop Areas* (in June)

	Area ('000 ha) 1993	Area ('000 ha) 1998	% Total Area 1998	%Crops and Grass (excl. R.G.) 1998
Wheat	1,759	2,045	11·0	17·5
Barley (% winter in brackets) ...	1,164	1,255 (61·5)	6·7	10·8
Oats	92	98	0·5	0·8
Other Grain (excl. maize) ...	16	22	0·1	0·2
Total Cereals	3,031	3,420	18·4	29·3
Potatoes	170	164	0·9	1·4
Sugar Beet	197	189	1·0	1·6
Oilseed Rape (non-SA) (% winter in brackets ...	377	506 (87·5)	2·7	4·3
Peas harvested dry ... ... }	244	102	0·5	0·9
Field Beans ... ... }		111	0·6	1·0
Linseed (non-SA)	150	100	0·5	0·9
Horticulture	187	177	1·0	1·5
Maize		103	0·6	0·9
Other Crops (non-SA) ... ... }	210	100	0·5	0·9
Bare Fallow ... ... }		34	0·2	0·3
Total Tillage	4,566	5,005	26·9	42·9
Temporary Grass (under 5 years old)	1,561	1,303	7·0	11·2
Total Arable	6,127	6,308	33·9	54·1
Permanent Grass (5 years old and over) ...	5,209	5,350	28·8	45·9
(Total Grass [excluding R.G.]) ...	(6,780)	(6,653)	(35·8)	(57·1)
Total Tillage and Grass (excl. R.G.)	11,335	11,658	62·7	100·0
Rough Grazing (R.G.)	5,840	5,845 *	31·4	
Other Land (inc. Set-Aside) ...	1,355	1,091 **	5·9	
Total Agricultural Area* ** ...	18,530	18,593	100·0	

(non-SA) = excluding crops grown on set-aside land
 * Including an estimated 1,221,000 ha of common grazing.
 ** All other land on agric. holdings, inc. woodland (490,000 ha) and set-aside (314,000 ha).
***Urban land and forest each approximately 2·0 million ha; other non-agricultural land approximately 1·5 million ha; total U.K. land area including inland waters: 24·1 million.

4. *Livestock Numbers* (in June; '000 head):

		1993	1998
Total Cattle and Calves		11,751	11,519
of which:	Dairy herd (inc. heifers in milk)	2,667	2,439
	Beef herd (inc. heifers in milk)	1,751	1,947
	Heifers in calf (first calf)	797	787
Total Sheep and Lambs		43,901	44,471
of which:	Female sheep used or to be used for breeding	N/A	21,260
	Rams and ram lambs	N/A	539
Total Pigs		7,756	8,146
of which:	Breeding herd (sows and gilts in pig)	802	778
Total Poultry		N/A	172,776
of which:	Table chicken	N/A	98,244
	Laying flock	N/A	29,483
	Breeding flock	N/A	10,023
	Growing pullets	10,653	9,860
Deer (farmed)		N/A	35
Goats		N/A	82

5. Size Structure
Number ('000) and Size distribution of holdings, 1996

Area (ha)	Total land area			Tillage and grass area		
	No.	%	% area	No.	%	% area
0·1 to 19·9	101·9	42·8	4·9	103·4	44·6	6·6
20 to 49·9	55·5	23·3	10·9	55·5	23·9	14·7
50 to 99·9	40·0	16·8	16·9	39·1	16·9	22·2
100 and over	40·4	17·0	67·4	33·8	14·6	56·5
Total	237·9	100·0	100·0	231·7	100·0	100·0

Average area (ha/[acres]) per holding: 71·0 (175); tillage and grass 53·8 (133).

Size of business (ESU)	No. of holdings ('000)	% of holdings	% of total ESU
Under 8	108·4	45·6	2·9
8 to under 40	65·7	27·6	15·4
40 to under 100	41·5	17·4	30·2
100 to under 200	16·0	6·7	24·8
200 and over	6·3	2·6	26·8
Total	237·9	100·0	100·0

Average size of holdings over 8 ESU (which is judged to be the minimum for full-time holdings, which are 53·4% of all holdings) = 65·8 ESU, 112·2 ha (277 acres). ESU = European Size Unit (the number provides a measure of the financial potential of the holding, based on standardised gross margins).

Number and Size distribution of holdings in England and Wales, 1996

Size Groups (ha)	By Total Area				By Crops and Grass Area			
	Holdings		Hectares		Holdings		Hectares	
	'000	%	'000,000	%	'000	%	'000,000	%
Under 10	46·8	26.9	0·22	2·0	46·4	28·0	0·21	2·4
10- 30	42·8	24·6	0·79	7·4	41·5	25·0	0·77	8·7
30- 50	23·8	13·7	0·93	8.7	24.1	14.5	0·94	10·7
50-100	30.6	17·6	2·18	20·3	29·8	18·0	2·11	24.0
100-200	19.2	11.1	2·65	24·7	16·8	10·1	2·31	26·2
200-300	5·4	3.1	1·30	12.1	4·0	2.4	0·97	11·0
300-500	3·4	2.0	1·29	12·0	2·3	1.4	0·85	9.6
500-700	0·9	0·5	0·54	5.0	0·5	0·3	0·31	3·5
700 and over	0·8	0·5	0·83	7.7	0·3	0·2	0·34	3·9
Total	173·7	100·0	10.74	100·0	165·8	100·0	8·80	100·0

6. Average Size of Enterprises

	1993	1998		1993	1998
	hectares			no.	
Crops and Grass	48·5	53·8	Dairy cows	64	66
Cereals	40·1	48·2	Beef cows	24	27
Oilseed Rape	24·6	29·1	Breeding sheep	217	242
Potatoes	7·6	9·7	Breeding pigs	68	78
Sugar Beet	19·6	20·4	Fattening pigs	398	505
			Laying fowls	1,035	1,214
			Broilers	30,641	45,469

7. Tenure

The following figures are for England and Wales, 1996; the areas are '000 hectares (percentages in brackets).

	No. of holdings	Area owned	Area rented
Wholly owned	115,948 (66·7)	5,184 (48·3)	—
Mainly owned	19,398 (11·2)	1,678 (15·6)	429 (4·0)
Wholly rented	24,817 (14·3)	—	1,998 (18·6)
Mainly rented	13,565 (7·8)	327 (3·0)	1,121 (10·4)
Total	173,728 (100)	7,189 (67·0)	3,548 (33·0)*

N.B. Mixed tenure holdings: mainly owned = over 50% owned; mainly rented = over 50% rented.
Wholly or mainly owned, 77·9% of holdings; wholly or mainly rented, 22·1%
*N.B. As the above figures for rented land include family arrangements (e.g. farmers, or family farming companies, renting from other members of the family, or family shareholders) the percentage of "truly" rented land is almost certainly a few percentage points less than the figures given above.

B. Finance

1. Expenditures and Outputs (1998 provisional, £ million).

Expenditures		Outputs		%
Feedingstuffs	2422	Wheat	1,647	(10·0)
Seeds	329	Barley	777	(4·7)
Fertilizers and lime	821	Oats and other cereals	68	(0·4)
Pesticides	652	Straw	185	(1·1)
Hired labour	1,945	Oilseed rape	399	(2·4)
Consumption of fixed		Linseed	67	(0·4)
capital*	2,548	Potatoes	639	(3·9)
Farm maintenance	352	Sugar beet	274	(1·7)
Machinery repairs	703	Peas/Beans for stockfeed	119	(0·7)
Machinery fuel and oil	382	Vegetables	1,022	(6·2)
Power and fuel	226	Fruit	216	(1·3)
Contract work	574	Ornamentals	658	(4·0)
Vet. and med	296	Finished cattle and calves	1,943	(11·8)
Straw for bedding	174	Finished sheep and lambs	1,142	(7·0)
Leasing of quota	110	Finished pigs	873	(5·3)
Imported livestock	15	Poultry	1,344	(8·2)
Net rent	195	Milk and milk products	2,729	(16·6)
Interest	711	Eggs	400	(2·4)
Miscellaneous**	1,786	Miscellaneous	1,912	(11·6)
Total Expenditures	14,241	Total Gross Output	16,414	(100)
Total Income From				
Farming	2,173	Total Crops	4,267	(26·0)
		Total Horticulture	1,903	(11·6)
	16,414	Total Livestock	5,457	(33·2)
		Total Livestock Products	3,180	(19·4)
		Other ,,	1,607	(9·8)
		Total Gross Output	16,414	(100)

*including 678 buildings and works and 1,331 plant, machinery and vehicles.
**less "other subsidies".
Note. The above layout of "expenditures" differs from that now published by MAFF.

2. U.K. Farming Income

Index of UK Farming Income* in Real Terms
(average 1940-69 = 100)

Year	Index	Year	Index
1940-49	101	1983	57
1950-59	100	1984	86
1960-69	99	1985	37
1970	95	1986	46
1971	96	1987	50
1972	110	1988	34
1973	138	1989	45
1974	103	1990	43
1975	98	1991	41
1976	113	1992	56
1977	98	1993	79
1978	89	1994	77
1979	73	1995	94
1980	56	1996	88
1981	66	1997	45
1982	77	1998 (provisional)	25

*The return to farmers and spouses for their labour, management, own land and own capital, after providing for depreciation. As this figure is no longer published by MAFF the figures for 1997 and 1998 are only approximate.

Indices of UK Farming Income and Total Income from Farming*
in Real Terms (1975 = 100)

Year	FI	TIFF	Year	FI	TIFF
1975	100	100	1987	51	58
1976	115	112	1988	35	55
1977	100	98	1989	46	57
1978	91	90	1990	44	49
1979	74	77	1991	42	49
1980	57	65	1992	57	60
1981	67	73	1993	81	81
1982	79	82	1994	79	83
1983	58	67	1995	96	95
1984	88	89	1996	90	87
1985	38	51	1997	46	54
1986	47	59	1998 (provisional)	26	37

*Farming income with the estimated value of the labour of family workers, non-principal partners and directors (and their spouses) added back. The calculation was changed in 1998; the revised figures for 1987 onwards have been published and incorporated above; the original 1975 figure has still been used as the base figure = 100.

3. Indices of Net Farm Income per Farm in Real Terms by main Types of Farming, UK: 6-year average 1977/8-1982/3 = 100.

	Dairy	LFA Cattle and Sheep	Lowland Cattle and Sheep	Specialist Cereals	Other Cropping	Pigs and Poultry
6-year average 1977/8-1982/3* ...	100	100	100	100	100	100
1983/84	69	94	63	134	137	50
1984/85	64	99	41	160	108	119
1985/86	70	80	18	16	23	82
1986/87	72	61	10	62	104	65
1987/88	94	100	22	10	43	47
1988/89	113	115	21	11	28	21
1989/90	98	77	10	24	128	91
1990/91	68	57	6	30	99	71
1991/92	71	67	9	30	83	43
1992/93	91	86	13	40	87	49
1993/94	98	98	15	38	108	15
1994/95	81	71	11	50	185	30
1995/96	96	98	11	77	210	62
1996/97	75	95	9	67	106	55
1997/98	47	47	1	22	45	19
1998/99 (provisional)	28	30	-3	14	71	-14

*i.e. 1980 is the centre year.

4. Balance Sheet of UK Agriculture (1997 provisional, £ mills.), and Ratios

Assets			£	£
Fixed:	Land and buildings...		52,853	
	Plant, machinery and vehicles		8,484	
	Breeding livestock		3,961	
	Total Fixed Assets			65,298
Current:	Trading livestock		2,719	
	Crops and stores		2,671	
	Debtors, cash deposits		3,685	
	Total Current Assets			9,075
	Total Assets			74,373

Liabilities

Long and medium-term:			£	£
	Bank loans		1,840	
	Other		2,085	
	Total long & medium-term			3,925
Short-term:	Bank Overdraft		2,541	
	Trade Credit		1,149	
	Hire Purchase and Leasing		827	
	Other		162	
	Total short-term			4,679
	Total Liabilities...			8,604
	Net Worth...			65,769

% Equity (Net Worth as % of Total Assets):
1980: 90·2   1990: 81·5   1997: 88·4

Net Worth as % of Total Assets, England, 1997/98, owner-occupied and tenanted land:
owned: 89·5   tenanted: 74·2

Total Income from Farming as % of Net Worth and Total Assets:

	% Net Worth	% Total Assets
1994	7·95	7·04
1995	7·63	6·50
1996	4·67	4·13

(Note, no charge has been made for the farmers' own labour or management, or interest on own capital.)

5. Bank Lending, Interest Payments and Investment

Bank Lending to Agriculture (£ mills. approx.):
1980: 2,900   1986: 6,000   1992: 6,925   1996: 6,625   1999: 7,500

Interest payments per annum (£ mills.):

	1979-81	1989-91	1998 provis.
Actual	417	962	711
At 1998 prices (approx.) ...	1030	1252	711

Gross fixed capital formation per annum (£ mills.):

			1997
Actual	1014	1090	2572
At 1998 prices (approx.)	2415	1420	2660

C. Miscellaneous

1. Crop Yields and Prices, 1994-98

Average Yields (tonnes/ha) (harvest years)

	1994	1995	1996	1997	1998	Average 1994/8
Wheat	7·35	7·70	8·15	7·38	7·55	7·63
Barley (all)	5·37	5·73	6·14	5·76	5·21	5·64
Winter	5·83	6·20	6·61	6·27	5·48	6·08
Spring	4·78	5·10	5·46	4·94	4·77	5·01
Oats	5·50	5·52	6·14	5·78	6·03	5·79
Oilseed Rape (excl. set-aside)	2·62	2·91	3·49	3·24	2·96	3·04
Linseed (excl. set-aside)	1·25	1·30	1·61	1·39	1·41	1·39
Field Beans (for stockfeed)	3·04	2·69	3·17	3·80	3·81	3·30
Dried Peas (for stockfeed)	3·91	3·77	3·84	3·79	3·80	3·82
Potatoes (all)	39·9	36·9	39·2	43·1	39.6	39.7
Early	21·4	22·6	23·5	23·8	18·8	22·02
Maincrop	41·8	38·9	42·1	45·0	42·2	42·0
Sugar Beet						
(adj. [16% SC] tonnes)	44·7	43·0	52·4	56·5	51·9	49·7

Average Prices per tonne (calendar years)

	1994	1995	1996	1997	1998
Wheat: milling	114	120	122	101	84
feed	102	110	111	89	75
Barley: malting	126	142	133	93	84
feed	102	105	101	79	70
Oats: milling	104	101	106	83	65
feed	101	99	104	76	61
Oilseed Rape (inc. set-aside	175	174	178	153	160
Linseed (inc. set-aside)	128	148	172	142	133
Field Beans (for stockfeed)	101	119	123	98	73
Dried Peas (for stockfeed)	106	118	121	98	71
Potatoes (all, inc. seed)	127	186	101	65	121
Early	188	156	97	74	152
Maincrop	122	190	98	63	118
Sugar Beet (less transport)	35·2	38·3	32·0	27·1	28·0

2. Self-Sufficiency (1998 provisional)

(a) Total Food:

all food and feed	68·1
indigenous type food	82·3

(b) Individual Products:

(Production as % of total new supply for use in the UK)

	1993	1998		1993	1998
Wheat	120	123	Beef and veal	100	80
Barley	115	125	Mutton and lamb	115	99
Oats	108	107	Pork	100	111
Total Cereals	108	114	Bacon and Ham	48	51
Oilseed rape	86	98	Poultrymeat	94	96
Linseed	135	139	Butter	71	78
Potatoes	90	89	Cheese	72	66
Sugar	65	64	Cream	136	146
Vegetables	N/A	72	Hen eggs	98	97
Fruit	N/A	9			

3. Food Consumption and Trends

Expenditure on food and drink as % of total consumers' expenditure (1998): household food, 10·3%; alcoholic drinks, 5·7%. (Eating and drinking out: an additional 4·7%).

Estimated Average Household Food Consumption (kg per person per year):

	1988	1993	1998
Milk and cream (equivalent pints) ...	209	199	187
Cheese	6·09	5·67	5·41
Fats	14·53	11·95	10·14
Eggs (number)	139	100	90
Meat and meat products ...	53·93	49·69	48·93
Fish	7·46	7·52	7·59
Fresh potatoes	53·69	45·51	37·18
Fresh green vegetables	15·36	12·47	12·79
Other fresh vegetables	24·78	24·81	25·27
Processed vegetables	28·64	29·20	29·02
Fresh fruit	30·98	32·06	37·23
Processed fruit and nuts ...	16·07	16·76	19·45
Sugar and preserves	12·96	10·05	8·11
Bread	44·63	39·35	38·58
Cakes and biscuits	13·19	13·55	13·78
Other cereals or cereal products ...	21·95	23·05	21·63
Beverages	3·92	3·29	3·02

Average expenditure, per person, per week, 1998	£
on household food	14·79
on food eaten out	4·78
total food	19·57
on household alcoholic drinks	1·33
on alcoholic drinks consumed outside household	1·52
total alcoholic drinks	2·85
on household soft drinks and confectionery	0·82
on soft drinks and confectionery consumed outside household	0·43
total soft drinks and confectionery	1·25
overall total	23·67

Total household £16·94; total outside household £6·73.

---

4. Percentage of Total Household Expenditure on Food and Drink, 1998:

Meat and meat products	27·8	Bread	5·2
Milk and cream	9·6	Cheese	3·7
Flour/cereals/cereal products	8·5	Beverages	3·5
Processed vegetables		Processed fruit and nuts	2·9
(inc. potatoes 3·7)	7·1	Fats	2·6
Fresh vegetables	6·8	Fresh potatoes	2·4
Fresh fruit	6·5	Eggs	1·2
Cakes and biscuits	5·5	Sugar and preserves	1·2
Fish	5·5		

Sources: Agriculture in the UK: 1998 (MAFF). All items except for the following:
A5 (part), A7: Other MAFF Statistics.
B4, Bank Lending: Bank of England, Financial Statistics Division.
C3 and C4: National Food Survey, 1997, MAFF.

11. RATE OF INFLATION; PRICE AND COST INDICES

1. *Retail Price Index* (all items)

	% increase on year earlier	Index* (1970 = 100)	Index (1980 = 100)
1970	—	100	
1971	9·5	109·5	
1972	7	117	
1973	9	128	
1974	16	148·5	
1975	24	184·5	
1976	16·5	215	
1977	16	249	
1978	8·3	270	
1979	13·4	306	
1980	18	361	100
1981	11·9	404	112
1982	8 6	439	122
1983	4·6	459	127
1984	5·0	482	133
1985	6·1	511	142
1986	3·4	528	146
1987	4·2	551	153
1988	4·9	578	160
1989	7·8	623	173
1990	9·5	682	189
1991	5·9	722	200
1992	3·7	749	207
1993	1·6	761	210
1994	2·4	779	215
1995	3·5	806	223
1996	2·4	825	228
1997	3·1	851	235
1998	3·4	880	243
1999 (estimated)	1·75	895	247
2000 (forecast)	1·75	911	252

*Index in 1965: 80.
„ „ 1962: 70. *Source: Economic Trends.*

2. *Price and Cost Indices 1998 (1990 = 131)*

(N.B. Retail Price Index: 129; RPI for Food only: 131)

(a) *Producer Prices*

Breadmaking Wheat	83·5	Dessert Apples	93·5
Other Milling Wheat	72·5	All Fresh Fruit	98·5
Feed Wheat	69	*All Crop Products*	88
Malting Barley	72	Calves	82
Feed Barley	68·5	Cattle	79·5
Milling Oats	63·5	Cows and Bulls	81
Feed Oats	63·5	Sheep	111·5
All Cereals	72·5	Wool	75
Early Potatoes	195	Pigs	72
Maincrop Potatoes	113	Poultry	92·5
Sugar Beet	88	Milk	104
Seeds	89·5	Eggs	85
Fresh Vegetables	106	*All Animals/Animal Products*	91·5
Flowers and Plants	109	*All Products*	90

(b) *Input Prices*

General Expenses	131	Animal Feedingstuffs	109
Seeds	127·5	Energy and Lubricants	112
Fertilisers	83	Maintce./Repair of Plant	150
Plant Protection Products	116	Machinery & Other Equipt.	125
Animals for Rearing/Prodn.	130	Farm Buildings	131

Source: MAFF Statistics.

12. METRIC CONVERSION FACTORS

Metric to Imperial		*Imperial to Metric*	
Area			
1 hectare	2·471 acres	1 acre	0·405 ha
1 square km	0·386 sq. mile	1 square mile	2·590 sq. km
1 square m	1·196 sq. yard	1 square yard	0·836 sq. m
1 square m	10·764 sq. feet	1 square foot	0·093 sq. m
	(m = metre, km = kilometre)		

Length			
1 mm	0·039 inch	1 inch	25·4 mm
1 cm	0·394 inch	1 inch	2·54 cm
1 m	3·281 feet	1 foot	0·305 m
1 m	1·094 yard	1 yard	0·914 m
1 km	0·6214 mile	1 mile	1·609 km
	(mm = millimetre, cm = centimetre)		

Volume			
1 millilitre	0·0352 fluid oz	1 fluid oz	28·413 ml
1 litre	35·2 fluid oz	1 fluid oz	0·028 litre
1 litre	1·76 pints	1 pint	0·568 litre
1 litre	0·22 gallon	1 gallon	4·546 litres
(Milk: 1 litre = 1·03 kg; 1 kg milk = 1·709 pints, 0·214 gal.; 1 tonne = 213·63 gal.)			
1 cubic m	35·31 cu feet	1 cubic foot	0·028 cu m
1 cubic m	1·307 cu yard	1 cubic yard	0·765 cu m
1 cubic m	220 gallons	1 gallon	0·005 cu m

Weight			
1 gram	0·0353 oz	1 oz	28·35 gm
1 kg	2·205 lb	1 lb	0·454 kg
1 tonne (1000 kg)	19·68 cwt	1 cwt	50·80 kg
1 tonne	0·984 ton	1 ton	1·016 tonne

Yields and Rates of Use			
1 tonne/ha	0·398 ton/acre	1 ton/acre	2·511 tonnes/ha
1 tonne/ha	7·95 cwt/acre	1 cwt/acre	0·125 tonne/ha
1 gram/ha	0·014 oz/acre	1 oz/acre	70·053 g/ha
1 kg/ha	0·892 lb/acre	1 lb/acre	1·121 g/ha
1 kg/ha	0·008 cwt/acre	1 cwt/acre	125·5 g/ha
1 kg/ha (fert.)	0·80 unit/acre	1 unit/acre	1·255 kg/ha
1 litre/ha	0·712 pint/acre	1 pint/acre	1·404 litre/ha
1 litre/ha	0·089 gal/acre	1 gal/acre	11·24 litres/ha

Power, Pressure, Temperature			
1 kW	1·341 hp	1 hp	0·746 kW
1 kilojoule	0·948 Btu	1 Btu	1·055 kilojoule
1 therm	10000 Btu	1 Btu	0·0001 therm
1 lb f ft	1·356 Nm	1 Nm	0·738 lb f ft
1 bar	14·705 psi	1 psi	0·068 bar
°C to °F	×1·8, +32	°F to °C	−32, ÷1·8

13. USEFUL ADDRESSES AND TELEPHONE NUMBERS*

1. GENERAL

ADAS (Agricultural Development and Advisory Service)
Headquarters: Oxford Spires Business Park, Boulevard,
Ford Lane, Kidlington, Oxford OX5 1NZ   01865   842742

Agricultural Central Trading Ltd. (ACT)
90 The Broadway, Chesham, Bucks. HP5 1EG   01494   784931

Agricultural Engineers' Association
Samuelson House, Paxton Road, Orton Centre, Peterborough,
Cambs. PE2 5LT   01733   371381

Agricultural Mortgage Corporation PLC (AMC)
AMC House, Chantry Street, Andover, Hants. SP10 1DD   01264   334344

Agricultural Wages Board
Nobel House, Room 716, 17 Smith Square, London SW1P 3JR   020 7238 6540

Association of Independent Crop Consultants
Agriculture House, Station Road, Liss, Hampshire GU33 7AR   01730   895354

Lantra National Training Organisation
National Agricultural Centre, Stoneleigh Park CV8 2LG   024 7669 6996

BBC Radio 4 Farming To-day
Room 648, Pebble Mill, Birmingham B5 7QQ   0121 432 9713

British Agricultural and Garden Machinery Association (BAGMA)
14-16 Church Street, Rickmansworth, Herts. WD3 1RQ   01923   720241

British Agrochemicals Association Ltd.
4 Lincoln Court, Lincoln Road, Peterborough, Cambs. PE1 2RP   01733   349225

British Cereal Exports
HGCA, Caledonia House, 223 Pentonville Road,
London N1 9HY   020 7520 3927

British Crop Protection Council
49 Downing Street, Farnham, Surrey GU9 7PH   01252   733072

British Deer Society
Burgate Manor, Fordingbridge, Hampshire SP6 1EF   01425   655434

British Grassland Society
University of Reading, 1 Earley Gate, Berks. RG6 6AT   0118 9318189

British Institute of Agricultural Consultants
The Estate Office, Torry Hill, Milstead, Sittingbourne,
Kent ME9 0SP   01795   830100

British Pig Association
7 Rickmansworth Road, Watford, Herts. WD1 7HE   01923   234377

British Potato Council
4300 Nash Court, John Smith Drive, Oxford Business Park
South, Oxford OX4 2RT   01865   714455

For a 680-page current directory of names, addresses and telephone numbers of UK agricultural firms and associations, with over 43,000 listings covering 70 categories and in 11 regions see **Green Pages**, *10th edition, available from 229 Acton Lane, London W4 5DD (tel. 0181-747 8028; fax. 0181-747 8054); price £16, including post and packing.*

British Poultry Meat Federation
7th Floor, Imperial House, 15/19 Kingsway,
London WC2B 6UA   020 7240 9889

British Sheep Dairying Association
Wield Wood, Upper Wield, Alresford, Hampshire S024 9RU   01420 563151

British Society of Plant Breeders
Woolpack Chambers, Market Street, Ely, Cambs. CB7 4ND   01353 653200

British Sugar
Oundle Road, Peterborough, Cambs. PE2 9QU   01733 563171

British Veterinary Association
7 Mansfield Street, London WlM OAT   020 7636 6544

British Wool Marketing Board
Wool House, Roydsdale Way, Euroway Trading Estate,
Bradford, West Yorkshire BD4 6SJ   01274 688666

CAB International
Wallingford, Oxon OX10 8DE   01491 832111

Central Association of Agricultural Valuers
Market Chambers, 35 Market Place, Coleford, Gloucestershire
GL16 8AA   01594 832979

Centre for Agricultural Strategy
University of Reading, P.O. Box 236, Earley Gate, Reading,
Berks. RG6 6AT   0118 931 8150

Council for the Protection of Rural England
Warwick House, 25 Buckingham Palace Road,
London SW1W 0PP   020 7976 6433

Country Landowners Association
16 Belgrave Square, London SWlX 8PQ   020 7235 0511

The Countryside Agency
John Dower House, Crescent Place, Cheltenham
Gloucestershire, GL50 3RA   01242 521381

Dairy Industry Federation
19 Cornwall Terrace, London NW1 4QP   020 7486 7244

Department of Agriculture, N. Ireland (DANI)
Dundonald House, Upper Newtownards Road, Belfast BT4 3SB   028 9052 0100

English Heritage
23 Savile Row, London WlX lAB   020 7973 3000

English Nature
Northminster House, Northminster, Peterborough PE1 lUA   01733 455000

English Tourist Board
Thames Tower, Blacks Road, London W6 9EL   020 8846 9000

Environment Agency
Rio House, Waterside Drive, Aztec West, Almonsbury, Bristol
BS12 4UD   01454-624400

European Commission
London Office, Jean Monnet House, 8 Storey's Gate, London
SW1P 3AT   020 7973 1992

Family Farmers' Association
Osborne Newton, Aveton Gifford, Kingsbridge, Devon TQ7 4PE   01548 852794

Farmers Club
3 Whitehall Court, London SWlA 2EL   020 7930 3751

Farmers Union of Wales
Llys Amaeth, Plas Gogerddon, Aberystwyth, Ceredigion
SY23 3BT   01970 820820

Farming and Agricultural Finance Limited
John Deere Credit House, Barnett Way, Barnwood,
Gloucester GL4 3RT   01452 376000

Farming and Rural Conservation Agency (FRCA)
Nobel House, 17 Smith Square, London SW1P 3JR   020 7238 5432

Farming and Wildlife Advisory Group (FWAG)
National Agricultural Centre, Stoneleigh Park, Warks. CV8 2RX 024 7669 6699

Federation of Agricultural Co-operatives (UK) Ltd.
164 Shaftesbury Avenue, London WC2H 8HL   020 7331 7216

The Fertilizer Manufacturers' Association Ltd.
Greenhill House, Thorpe Road, Peterborough PE3 6GF   01733 331303

Food and Farming Education Service
National Agricultural Centre, Stoneleigh Park, Warks. CV8 2LZ 024 7653 5707

Food from Britain
123 Buckingham Palace Road, London SW1W 9SA   020 7233 5111

Food and Drink Federation
Federation House, 6 Catherine Street, London WC2B 5JJ   020 7836 2460

Forestry Commission
231 Corstorphine Road, Edinburgh EH12 7AT   0131-334 0303

Grain and Feed Trade Association (GAFTA)
GAFTA House, 6 Chapel Place, Rivington Street,
London EC3A 3SH   020 7814 9666

Health and Safety Executive
Information Centre, Broad Lane, Sheffield S3 7HQ   0114 289 2345

Home Grown Cereals Authority
Caledonia House, 223 Pentonville Road, London N1 9PG   020 7520 3904
Price Information Service   020 7520 3972

Horticultural Development Council
Bradbourne House, Stable Block, East Malling, Kent ME19 6DZ 01732 848383

Institution of Agricultural Engineers
West End Road, Silsoe, Bedford MK45 4DU   01525 861096

Institute of Agricultural Management
Farm Management Unit, University of Reading, PO Box 236,
Reading RG6 6AT   0118 935 1458

Institute of Agricultural Secretaries and Administrators
National Agricultural Centre, Stoneleigh Park, Warks. CV8 2LZ 01203 696592

Institute of Chartered Foresters
7a St. Colme Street, Edinburgh EH3 6AA   0131 225 2705

International Grains Council
1 Canada Square, Canary Wharf, London E14 5AE   020 7513 1122

Intervention Board Executive Agency
Kings House, 33 Kings Road, Reading RG1 3BU   0118 958 3626

Land Drainage Contractors Association
National Agricultural Centre, Stoneleigh Park, Warks. CV8 2LG 01327 263264

Land Heritage
Pounds Corner, Whitestone, Exeter, Devon EX4 2HP   01647 61099

Lands Improvement Holdings PLC
1 Buckingham Place, London SW1E 6HR   020 7222 5331

Liffe Commodity Products
1 Commodity Quay, St. Katherine Dock, London E1 9AX   020 7481 2080

Meat and Livestock Commission
PO Box 44, Winterhill House, Snowdon Drive, Milton Keynes
MK6 1AX   01908 677577

Milk Development Council
5-7 John Princes Street, London W1M 0AP   020 7629 7262

Ministry of Agriculture, Fisheries and Food (Helpline)
3 Whitehall Place, London SW1A 2HH   0645-335577

National Agricultural Centre
Stoneleigh Park, Warks. CV8 2LZ   024 7669 6969

National Association of Agricultural Contractors
1st Floor, 8 High Street, Maldon, Essex CM9 5PJ   01621 841675

National Association of British & Irish Millers (NABIM)
21 Arlington Street, London SW1A 1RN   020 7493 2521

National Association of Farmers' Markets
Bath Environmental Centre, 24 Milsom Street, Bath BA 1DG   01225 460620

National Cattle Association
Scotsbridge House, Scots Hill, Rickmansworth, Hertfordshire
WD3 3BB   01926 889965

National Dairy Council
5-7 John Princes Street, London W1M OAP   020 7499 7822

National Farmers' Union
Agriculture House, 164 Shaftesbury Avenue,
London WC2H 8HL   020 7331 7200

National Farmers Union of Scotland
Rural Centre, West Mains, Ingliston, Newbridge, Midlothian
EH28 8LT   0131-472 4000

National Federation of Young Farmers Clubs
YFC Centre, National Agricultural Centre, Stoneleigh Park,
Warks. CV8 2LG   01203 857200

National Office of Animal Health (NOAH)
3 Crossfield Chambers, Gladbeck Way, Enfield,
Middlesex EN2 7HF   020 8367 3131

National Sheep Association
The Sheep Centre, Malvern, Worcs. WR13 6PH   01684 892661

National Trust
36 Queen Anne's Gate, London SW1H 9AS   020 7222 9251

Processed Vegetable Growers' Association Limited (PGVA)
133 Eastgate, Louth, Lincolnshire LN11 9QG   01507 602427

Royal Agricultural Benevolent Institution (RABI)
Shaw House, 27 West Way, Oxford OX2 OQH   01865 724931

Royal Agricultural Society of England (RASE)
National Agricultural Centre, Stoneleigh Park, Warks. CV8 2LZ   024 7669 6969

Royal Association of British Dairy Farmers
Dairy House, 60 Kenilworth Road, Leamington Spa, Warwicks
CV32 6JX   01926 887477

Royal Forestry Society
102 High Street, Tring, Herts. HP23 4AF   01442 822028

Royal Highland and Agricultural Society of Scotland
Ingliston, Edinburgh EH28 8NF   0131-335 6200

Royal Horticultural Society
80 Vincent Square, London SW1P 2PE   020 7834 4333

Royal Institution of Chartered Surveyors (RICS)
12 Great George Street, Parliament Square, London SW1P 3AD 020 7222 7000

Royal Welsh Agricultural Society
Llanelwedd, Builth Wells, Powys LD2 3SY   01982 553683

Rural, Agricultural and Allied Workers Trade Group (TGWU)
Transport House, 16 Palace Street, Victoria, London SW1E 5JD 020 7828 7788

Rural Development Commission
141 Castle Street, Salisbury, Wiltshire SP1 3TP   01722 336255

Scottish Executive Environment Group
Environment Protection Unit, Victoria Quay,
Edinburgh EH6 6QQ   0131-556 8400

Tenant Farmers' Association
7 Brewery Court, Theale, Reading, Berks. RG7 5AJ   0118 9306130

The Stationery Office
The Publications Centre, PO Box 276, London SW8 5DT   020 7873 0011

Ulster Farmers Union
475 Antrim Road, Belfast BT15 3DA   028 9037 0222

United Farmers Trading Agency (U.F.T.A.)
Hancock House, Smallgate, Beccles, Suffolk NR34 9AE.   01502 717877

UK Agricultural Supply Trade Association (UKASTA)
3 Whitehall Court, London SW1A 2EQ   020 7930 3611

UK Register of Organic Food Standards (UKROFS)
Nobel House, Room G43, 17 Smith Square, London SW1P 3JR 020 7238 5915

National Assembly for Wales
Crown Buildings, Cathays Park, Cardiff CF1 3NQ   029 2082 5111

Women's Food and Farming Union
National Agricultural Centre, Stoneleigh Park, Warks. CV8 2LZ 024 7669 3171

2. UNIVERSITY AGRICULTURAL ECONOMISTS
(Farm Business Survey work)

ENGLAND AND WALES

Northern: Department of Agricultural Economics and Food
Marketing, University of Newcastle-upon-Tyne,
Newcastle-upon-Tyne NE1 7RU   0191 222 6902

North Eastern: Rural Business Research Unit, Askham Bryan
College, Askham Bryan, York YO23 3FR   01904 772233

North Western: Farm Business Unit, School of Economic Studies,
The University of Manchester, Manchester
M13 9PL   0161 275 4799

East Midland: Rural Business Research Unit, University of Nottingham,
Sutton Bonington Campus, Loughborough
LE12 5RD   0115 9516070

Eastern: Rural Business Unit, Department of
Land Economy, University of Cambridge
19 Silver Street, Cambridge CB3 9EP   01223 337166

South Eastern: Farm Business Unit, Department of Agricultural
Economics and Business Management,
Wye College (University of London),
Ashford, Kent TN25 5AH   01233 812401

Southern: Department of Agricultural and Food Economics
University of Reading, 4 Earley Gate, Whiteknights
Road, PO Box 237, Reading RG6 6AR   0118 931 8960

South Western: Agricultural Economics Unit, University of
Exeter, Lafrowda House, St. German's Road,
Exeter EX4 6TL   01392 263839

Wales: Welsh Institute of Rural Studies,
Llanbadarn Campus,
Aberystwyth, Ceredigion SY23 3AL   01970 622253

SCOTLAND (Advisory Services also)
Scottish Agricultural College
Rural Resource Management Department, Kings Buildings,
West Mains Road, Edinburgh EH9 3JG   0131-667 1041

Regional Offices:
North: SAC Aberdeen, Craibstone, Bucksburn, Aberdeen AB21 9YA
     01224 711000
East: SAC Edinburgh, West Mains Road, Edinburgh EH9 3JG 0131-667 1041
West: SAC Auchincruive, Ayr KA6 5HW   01292 520331

NORTHERN IRELAND (Advisory Services also)
Economics & Statistics Division, Department of Agriculture, Dundonald House,
Upper Newtownards Road, Belfast BT4 3SB   028 9052 0100

4. COMMERCIAL BANKS: AGRICULTURAL DEPARTMENTS

Barclays Bank PLC
Barclays Agricultural Banking, St. Swithin's House, 11/12 St. Swithin's
Lane, London EC4N 8AS   020 7929 4080

Clydesdale Bank PLC
Business Banking Centre, 10 Fleet Place, London EC4M 7RB   020 7395 5662

Lloyds TSB Group PLC
Business Banking, Agricultural Finance, PO Box 112,
Bristol BS99 7LB   0117 9433433

Midland Bank (HSBC) PLC
Midland Agriculture, 27 Poultry, London EC2P 2BX   020 7260 6800

Natwest
Agricultural Office, Ground Floor, National Westminster House,
73a Commercial Road, Swindon SN1 5NX   01793 422891

The Royal Bank of Scotland PLC
Agricultural Services, PO Box 31, 42 St. Andrew Square, Edinburgh
EH2 2YE   0131-523 2227

5. RESEARCH ORGANISATIONS

Biotechnology and Biological Sciences Research Council
Polaris House, North Star Avenue, Swindon, Wilts. SN2 IUH   01793 413253

Arable Research Centres
Manor Farm, Daglingworth, Cirencester, Glos. GL7 7AH   01285 652184

Babraham Institute
Babraham, Cambridge CB2 4AT   01223 496000

Broom's Barn (IACR)
Higham, Bury St. Edmunds, Suffolk IP28 6NP   01284 812200

CEDAR (Centre for Dairy Research)
Arborfield Hall Farm, Reading Road, Arborfield, Reading,
RG2 9HX   0118 9760964

Hannah Research Institute
Ayr, Scotland KA6 5HL   01292 674000

Institute for Animal Health
Compton, Newbury, Berks. RG20 7NN   01635 578411

Institute of Food Research
Norwich Research Park, Colney, Norwich NR4 7UA   01603 255000
Earley Gate, Whiteknights Road, Reading RG6 6BZ   0118 935 7000

Institute of Grassland and Environmental Research (IGER)
Aberystwyth Research Centre, Plas Gogerddan, Aberystwyth,
Ceredigion SY23 3EB   01970 828255

North Wyke Research Station, Okehampton, Devon EX20 2SB   01837 82558

Kingshay Farming Trust
Henley Manor, Crewkerne, Somerset TA18 8PH   01460 72977

Long Ashton Research Station (IACR)
Long Ashton, Bristol BS41 9AF   01275 392181

Macauley Land Use Research Institute
Craigiebuckler, Aberdeen AB15 8QH   01224 318611

Morley Research Centre
Morley St. Botolph, Wymondham, Norfolk NR18 9DB   01953 605511

National Institute of Agricultural Botany (NIAB)
Huntingdon Road, Cambridge CB3 0LE   01223 276381

Pea Growers Research Organisation (PGRO)
The Research Station, Great North Road, Thornhaugh,
Peterborough PE8 6HJ   01780 782585

Roslin Institute
Roslin, Midlothian EH25 9PS   0131 527 4200

IACR – Rothamsted
Harpenden, Hertfordshire AL5 2JQ   01582 763133

Rowett Research Institute
Bucksburn, Aberdeen AB21 9SB   01224 712751

Scottish Crop Research Institute (SCRI)
Invergowrie, Dundee DD2 5DA   01382 562731

Silsoe Research Institute
Wrest Park, Silsoe, Bedford MK45 4HS   01525 860000

6. NATIONAL AGRICULTURAL COLLEGES

Cranfield University, Silsoe Campus
Silsoe, Bedford MK45 4DT   01525 863000

Harper Adams Agricultural College
Edgmond, Newport, Shropshire TF10 8NB   01952 820280

Royal Agricultural College
Stroud Road, Cirencester, Glos. GL7 6JS   01285 652531

Seale-Hayne Faculty (University of Plymouth)
Newton Abbot, Devon TQ12 6NQ   01626 325800

Shuttleworth College
Old Warden Park, Biggleswade, Beds. SG18 9EA   01767 626200

Welsh Institute of Rural Studies
Llanbadarn, Aberystwyth, Ceredigion SY23 3AL   01970 622253

Writtle College
Lordship Road, Writtle, Chelmsford, Essex CM1 3RR   01245 424200

N.B. The **Scottish Agricultural College** and its regional offices are listed on page 238.

INDEX

ALSO AVAILABLE